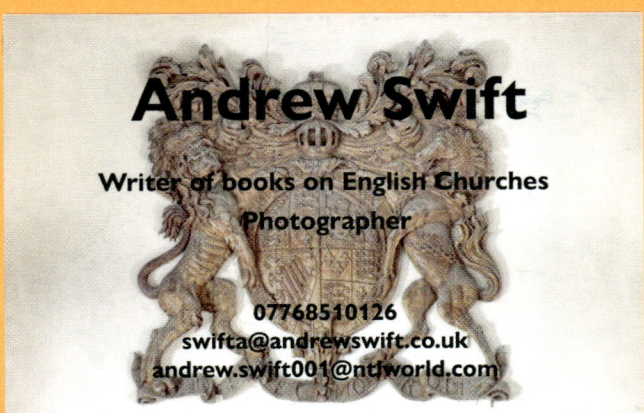

Andrew Swift

Writer of books on English Churches
Photographer

07768510126
swifta@andrewswift.co.uk
andrew.swift001@ntlworld.com

102A The Street
Rockland St Mary
Norwich
NR14 7HQ

May 28th 2020

Mr Tim Grimshaw
5 Chirton Dene Quays
NORTH SHIELDS
NE29 6YW

Dear Tim,

Many thanks for your lovely note. I hope the book gives you much pleasure. I was very interested to hear of your church visiting, you have a very impressive record! Hopefully you will remember the ones in the book that you visited in Suffolk. Your note had an illustration of Ellingham church in Northumberland, I was there only last year en route to Orkney, we stayed a night in the pub and naturally took in the church. We thought the area was grand and now want to go again, although many years ago I did some geological work in the north east and saw some of the picturesque spots like Seahouses and Beadnell. I stayed in Peterlee, which wasn't quite as scenic!

As you say, the lockdown is a pain but it seems we are (officially and unofficially) coming out of it gradually. Fortunately when we were shuttered up I was in the midst of writing a third Norfolk book, so haven't needed to go out after churches. I'm about half way through it now, should be out early next year at the latest.

Many thanks for getting in touch.

Best wishes,

Andrew

Holy Innocents, Gt. Barton, Suffolk

St Mary, Helmingham, Suffolk

St. Mary, Barking, Suffolk.

125 Suffolk Churches of Village and Countryside

125 Suffolk Churches of Village and Countryside

Andrew Swift

Foreword by
Clare, Countess of Euston
Lord Lieutenant of Suffolk

First published 2019 by Velox Books
102A The Street, Rockland St Mary. Norwich NR14 7HQ

Copyright © Andrew Swift 2019

Text, design, photographs and illustrations © Andrew Swift 2019

All rights reserved. No part of this book may be reproduced or utilized in any form or by any means, electronic or mechanical, including photocopying, recording or by information storage or retrieval systems, without permission in writing from Velox Books.

Photographs

Cover: Lackford St Lawrence
Frontispiece: Withersfield St Mary the Virgin
This page: Worlington All Saints

ISBN 978-0-9575701-6-0

Produced by Biddles Books, King's Lynn PE32 1SF

Foreword

It is my very great privilege as Her Majesty the Queen's Lord Lieutenant of Suffolk and Patron of the Suffolk Historic Churches Trust, to write this Foreword to Andrew Swift's lovely book. It is a work of true scholarship.

Suffolk's historic churches are one of the great glories of England, reflecting in their beauty and sheer number the importance of this county to the Christian Heritage of the British Isles. Holy Suffolk, Seely Suffolk, the home of Edmund, King and Martyr, who for hundreds of years held sway as England's Patron Saint. We are on the cusp of celebrating the Millennium of King Canute's visit to Bury St Edmunds to found the great Abbey in St Edmund's honour. The publication of this wonderful book could not be more timely.

It is salutary to remind ourselves that at the time of the Black Death, Suffolk's churches great and small were full of worshippers, and I often think that the calm spirituality that greets a visitor today as they walk through the porch of these beautiful buildings, is the result of hundreds of years of prayer and the love of God that has somehow become part of the old stones themselves.

Andrew Swift does not discuss the better-known urban churches or the mighty buildings in our wealthier market towns, enriched beyond imagination by the wool trade of the Middle Ages. They are in a league of their own.

Instead, he tells us the story of 125 carefully chosen Suffolk churches of village and countryside, all so different in little ways, so representative of the spirit of a truly free minded people. We are so fortunate that so many of them still remain, loved and cherished in parish after parish across the county.

I am deeply grateful to Andrew Swift for this great work, and on an even more practical note for explaining where to find the keys! This book will swiftly become the first port of call for all eager church visitors like myself.

Clare, Countess of Euston
H.M. Lord Lieutenant of Suffolk

Introduction

This book constitutes the third in my series of 100 Churches of Village and Countryside books, but astute readers will have noticed that this one for Suffolk contains 125 churches. The reason is that it is unlikely that there will be more Suffolk books in the future, so I thought it was a good idea to cover a greater number of churches in this single volume. As to the choice of churches I have made, I have remained true to the original intention in my earlier books and have chosen churches with rural settings; city and town churches were not considered. Also, I have avoided churches that have been the subject of a lot of previous attention in the literature and have concentrated on those that are lesser known and frequently overlooked. Two relatively recent publications by Tilbrook, Tricker and Pipe (1998) and Stanford (2005) cover a good selection of Suffolk churches in words and excellent photographs, and their featured examples are not duplicated here. Tricker (1983) is scantily illustrated, but the featured churches are very well described, so these churches will not be found here either. Churches featured in Simon Jenkins popular book of his choice of the thousand best English churches (2009) were also not considered. Only active, working Anglican churches are included, although Darmsden is not on the Church of England official list. Practically all the churches in this book are open at all reasonable times, as there is little point in directing potential visitors to a locked church, but thankfully more and more are being opened as I write. However, there are still many churches that are habitually kept locked, and I have included a few of these in order to present a broad geographical coverage of entries across Suffolk. In most cases locked churches can be accessed via keyholders or churchwardens.

I have greatly enjoyed my explorations amongst, and discoveries within, the churches of Suffolk. Each and every one has its merits and rewards for the visitor, and all share an indefinable atmosphere of peace and reflection found only in parish churches. It almost goes without saying that Suffolk is a marvellous county, but especially it is a grand place to discover and appreciate rural church buildings. That is mostly due to the mellow and timeless countryside in which they are set and which has inspired poets, artists and writers throughout the ages. Many words of praise and glowing testimonials have been lavished on Suffolk's considerable assets, all deserved, and I am happy to add more.

It is remarkable that so many different landscapes can be experienced in Suffolk, from the deeply incised maritime and riverine inlets and their intervening peninsulas of the south east, to the heathy Sandlings area of the east, the hilly country south east of Bury St Edmunds, and delightful rolling scenery of High Suffolk in the north and centre. And can anyone who has visited the area in the south containing the fine old towns of Lavenham, Long Melford, Sudbury, Cavendish and others, ever forget it? Each part of the county is imbued with its own unique atmosphere, and this is absorbed into the churches of each one, giving a special 'difference' to pique the senses of anyone who goes to see them.

Many churches are very old, but almost all were subsequently modified and added to in succeeding centuries, and it is rare to find evidence of buildings built in or before the C11th, except for one factor. That is the presence of distinctive and intriguing round towers at something like 42 of Suffolk's churches. No aspect of East Anglian church architecture has prompted so much argument amongst church enthusiasts as these mysterious structures, and a book introduction is no place to set out the pros and cons, but there is still no consensus as to why they are round and how old they are. Nevertheless, a significant body of opinion would have it that some part of certain of these towers is Anglo-Saxon in age; there are nine round tower churches to admire in this book. The following period of Norman architecture is much better represented and many churches have prominent Romanesque features, particularly doorways and arcades. The heavy, monolithic conception of Norman work is confounded by the skilful and expressive carving of doorways at Mettingham and Great Bradley, for example.

The Early English, Decorated and Perpendicular periods that followed, collectively known as the Gothic interval, saw the greatest church building and reconfiguration programmes in British history, and it was in the C13th–C15th that the majority of Suffolk churches were constructed, many on the same ground once occupied by earlier churches, some of whose features were incorporated in the new buildings. In the Perpendicular period most work took the form of restructuring and embellishment of the earlier Gothic churches. Thereafter for 300 years or so, the building impetus slackened, and there are few churches of post-Perpendicular age in Suffolk until the great Anglican and religious revival in the middle years of the C19th, masterminded and urged forward initially by medievalists in societies at Oxford and Cambridge, but soon embraced by the majority of churchmen in Britain. In essence, this movement promoted a return to medieval, pre-Reformation church ritual, architecture and furnishings. It was remarkably effective and pervasive, sweeping virtually the whole country, and exciting religious fervour. The result in Suffolk, like everywhere else, was the building of new churches to Gothic templates, but a far greater impact was made by a tidal wave of restorations which affected nearly every Anglican church. Out went much of the medieval and in came nouveau Gothic structures, furnishings and reorderings which still dominate very many churches today, inside and out, in Suffolk as elsewhere.

The tide of evangelical zeal gradually lessened in the late C19th and early C20th and with most churches restored, new church buildings and modifications were not necessary, but nevertheless church building did continue at a modest level and does so to the present day. Right now, we are in the midst of a low-key equivalent of the Victorian restoration programme which so radically changed the appearance of their churches. In a great number of today's buildings the old C19th furnishings have been, or soon will be, removed, often wholesale, to make way for modern facilities like kitchens, toilets and social areas. Modern seating and heating are being introduced and other furnishings upgraded, reflecting the needs and demands of C21st churchgoers. This process will continue and gain momentum as finances permit, and I wonder what this book would look like if I were to write it in 2050. Which I suggest adds an extra poignancy to the photographs and text within, *transeundum omnia*!

To the many people I met on my visits to Suffolk's churches, people who keep the church alive and who helped me in my quest, grateful thanks. I am delighted to offer special thanks to the Patron of the Suffolk Historic Churches Trust, Clare, Countess of Euston, the Lord Lieutenant of Suffolk, for her Foreword. As ever, my deep appreciation to Dr Joanne E. Norris for driving, proof reading and much else.

Andrew Swift, Rockland St Mary. Norfolk   September 2019

About the author

Andrew Swift was born in Leicestershire and lived there until 2012 when a quirk of fate resulted in an unexpected move to Norfolk, a move he has never regretted. Already a keen interest in churches had led to a two volume book on Leicestershire churches and another on Rutland churches. Now with the greatest concentration of medieval churches on the doorstep the author began the immensely pleasurable task of visiting as many as possible. In due course two volumes each featuring 100 lesser known rural churches of Norfolk were published. This book on Suffolk churches continues the theme begun in the larger county, only this time with 125 churches. Andrew Swift was a university geologist until 2005 and remains passionate about the subject. His many other interests include all aspects of natural history, the British landscape, numismatics, the 1st World War, music and book collecting.

The author at Alderton St Andrew

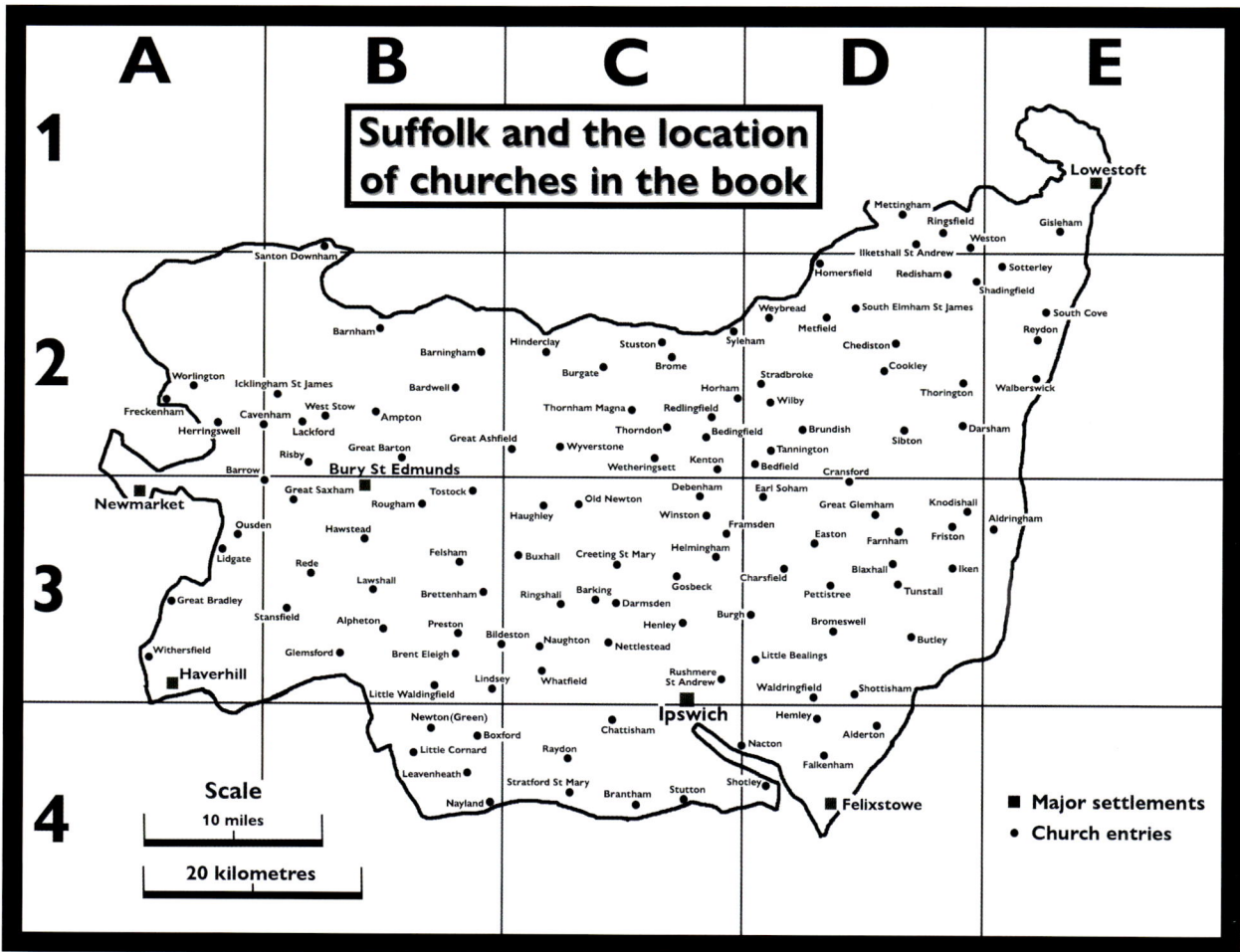

In the text churches are located by a letter/number reference to this map, and also by an ordnance survey grid reference

The Churches

Alderton, Aldringham, Alpheton, Ampton, Bardwell, Barking, Barnham, Barningham, Barrow, Bedfield, Bedingfield, Bildeston, Blaxhall, Boxford, Brantham, Brent Eleigh, Brettenham, Brome, Bromeswell, Brundish, Burgate, Burgh, Butley, Buxhall, Cavenham, Charsfield, Chattisham, Chediston, Cookley, Cransford, Creeting St Mary, Darmsden, Darsham, Debenham, Earl Soham, Easton, Falkenham, Farnham, Felsham, Framsden, Freckenham, Friston, Gisleham, Glemsford, Gosbeck, Great Ashfield, Great Barton, Great Bradley, Great Glemham, Great Saxham, Haughley, Hawstead, Helmingham, Hemley, Henley, Herringswell, Hinderclay, Homersfield, Horham, Icklingham St James, Iken, Ilketshall St Andrew, Kenton, Knodishall, Lackford, Lawshall, Leavenheath, Lidgate, Lindsey, Little Bealings, Little Cornard, Little Waldingfield, Metfield, Mettingham, Nacton, Naughton, Nayland, Nettlestead, Newton (Green), Old Newton, Ousden, Pettistree, Preston, Raydon, Rede, Redisham, Redlingfield, Reydon, Ringsfield, Ringshall, Risby, Rougham, Rushmere St Andrew, Santon Downham, Shadingfield, Shotley, Shottisham, Sibton, Sotterley, South Cove, South Elmham St James, Stansfield, Stradbroke, Stratford St Mary, Stuston, Stutton, Syleham, Tannington, Thorington, Thorndon, Thornham Magna, Tostock, Tunstall, Walberswick, Waldringfield, West Stow, Weston, Wetheringsett, Weybread, Whatfield, Wilby, Winston, Withersfield, Worlington, Wyverstone

Brettenham St Mary the Virgin

ALDERTON ST ANDREW

D4, TM 342 416

St Andrew bathes in winter sunshine

Alderton is situated on one of the many distinctive tracts of land defined by the river valleys and estuaries of south east Suffolk. To the southwest of the village is the broad River Deben, and to the east, the sea. That geographical setting of being 'out on a limb' imparts itself onto the villages hereabouts and all have an individual atmosphere. St Andrew has a spacious interior despite the lack of aisles, but for many years was subject to neglect through lack of funds for renewal, during which time the once proud C15th tower collapsed in stages, leaving the eerie, ivy-shrouded, jagged stub we see today. One of its bells survived and was hung in a cradle on the grass west of the tower as a Millennium project. The chancel fell into decay quite early on and by the late C18th had disappeared. The nave was also in a parlous state when at last help arrived in 1862 in the form of architect Sir Arthur Blomfield, who oversaw an almost complete rebuilding of the church. The chancel was renewed entirely and the rest except for a small portion of the north nave wall was also reconstructed. The north porch is the last testament to the undoubtedly grand medieval church, but despite being spared at the time of the rebuilding, it too is in poor condition today. However, there are many indications of its previous grandeur in the frieze of Marian monograms and other motifs, flushwork, niches and deeply moulded outer doorway with spandrel figures. The visitor steps into the huge echoing space of the nave, that the fittings struggle to fill. A glance to the right reveals the imposing tower arch, telling of St Andrew's earlier heyday. The medieval font presumably disappeared at the time of the rebuilding, perhaps before, but the Victorian replacement lacks distinction. Older fittings can be found in the nave south east corner, spared and refitted; these are a C14th piscina lacking its internal cusping with, above, in a window embrasure, a curious thin niche. This has an ornate head and is also probably C14th. A chapel must once have been present here. In the opposite nave wall is an old, blocked doorway which presumably once led into a transept, long removed. The George III royal arms was restored in recent times, and looks well. The church has several wall tablets, but none are in the first rank, or are particularly old. The oldest, dated 1769, is for Robert Biggs, and the best is the Pytches tablet of the early C19th, despite the blank area meant for later deceased members of the family. New bench seating was recently installed in the nave.

Remains of the tower, and bell

St Andrew from the north west

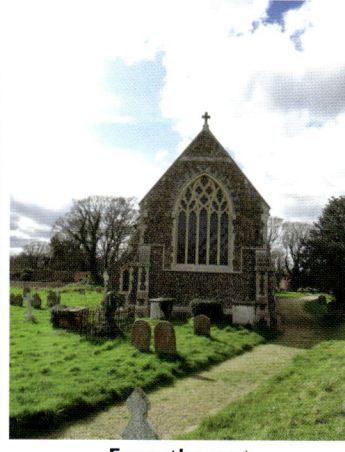
From the east

Views to the east and west

The chancel

Tower arch

Chancel north wall details

Piscina, niche, tablets

C14th niche

The font

George III royal arms

Oil lamp

Lithograph, war memorial, tablet

11

ALDRINGHAM ST ANDREW E3, TM 451 602

St Andrew from the south west

St Andrew has an enviable setting, in the midst of heath and heathy woodland; the village of Aldringham is over a mile distant. The church stands on elevated ground which drops down to the west, with pleasantly undulating countryside beyond. Many fine walks criss-cross the neighbourhood, particularly on the nearby Aldringham Common. The church has had a chequered career since its early foundation in the C12th, culminating in semi-ruination in the middle of the C19th, when the square tower had mostly collapsed, together with the western section of the nave. The chancel remained in use and indeed still shows its C12th origins today, the fabric containing a wide range of irregular stones, including Coralline Crag (which crops out in the area), flint, quartzite and brick. A much needed series of repairs began around 1843, more followed in the 1870's and refurnishing continued into the 1890's. The end result was a substantial restoration, which included a shortened nave with a bellcote at the west apex, south porch, north vestry, and almost complete refitting of the interior. Several old details were retained in the south wall, in particular a C13th priest's doorway with round-headed interior arch, lancet window of similar age and the external expression of the stairway for the long-vanished rood loft. A painting inside the church shows the state of the church in 1842, before restoration. The C19th north vestry now links the church to a recent extension housing modern facilities. The south doorway appears to be medieval and the two head stops on the external hood mould are certainly of that age. The interior is a late Victorian showpiece, and very little changed since those days. At the west end is tiered seating, and the wooden openwork pulpit, reading desk and lectern of 1895 are high quality features by Alexander Gibbs. The lovely reredos, also by Gibbs, is topped by a finely carved entablature with arches below housing the Decalogue, Lord's Prayer and Creed. The Gibbs workshop was also responsible for the outstanding glass of the east and west windows. 1940's glass depicting St Andrew fills the south wall lancet window, commemmorating Edward Fraser Stanford, who from 1917-44 was top man for Stanfords, the famous map makers and retailers. Two medieval features remain, one is a super C15th font of familiar design with Evangelists symbols and angels on the bowl, and in the chancel are elements of a C13th pillar piscina. The attractive churchyard contains several striking gravestones.

South wall details

From the north east

Chancel fabric

Looking east and west along the church

The sanctuary

The font

Pillar piscina

Priest's doorway

The pulpit

Painting, war memorial, tablet

St Andrew

East window glass detail

Garrett wall tablet

ALPHETON ST PETER & ST PAUL   B3, TL 873 504

Perfectly set in its hollow, Alpheton St Peter & St Paul

St Peter & St Paul is set in a very special spot, steeped in history and beauty. The associated C13th barns are amongst the oldest still in use or indeed in existence, and the mostly C17th and C18th Hall nearby sits on the site of a much older one. All these elements have been in place as a manor farm complex probably since Saxon days. The site now has a new lease of life as a wedding venue, which in turn has kick-started life in the church, which is a partner in the enterprise. The church is worthy of its site, being very attractively composed, without aisles but possessing a pretty timbered C15th porch and bold, roughly contemporary tower. The roots of the rest of the building certainly pre-date the tower and may be very early. The south and priest's doorway are roughly contemporary, with varied paterae around the mouldings. To the right of the south doorway is a composite stoup. The interior is a delight and full of interest. The plain font is undistinguished but it sits on an older C13th Purbeck Marble base which once had four pillars. On the south wall is an excellent, if rustic, royal arms for Charles I, recently restored. Opposite on the north wall is a very degraded St Christopher painting. Some rather worn C15th canopy glass can be seen in the heads of some nave windows. The handsome pulpit, now set on a modern base, is a classic Jacobean design, and next to it is the lower doorway to the rood stairs, which are still in situ, twisting their way to the upper doorway above. Below this doorway is a fascinating medieval niche with vaulting and a Bacchanalian head at its apex, and below that is a large squint installed in the C19th; this was responsible for subsequent foundering of the northern section of the chancel arch. A complementary, but less well-preserved niche can be seen on the south side of the chancel arch. That one has some original colour. The chancel boasts a striking C14th piscina and single sedile, both intricately carved with ogee arches, pinnacles, crockets, cusping, medallions and figures on the sedile, including a crowned man. Another more modest piscina is set in the nave south wall. The east window glass was renewed in 2000 for the Millennium with an inspired modern design by Pippa Blackall, of the Risen Christ, which also depicts local figures and themes. There is some old woodwork in the chancel, including a misericord. One or two of the sparse poppyheads in the nave are also old. There are three box pews at the west end. See the tablet of John Shepherd (d.1815) for a Nelson connection.

St Peter's tower

The church from the south

South doorway and stoup

Views east and north west along the church

Chancel piscina and sedilia

Pulpit, rood stairs & doorways

Rood stairs & lower doorway

The font

Nave piscina, niche, lamps

Charles I royal arms

East window by Pippa Blackall

St Christopher painting

C15th glass, poppyheads

AMPTON ST PETER

B2, TL 866 711

St Peter sits demurely in its narrow churchyard, the super interior unsuspected

To do this remarkable little church justice would considerably exceed the space available, yet little would be expected from the simple, modest exterior and plan. Despite being customarily locked, seeking access is strongly recommended. Most of the building is C14th or C15th, but the south doorway is C13th and coursed flints at the base of the nave south wall also point to pre-C14th foundation. A blocked window in the chancel south wall has a rugged, crude square frame which also speaks of older days. On the nave north side see how a C15th chantrey chapel partially blocks an earlier intersecting window. Exuberant architect S. S. Teulon effected one of his more restrained makeovers in 1846, and there was another restoration in 1889. The considerable number of exciting items inside will take some time to appreciate. At the west end above the plain Victorian font a rare, but distressed, fretwork royal arms for Charles I is mounted across the tower arch, flanked by two thistles. On the walls by the arch are two very worn consecration crosses. By the door is a battered stoup. On the floors, mounted on walls or propped up against them is an array of C15th brasses, all missing some elements. The best is in the nave floor and depicts the Coket family, minus male children. The wall memorials and tablets are exceptional, most are for members of the Calthorpe family. The two largest and most important are in the chancel, a huge monolithic extravaganza of c.1640 by the Christmas brothers is for Henry and Dorothy Calthorpe, while to the east of it is a fine memorial of 1629 by Nicholas Stone for William Whettell, with refined modelling. Above these model citizens of the past is a restored C15th chancel roof, with a colourful and singular C17th painting scheme. Also in the chancel is a small, probably C13th piscina; another, of C15th date and much damaged, resides in the chantrey chapel. The pulpit is a bold, distinguished C18th example with grand tester, also C18th are the elegant communion rails. The chapel, though a little neglected, houses some excellent items. The coffin lid against the wall is C13th, while above it in the window, and in other windows, is a range of armorial and other old glass. The north wall bears a weighty, extravagant, (and dirty) Calthorpe tablet of the early C18th. In short, also see the chapel arch and two handsome C20th mosaics in its jambs, east window glass by Burlison and Grylls, two hatchments under the tower, an old prayer desk, C19th iron stove, rood stair doorways and a wonderful old chest.

The church from the west and north west

North chapel obscuring earlier window

Looking east and west along the church

Entrance to chantrey chapel

Organ, pulpit, rood stair doorways

Calthorpe (c.1640) and Whettell (1629) memorials

Brasses, all C15th

The font

Chapel glass

Charles 1st royal arms, hatchment, St George

Communion rails

Ancient chest

BARDWELL ST PETER & ST PAUL B2, TL 941 736

St Peter & St Paul's tower peers from the tree cover

St Peter & St Paul is an exceptional church lurking in the backwoods of north Suffolk. The building stands in a fairly tight churchyard (with a later extension to the north east) hemmed in by trees, and this makes it difficult to obtain an uninterrupted view of the whole church. Only the bold, tall C15th tower is immediately prominent and it soars giddily over visitors as they thread their way up the gentle climb to the south door. The tower is an undoubted highlight, with flushwork and a good ensemble of west doorway with narrow Perpendicular window above, also a dainty Hertfordshire-type mini-spire, but the porch, also C15th, is outstanding too. This has diverse flushwork, niches, an arms for major donor Sir William Berdewell (d.1434), impressive side windows and an entrance arch decorated with fleurons. The chancel was largely rebuilt with whole flint nodules in 1852-3 at a time when much other refurbishing was carried out. Inside, the hammerbeam nave roof is a tour-de-force, regardless of the ruthless removal (and no doubt burning) of all but four of the hammerbeam angels, probably in the C17th. It retains most of its painting and a superb set of bosses, and one of the four angels carries the date 1421, thus dating the structure. Two nave windows contain fine arrays of C15th glass, including some excellent full figures, almost certainly donors, including Sir William Berdewell. Amongst many other pieces is a vivid Pietà and charming birds and fruit, these being later in date. As well as the old glass also see high-quality C19th glass by the O'Connor workshop and W. G. Taylor. Five consecration crosses and wall paintings were revealed during Victorian restoration. The latter were recorded and rapidly re-covered; a few, re-exposed later, are visible in the nave. The nicely restored royal arms are for George II, whilst the plain font with slender stem is C14th. In the north east corner of the nave both rood stair openings and stairs survive. Nearby is a piscina, denoting the former presence of a chapel. In the walls to either side of the chancel arch are squints. Some panels from the old rood screen stand in the nave north east corner, and show fine workmanship, the wood mellowed to a silvery hue. The church is dignified by a large number of splendid wall memorials, particularly in the chancel, where there are two formidable C17th examples for members of the Read family. Of the rest, see a tomb chest cut in two with the halves embedded in the chancel north and south walls; also Suffolk's only Boer War memorial.

Tower west face

The church from the south west

The porch

Looking west

The church from the west end, with font

The chancel

C15th glass, figures of donors

Old glass (top), wall tablets (below)

Read memorials (1652, 1678)

Nave roof

Boss and two roof figures

George II royal arms

Wall paintings

19

BARKING ST MARY

C3, TM 076 535

A church enthusiast's wonderland

St Mary is a superb church for the church lover, distinguished by outstanding features and architecture from many ages and periods. There is not the space to do the church full justice here, and although listing and compression are undesirable, they were necessary in order to include at least the most important items and structures. To begin with, the setting is delightful. St Mary is reached by a shady lane and stands elevated above its straggling village, which is strung out below along the valley of the Gipping. Cedars of Lebanon and the charming old rectory enhance the surroundings. The building is of grand proportions, mostly C14th and C15th but the chancel and porch, also possibly the two-storey vestry/sacristy and base of the tower may be C13th. There are two crenellated aisles, battlements also on the north clerestory and vestry. Most windows are Perpendicular replacements, but the intersecting and cusped east window is early C14th. One in the south aisle and the tower west window are also Decorated. The late Perpendicular westernmost window of the north aisle north wall, unusually, is partially fabricated with terracotta mouldings (perhaps from Shrubland Old Hall, Coddenham). Set into the internal reveals of the same window are beautifully worked strips of the same material. The west, south and internal vestry doors are also finely carved. The porch is low and long, and the inner doorway is flanked by a stoup with a damaged C17th text above. Two small, ancient lancets are set in the vestry north wall. Grand gargoyles glare down from the north aisle; there are others elsewhere. Treasures of the nave and aisles include fine, partly restored, C15th/C16th roofs (the nave has kingposts), handsome rood screen with outstanding carvings and remains of coving and colouring, two superb parcloses north and south enclosing chapels, benches with significant medieval components, excellent C15th font with nice details and exuberant cover, Charles II royal arms, rood stair doorways, gracious wall tablets, piscinas, medieval glass fragments, C17th Flemish carving incorporated into the modern pulpit, two redundant old braziers, C19th bier, huge C14th chest and C18th Lord's Prayer, Decalogue and Creed boards. In the chancel a large pew incorporating old panels and enclosing C16th benches, C17th barley twist altar rails, restored medieval piscina and drop-sill sedilia. St Mary is a church to savour.

St Mary, s. doorway, vestry windows, gargoyle | From the north east | Thurston tomb, north aisle

Interior looking east | Chancel screen | The chancel

The church looking west | North chapel parclose | Charles II arms, rood stair doorway | Old benches

Pulpit, north parclose, nave roof | Tomb side?, font, chapel, moulding | Medieval glass fragments | Tablets, Commandments board

BARNHAM ST GREGORY

B2, TL 871 792

St Gregory from the south

Barnham lies in the north west of Suffolk, in an area containing few churches. In the early 1860's the 5th Earl of Grafton and his successor the 6th Earl funded and oversaw a sweeping restoration of St Gregory. So pervasive was this overhaul, together with an earlier one in 1840, that most medieval features and fittings were swept away, leaving a neat, but ultimately rather uninspiring interior. It is thought that J.H. Hakewill, who restored many East Anglian churches, was responsible for the work. The 6th Earl reinforced links with the main family church at Euston, including fitting stained glass featuring the patron saint of that church, St Genevieve. During the 1860's restoration a new north aisle was added, possibly also the north transept, although this latter is also attributed to the earlier restoration in 1840. Most windows were renewed in the Early English style, but the priest's doorway into the chancel is original C13th, and dates the chancel. The nave is probably of similar age, but the tower was added in the C14th. It contains an unusual external doorway to the north which accesses the tower stairs. The modest, crenellated south porch is difficult to date, but may be pre-C19th. The main impression of the interior is the plainness of the furnishings and fittings, almost all of them dating from the C19th. Near the door resides a small, octagonal, C13th font. Like its later surroundings, it is simple and unadorned. Another C13th survivor is found in the chancel, an elegant piscina, with engaged shafts and tracery featuring a curious design of conjoined trefoils, and an embellished drain. Mounted on the nave south wall near the south doorway is a large, rare royal arms for William III. It has acquired a dark patina with age. Of a more recent vintage is a remarkable map of Barnham that usually hangs on the north wall of the aisle. It is a collage and shows, with photographs and articles, the houses of the village and their occupants at the time of the 1911 census, with especial regard to those affected by the 1st World War. The organ is located in the north aisle and is a typical, muscular Victorian example; nearby is another modern item, the attractive pulpit. But the highlights of the interior are two very fine, early C20th windows, the east and nave south east, by renowned stained glass artist A.K. Nicholson. The east window shows a Crucifixion scene and the nave St Gregory and St Genevieve. Below the latter two figures are roundels in C16th/17th Flemish style. Both windows are refined, sparkling and intense.

The porch

View from the east

Doorways – tower, chancel, nave

The church looking east

The chancel

East window, Nicholson glass

Details of the Nicholson glass

Chancel south east

The piscina

Wall brass and floor tablet

North west across the church

Looking south across the nave

Font, war memorial model

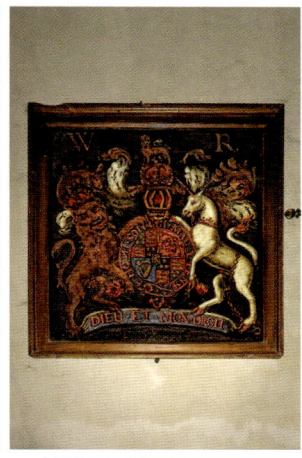
William III royal arms

23

BARNINGHAM ST ANDREW

B2, TL 968 769

St Andrew from Church Road in Barningham

A special pleasure attends discovering and exploring the churches of north Suffolk. Here there are no Lavenhams, Southwolds or Long Melfords, but instead we have a mellow landscape populated by characterful churches that speak eloquently of days past. Due to their relative obscurity, few people are aware of the treasures tucked away in these buildings, and Barningham is a case in point, as we shall see. But first the exterior: the windows of the chancel mark it out as Decorated, with pretty tracery in the east window and a low-side window to the south, with a larger thin window above. The nave windows, in contrast, are Perpendicular. However, it is hard to establish whether these replaced earlier ones; possibly the nave is contemporary with the chancel. However, the bold south porch is undoubtedly C15th, as is the tower, dated by a bequest of 1439. This tower has stepped battlements, a prominent stair turret to the south and panelling at the base; the buttresses stop a little way up the final stage. To the north the chancel is supported by substantial buttresses. Inside, the treasure alluded to earlier, an exquisite set of medieval benches that fill the nave. Elsewhere these would receive far more attention. There is superb carving on the ends, flamboyant poppyheads and intricately worked backs to the benches, but the icing on the cake is the remarkable suite of arm rest figures, animal and human, real and imaginary. Most have some damage, but overall are in good order. The panelling around the nave walls is worthy of note too. There is excellent woodwork elsewhere, like the well-preserved C15th screen with its intricate tracery and C17th doors. The nice pulpit appears to be a hybrid of early C17th tester and C18th box below. Admire too the C19th wall post figures with shields carrying Virtues in the chancel. Also in the chancel is a medieval angle piscina and drop-sill sedilia, plus a wall-mounted brass of 1499 for William Goche. The font is C14th with unusual tracery patterns around the bowl and a robust, somewhat later, cover. The royal arms is for Victoria, but may be adapted from an earlier set. An impressive open rood stair ascends the embrasure of the nave south east window and ends in two doorways; at its base is an enigmatic stone head and nearby, a good piscina. The Last Supper behind the altar was painted by a rector's wife in 1877. There is a little old glass and some very good C19th work, including the east window by Heaton, Butler and Bayne.

Tower and south porch

From the north east

Chancel details

West along the nave

St Andrew's superb woodwork

The chancel

Sanctuary south east corner

Rood stairs & doorways, piscina

The font and cover

The pulpit

Goche brass 1499

Old (top) & C19th glass (bottom)

Victoria royal arms, head

BARROW ALL SAINTS A/B3, TL 760 646

Barrow All Saints from the south west

All Saints might be adrift from its village in a physical sense, but the church is clearly loved and looked after, and is a credit to the parish. Most East Anglian churches enjoy a large degree of anonymity and are rarely newsworthy beyond the benefice they are in, but a few years ago the vicar of All Saints, Father Peter MacLeod-Miller, attracted wider attention through his colourful personality and habit of bringing members of his menagerie to church services. These days things have settled down and the good Father now ministers in Australia, but this fine church is still worthy of attention. There's not much of it, but evidence of Norman origins exists in the small Norman window in the nave north wall and also, perhaps, in the tower where there are two crude, blocked windows, unfortunately missing their heads, with small slit windows set in the fillings to light the internal tower stairs. The blocked windows may be pre-C13th. The unbuttressed tower is otherwise C13th with a later battlemented parapet, and the rest of the church is C13th-C15th. It was given a considerable Victorian restoration in the mid-C19th by L.N. Cottingham and his son. The east window is interesting and consists of three lancets within an overall frame, a later Early English motif. The window has been renewed but may faithfully follow an original. The interior balances the old and the Victorian extremely well and there are excellent examples of features from many periods. The very old is represented by the chancel double piscina, sedilia and aumbrys which are C13th, as is the impressive double piscina in the south aisle east wall. Next to the latter is a C14th tomb recess and next to that, sedilia. Most of these features have been restored. In the splay of the Norman window in the north wall are washed-out paintings said to be dancers or musicians, which could be any age from C12th-C16th. One of the church highlights is a superb tomb chest cum Easter sepulchre in the chancel, generally Rennaisance in style and enhanced with shields in lozenges and in quatrefoils. The brasses for Sir Clement Heigham on the back wall probably don't belong with the chest. Parts of other brasses are mounted on boards near the south door. The choir stalls incorporate parts from older examples, including striking poppyheads and arm rest figures, and there are two old benches with traceried ends and carved backs in the south aisle. There are some excellent wall memorials, the Heigham family being well represented. The C15th font has painted shields on the bowl.

All Saints from the west   Tower and porch   Slits within older window   Norman window

Looking west from the chancel, east from the nave and east into the chancel

Chancel piscina, sedilia, wall tablets   The south chapel   Tomb chest of c.1500, with brasses   Heigham wall memorial of 1634

For Susan Heigham, d.1695   The font   Paintings in the Norman window splay   Woodwork and faces

BEDFIELD ST NICHOLAS D2, TM 227 663

Quiet and secluded, St Nicholas is the quintessential country church

Deep in the countryside, down a rustic track at some little distance from its village, Bedfield St Nicholas bristles with atmosphere and mystique. The church's great age is testified to by the north doorway, which is immediately apparent as the visitor enters the wild churchyard. It is Norman, with chevrons and bobbins in the head and a shaft either side. Further investigation on the north side will reveal coursed flint fabric which also indicates a C12th origin. This style of coursing terminates abruptly in the middle of the chancel wall, with the portion eastwards representing a C13th extension. The C14th/C15th tower has a busy western face with flushwork arcading at the base, a good west doorway with fleurons in the mouldings, succeeded upwards by a Perpendicular window flanked by two ornate niches, with another niche above. There is further flushwork on the battlemented parapet, worked into quatrefoils on the crenels and two-arch arcades on the merlons. Above the quatrefoils is chequerboard flushwork. To the south is a stair turret with the arms of the important Ufford family near the top. The ramshackle C15th porch has a leaning facade and blocked side windows, but also great charm. There are no aisles or other extensions, yet the interior does not feel cramped. The font is an assertive early Perpendicular example, with bold tracery and Ufford arms on the deep bowl. Surmounting it is an equally imposing C17th cover, cleverly designed to allow access to the priest and also views to the christening party. The pulpit is the remnant of a C17th two or three-decker, but retains some of the majesty of the original, and is topped with a sturdy book ledge with prominent brackets. The pulpit partially obscures a medieval niche to the north of the chancel arch, which is matched by another to the south; these indicate the earlier presence of chapels. The dado of a medieval screen is of great interest, as it retains paintings of prophets, two of which escaped despoilment by being concealed behind the pulpit for many years. These are Joel and Baruch, the names of others on the north side have been scratched out, but the figures have benefitted from recent cleaning. C17th rustic benches at the west end of the church have scrolled heads and unusual decoration. The old rood stairs are clearly seen in the splay of the south east nave window, also their doorways. The medieval chancel piscina is plain. Curiosities include a copy of the C16th Paraphrase of Erasmus book and framed examples of worked lead from the nave roof.

The tower from the west | St Nicholas from the north west | The porch | Norman north door

Interior looking east | The pulpit | Screen and details | Screen north side

Rood stairs and doorways | The chancel | Chancel piscina | Interior from the sanctuary

West from the screen | The font | Old benches | Paraphrase of Erasmus, worked lead, niche

BEDINGFIELD ST MARY　　C2, TM 179 687

St Mary from the south east

One of Suffolk's shyest churches, St Mary hides behind a screen of lush garden foliage and trees, which form an effective barrier to observation, particularly in summer. Coming through the aisle of trees from the main gate on Park Road is like entering a secret country, an excellent introduction to an enjoyable church. Most of the C13th–C15th body of the church is rendered, except for the nave north wall, which may have lost its coating over time. It is here that it can be seen that the nave walls were heightened in brick (?C17th). This can also be seen in the west gable of the nave. The tower is of moderate height and the fabric reveals the varied evolution of its building, with the bottom parts being perhaps C13th and the top, C14th. The belfry window tracery, where preserved, is Decorated. Oddly, buttressing is only employed above the bottom stage of the tower. Perhaps the top part had to be rebuilt or supported after becoming unsafe. The long, low porch is C15th, with a curious roof. The C14th inner door is flanked high to the east by a small, yet finely worked niche. The north vestry was built during the short reign of William IV, in 1834. Windows are a mixture of Decorated and Perpendicular forms (one of the latter to the south has bold tracery and transoms), but with a C13th lancet in the chancel north wall and an odd round window to the west of the porch. That may have started life as a Saxon opening. The Victorians were certainly busy inside, but a sense of the antique was retained, mainly via the old benches in the nave. A few are C19th, but the majority are early C17th, with poppyheads embellished with scrolls with flowers at their centre and finials, little scrolls also on the elbows. Some C15th bench ends are mounted on the wall ends of the later benches, with quite different poppyheads and very battered elbow figures. The font is a neat C15th example, with tracery and quatrefoils around the bowl and a stem with a large central pillar and four slimmer ones attached. On the north nave wall near the chancel arch a rood loft doorway and stairs are preserved. A royal arms for Victoria is mounted above the tower arch, while below it under the arch is a massive old chest, bristling with ironwork and locks. The chancel is almost all Victorian, but retains an old piscina. The hatchment of 1853 on the chancel wall is for a member of the Bedingfield family. Excellent C19th and C20th glass adorns several windows, including work from the Morris factory. The nave hammerbeam roof is impressive.

Church west end from the north

St Mary from the south west

South doorway

Interior looking east

The pulpit

Rood loft doorway and stairs

Benches and details

The east end

Chancel south east corner

Chancel piscina

Bedingfield hatchment (1853)

West from the chancel

The font

Victoria royal arms

Old chest

BILDESTON ST MARY MAGDALENE   B/C3, TL 985 492

St Mary from Church Lane

St Mary is a large, imposing, C14th-C16th church, sure to please its visitors. Nave and chancel are under one roof. The chancel, some windows and other details are Decorated, but a considerable Victorian restoration may have introduced non-original work in the Decorated style. However, the overall impression is of a classic Perpendicular church, with striking 2-storey porch, bold windows and a lovely clerestory. The setting on high land away from the village adds to St Mary's impressive credentials. Until 1975 a conventional medieval tower stood at the west end, but in that year most of the top half of the tower collapsed, taking the south west part of the nave with it. It wasn't until the turn of the C21st that a replacement top half of the tower and repairs were completed. Even today, this new tower and its mini-spike give rise to strong sentiments, and it is true to say the structure has few supporters. However, the rest of the church has plenty of consolations. The C15th porch is highly decorated with flushwork and niches. The entrance arch is ornamented with fleurons and the south doorway within is embellished with shields and fleurons, with an angel at the apex. There are spandrels with shields and two large, self-assured lions as hoodmould stops. The fine door itself is old, with Perpendicular tracery and a vine trail around it. Inside, the aforementioned C19th reconfigurations left an impressive space and quality furniture, but most medieval features were swept away. The arcades are superb and some capitals are enhanced with carved heads. The font is a chunky, characteristic C15th example, and has been in the wars, but like many fonts, its war wounds add character. In the south aisle is another battered survivor, a C14th piscina with crocketed canopy. Also in the south aisle are the altar table, rails and part of the rood screen from the redundant Wattisham church; the old screen sees service as a reredos, but today its saints are of Victorian vintage. Between the two parts of the reredos are C17th grave markers, the highest one apparently re-used. A brass of 1599 is mounted on the chancel wall, it is an outstanding example despite losing one of its figures. Some fine glass adorns the church, particularly the Kempe window of 1892 in the south aisle, and a 1981 depiction of the Crucifixion attended by the church's patron saint, by Pippa Blackall. See also the old misericords, striking C19th sedilia and Stuart altar rails in the chancel, a number of good wall tablets and the brightly painted angels in the nave roof.

The church from the north

The porch

South doorway

Looking east and west along the church

The south chapel

South aisle piscina

Chancel sedilia

Arcade capital

The font

Kempe and Blackall glass

Wade brass (1599)

The nave roof

Parker (1858) & Wilson (1837) tablets

BLAXHALL ST PETER

D3, TM 356 569

The first day of Spring finds rooks busy around St Peter

Blaxhall has some fame out of proportion to its modest size (population c.200). That is due to two things, firstly the local pub, The Ship, has a long history of traditional singing, and its more prominent practitioners of the past were recorded in action in the pub. The singing (and dancing) tradition continues today. The village can also boast an important family of C19th and C20th artists and artisans, the Ropes, whose descendants still live at Grove Farm. Edwin James Rope was responsible for the distinctive organ chamber built off the chancel north wall; of the work of the women of the family, more later. St Peter's C15th tower is much repaired in brick, but has a lot to recommend it, particularly the west doorway with its large lion stops, spandrel carvings of a green man and an angel, fleurons around the mouldings, panelled flushwork frieze at the base and another above the doorway. Flushwork too on the buttresses. North and south nave wall lancets indicate a C13th age, whilst the rest of the windows are early C14th Y-, intersecting Y- and intersecting Y- with cusping (east window). Some of the windows were replaced in brick in the C16th, but the early C14th designs were retained. There are no aisles, but the C15th south porch is delightfully adorned with flushwork and monograms. Inside, the C15th font has busy tracery and shield designs on the bowl and an impressive stem, and there is a stoup with trefoil head near the door. On the west wall is a worn piece of Saxon carving, probably from a cross. Also on that wall are two paintings made to look like tablets, for churchwardens of different periods. The first of the items by women of the Rope family, a dignified bronze war memorial by sculptor E.M. Rope is set on the north wall. A little further east on the same wall is a white commemmorative wall tablet and, further east, another in a window embrasure; another is mounted on the chancel north wall. These are by D.A.A. and E.M. Rope and take the form of carved, sentimental scenes. M.E. Rope and M.A. Rope were responsible for the inspired east window glass, while the affecting scene of Sunday School children in the porch was designed by E.M. Rope but made-up by one of the glass-making family members. There is an excellent C16th hammerbeam nave roof, with traceried spandrels and wooden, book-holding angels below the wall plates. Both rood stair doorways are still extant and in the chancel is a medieval piscina with ogee arch, and drop-sill sedilia. The C17th Saunders wall tablet is striking.

St Peter from the north west and south east   **West doorway**

Looking east   **The chancel**   **Looking west from the sanctuary**   **Roofs**

Wall plate angels   **The pulpit**   **East window**   **Porch window**

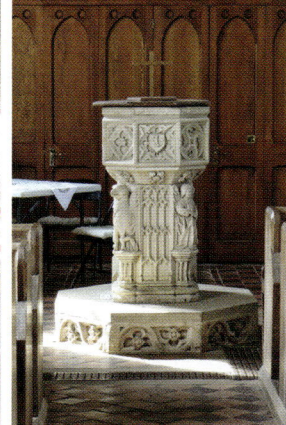

Rood stairs doorways   **The font**   **Skull, piscina, stoup**   **Tablets, Ropper painting**

BOXFORD ST MARY

B4, TL 962 404

A symbol of medieval prosperity. St Mary from the south east

Boxford is a charming village with a population of around 1225, making it quite large by East Anglian standards. In fact, it has the feel of a larger, more important place, reflecting its medieval history as a market and wool town. It lies in a very desirable part of the world, near 'Constable Country' and in the midst of wonderfully evocative English countryside. St Mary also testifies to the village's more expansive past, being a large church with an especially grand and ornate mid-C15th south porch. There are two aisles, extended as chancel chapels, a bold and enriched C14th tower with a self-important little lantern/spirelet on top, and, secreted on the north side, an important and very early C14th wooden porch, skeletal and dark. The rest is largely C15th with much fine Perpendicular work, and in 1886-7 the church was reseated and a new chancel roof installed. The interior is distinguished by stately arcades and a pleasing sense of order and dedicated care. Many fine objects are housed here. Both north and south doorways are often open, but entering from the north is recommended in order to pass through the rare wooden porch. An upper room in the tower is fronted by a venerable set of rails on a stout carved beam. Against a pillar facing the south doorway is a traceried C15th font, but examination reveals that it is just a stem, the bowl is missing. The C17th cover is more interesting, as it opens out via folding doors to reveal a painted interior, with texts on banners. The C18th pulpit is a handsome specimen, with particularly attractive steps with balusters; the elegant communion rails are also C18th. The upper rood stair doorway is sealed with a wooden door. Several nice C16th and C17th brasses adorn St Mary, most inscription only, but the one of 1606 for baby David Birde is supported by a poignant engraving of him asleep in his cot. The south chancel chapel has tall, canopied niches, with much original red colouration, flanking the altar, with, next to the left hand pair, a wall painting of King Edmund holding an arrow. The niches house faint paintings, better seen in the larger, more ornate northern set. There are paintings too above the chancel arch, a very small seated Christ flanked by much larger angels, the whole now faded. The south chapel piscina has a fine ogee arch with shields either side in the square head. Several corbel heads are worth seeking out, as are two distinctive wooden charity boards. The east window displays a vivid modern representation of the Transfiguration designed by Rosemary Rutherford.

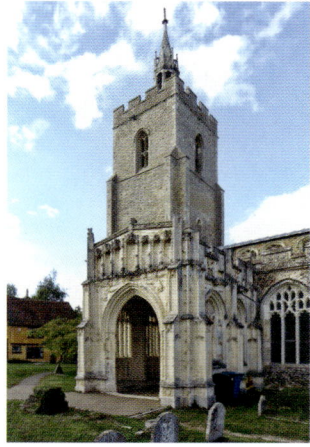
South porch and tower

St Mary from the south

The medieval north porch

Looking east along the church

The chancel

The church looking west

Chancel south chapel

Pulpit, rood loft doorway

The font and cover

Chancel arch & chapel paintings, piscina

Four of St Mary's fine brasses

Rosemary Rutherford glass, east window

Charity boards, corbel head

BRANTHAM ST MICHAEL the ARCHANGEL C4, TM 112 341

The view from the south east shows St Michael at its best

There's more than a hint of Essex at Brantham, the village stands very close to Suffolk's border with that county. The settlement has grown considerably in recent years as more and more dormitory housing and industrial areas have sprung up, but a gentler Brantham stills exists around St Michael in a haven of peace and greenery. And the church looks very well in its big churchyard. St Michael's C14th origins were largely submerged or removed by renovations in 1800 and a considerable overhaul by E.C. Hakewill in 1869, which amounted to complete rebuilding except for the nave and lower part of the tower. The architect fitted a sweeping roof which pitches down to embrace a new north aisle. On the south side a porch was demolished in 1869 but on the same spot a choir vestry was built in 1957; this was later converted to house modern facilities. A quaint and appealing touch is Hakewill's 'Hansel and Gretel' cottage tucked into the angle of nave and chancel to the south, which serves as a vicar's vestry. The nave windows were largely renewed, but their Decorated style may derive from the originals. The distinctive weathervane came from the demolished St Michael in Manningtree. The arts and crafts style lych gate of 1897, by E.S. Prior, is delightful, with a pretty, curving roofline. The interior is larger than suspected from outside and on entering from the north the first object to attract attention is the considerable organ loft on the south wall. Beneath it is the doorway to the converted old choir vestry. The font stands just in front of the tower arch and is C14th. It is not native to St Michael and was brought here from St Martin at Palace Plain in Norwich. It has quatrefoils on the octagonal bowl and slim pillars enclosing tracery panels on the stem. The C14th nave piscina, marking the site of a guild altar, is of angle type. Another angle piscina in the chancel is identical to the nave example, but appears to be a Victorian copy. In a nave window near to the piscina is a composite panel of C15th glass with two well-defined part-figures and other bits and pieces, it is said to have come from Dodnash Priory, to which St Michael was allied. Vibrant modern glass of a scene with John the Baptist by Hall and Sons can be seen in the west window. The pulpit of c.1900 is an outstanding feature, with vivacious carving of the Glastonbury Holy Thorn Tree. Striking corbel figures of Ss Michael and Gabriel distinguish the chancel arch. The royal arms is for George III.

The north side of the church

View from the north east

The lych gate of 1897

Interior from the west

The chancel

Interior from the east

The font

Medieval angle piscina

St Michael

Pulpit, c.1900

Bench end figures

George III royal arms, ledger slab

Medieval and 1946 glass

BRENT ELEIGH ST MARY

B3, TL 942 482

St Mary is a jewel in Suffolk's crown of churches

Very near to Brent Eleigh is the fabulous pile and tourist trap that is Lavenham St Peter and St Paul, but the smaller village has something that Lavenham would give its eye teeth to have. This is a trio of wall paintings on the east wall of great rarity and beauty, at least what you can see of them, for one of the paintings is very indistinct and the blue of another has oxidised to a rather unpleasant sooty colour. It is the painting that forms the centrepiece that is the real gem, it is a crucifixion scene, with Christ flanked by St John and the Virgin Mary. It formed the reredos in the early church, and, as such, is incredibly rare. The style is typical of its period, and the figures are reminiscent of those on the famed Thornham Parva retable. The figures are slender and willowy, and appear to sway gently, whilst the colours are pastel and dream-like. The age of the paintings is gauged to be late C13th into early C14th. Recent mindless vandalism when areas of the paintings were gouged with a knife or similar sent shudders of revulsion through not only the local area, but nationwide. Thankfully, restoration is now complete and the hope must be that it never happens again. If the paintings were all St Mary offered, it would be enough, but there is much more here. The bulk of the church is C14th and C15th, but the chancel is older and there is a C14th south aisle, also a nice south porch and C19th vestry to the north. The interior exudes a sharp tang of the past and it seems to have quietly passed through the C19th without attracting the attention of the restorers. There is much old woodwork. C17th and C18th box pews fill the nave, and there is older seating too. The pulpit is a fine Jacobean example. The three-side chunky C18th altar rails form a handsome set. The C13th font is of Purbeck Marble and has the familiar arcaded bowl. The cover is another Jacobean piece, of pleasing design. The chancel houses a very substantial marble monument of 1743 for Edward Colman, with reclining figure, pediment and putti, while around it a group of good C18th and C19th wall tablets complete the picture. Patina'd parclose screening of great character encloses the east end of the aisle; inside is a C14th piscina indicating the area's earlier use as a chapel. Venerable ledger slabs stud the ancient pamment and tile floors. Both rood stair openings are still open, as are the stairs between them. The big royal arms is for George I, but the achievement is that of Queen Anne. The church's single hatchment is set on the north side of the arcade, west end.

St Mary from the east

Tower from the south

Tower west door & window

Colman tomb

Nave looking east and box pews

Pulpit, rood stairs doorways

Interior looking west

Chancel and paintings

Painted C13th reredos

Colman monument (1743)

The font

George I royal arms

South aisle piscina

BRETTENHAM ST MARY the VIRGIN — B3, TL 967 542

The south west tower adds a distinctive touch to St Mary

Brettenham lies in an extensive area of unspoilt Suffolk countryside between the north-south running A134 and A14 trunk roads. A place of timeless villages and gentle, evocative scenery. There is no missing St Mary, it stands proudly at the main road junction in the village, with its rare south west tower as the focal point. Like most of these towers, it doubles as the porch and main entrance. There is an impressive outer doorway with recessive mouldings and a worn niche above. At the base is flushwork and at the top, battlements. The inner doorway has medieval doors with foliage carving around the outside, a stoup stands to the east. The tower is C14th, and the belfry windows have Decorated tracery; the rest of the church is also largely C14th. There are no aisles or other buildings off the main structure. The nave boasts windows with good Decorated tracery, including mouchette designs, but the chancel has Perpendicular windows and may post-date the nave or be an earlier structure with windows renewed in the C15th. An expanse of uninspired Victorian benches in the nave greets the visitor inside, just a part of much renewal undertaken here in the C19th, but the chancel is attractively laid out with several good features. The font is an excellent, octagonal late C14th example mounted on a substantial two-step plinth. On the bowl panels are intricate carvings of ogee arches with crockets and cusps, and the rim is crenelated and incised with crosses. Below the bowl the heads have been vigorously defaced. Surmounting the font is a delightful C17th conical cover. In the nave south east corner is a medieval piscina, indicating that a chapel was once in place there. Nearby is an exemplary war memorial with flags. The pulpit is Victorian, but the reading desk to the south incorporates some old parts. In the north wall by the pulpit is the sealed lower doorway to the rood loft. Most of the church's glass is C19th and by Ward and Hughes, and, although the quality is reasonable, some deterioration is now apparent. In the chancel is a window containing C15th glass fragments. The C14th chancel angle piscina is a fine example and its carvings, in part, bear similarities to those of the font; they are probably contemporary. By the piscina are drop-sill sedilia. To the north of the altar is an excellent inscription brass of 1611 for Thomas Weniffe and on the chancel south wall is a tablet of 1658 for a relative, Edoardus Wenyeve. On the east wall are two unusual, large paintings of 1881, with biblical themes. The attractive barley-twist altar rails are C17th.

Tower from the south | View from the north west | From the east | Chancel doorway

Interior looking north east | Blocked rood loft doorway | War memorial | Ward & Hughes glass (1866)

Chancel arch and chancel | Chancel & Thomas Weniffe brass (1611) | Painting on tin in chancel | Chancel angle piscina

Old glass in chancel window | Edoardus Wenyeve tablet (1658) | Nave looking west | The font

BROME ST MARY

C2, TM 145 764

Brome St Mary, a vision of Victorian Gothic

Time changes everything. A familiar observation, but very apposite for Brome St Mary. Not too long ago it suffered from the anti-everything Victorian attitude that was prevalent until the late C20th. Now we look on the works of C19th artists, builders and fabricators with altogether different eyes, and are able to appreciate St Mary for the wonderful building it is. The reconfigurations wrought here in the late 1800's almost entirely removed the medieval face of the church, which was founded in at least Norman times. The round bottom half of the tower remains from those times, but the only other recognisable old element is the lovely C15th south porch. However, though not at all obvious, the core of the church (nave, chancel, north aisle) remains from the medieval building. Several architects and designers had a hand in the restorations, but by far the greatest contribution was made by Thomas Jeckyll (1827-1881), a man whose star has been rising in recent times as his brilliant legacy becomes better known and appreciated. Jeckyll worked on fewer than 20 East Anglian churches, but his work here is some of his most substantial and striking. He provided a new north transept, substantially rebuilt the aisle, remade the nave and chancel roofs, designed a number of furnishings and fittings, and refreshed the stonework throughout. His great flair can be seen in the details, like the angels on the transept and duotone arches above certain windows. Jeckyll's inspired designs for the pulpit, reading desk, chancel piscina and sedilia, reredos and altar rails, were realised by stonemason James Williams of Ipswich. The typical C15th font is possibly original, but its undamaged condition and finish suggest it is also William's work, as is the elaborate cover. Jeckyll was an ardent medievalist and St Mary offers a privileged view of his beliefs, imaginative mind and abilities. Yet there is more to see inside, from an earlier age, when local magnates the Cornwallis's of Brome Hall exercised their influence over the church and housed their memorials within it. These are mostly in the Cornwallis chapel, part of the north aisle. Pride of place goes to two grand tomb chests, the oldest for Sir John Cornwallis (d.1544) and his wife. The other is for his son, Thomas (d.1604) and wife Anne, and is based very firmly on the design of his father's tomb. Both are ornate and attractive. On the wall are three grandiloquent monuments to Cornwallis's, the oldest is for Henry (d.1598), with further lavish examples for Frederick (d.1662) and Elizabeth (d.1681).

| Transept angel and tower | St Mary from the south west | The other transept angel |

| The interior looking east and west | | The font and baptistry |

| The sanctuary and reredos | Sanctuary fittings | More fine objects | Henry Cornwallis, d.1598 |

Tomb chests and wall monument for Sir John, Thomas and Elizabeth Cornwallis — Nave seating

BROMESWELL ST EDMUND

D3, TM 302 506

A dull day at Bromeswell St Edmund

A first assessment of St Edmund might be coloured by the chancel of the mid-C19th, the late C20th extension to the north and the C16th porch (all of brick), but there is a much older church at the heart of the building. The nave is Norman and retains its steeply pitched roof, originally thatched. Its C12th structure is relatively untouched except for later windows. The south doorway is also Norman, and despite being less ornate than often seen, is still attractive. There is a blocked round-headed Norman window in the nave north wall, now occupied by a war memorial. The blocked nave north doorway would also appear to be Norman, despite a later pointed arch. The chancel was entirely replaced around 1850 by a brick structure, and it appears that a portion of the nave was absorbed at that time, for the chancel arch is gone and the higher of the two rood loft doorways is now flush with the end of the new chancel. The tower is C15th, with a flushwork panelled frieze at the base, with further flushwork on the parapet and buttresses. On a dark day inside the nave feels bewitchingly ancient, an impression carried over into the rest of the building, despite its much more recent origins. Several knarled and worn C15th benches still see service in the nave, though they are very frail these days. The poppyheads have been attacked by boring insects and most arm rest figures have gone. Those remaining are very badly eroded, but all that wear and tear simply adds to the stimulating atmosphere. The C15th octagonal font with its familiar design of evangelist symbols and angels on the bowl, and lions around the stem, has also been attacked, but mostly by human agency. The font sits in the shadow of a notably high and narrow tower arch. The C17th pulpit is prim and elegant, and is ornamented with characteristic arcade carving; it stands on an unfeasibly thin stem. More super C17th woodwork can be found in the chancel, in the form of robust, well-made altar rails and a most attractive communion table. The nave roof is of hammerbeam type, but is a modest construction. In all probability the Puritans removed its medieval angels, but very adequate C20th replacements hang in their place, two or three of wood and the rest plastic. The C19th stained glass is of good quality, some designed by the gifted William Wailes, although there are few windows to accommodate it. In the belfry is a rather special bell, made in Belgium in 1530 and beautified with small medallions depicting biblical scenes.

St Edmund from the north west and south west — Norman south doorway

The interior looking east — The west end — Communion rails and table

Rood loft opening — Nave roof — Roof angel — Jacobean pulpit

   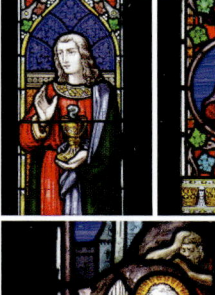 

Medieval benches in the nave — The font — C19th glass by Wailes & others

BRUNDISH ST LAWRENCE   D2, TM 271 695

Crystal clear late afternoon sunlight illuminates St Lawrence

St Lawrence stands alone and serene in a beautiful setting off tiny country lanes, a wonderful stillness all around. Brundish is much depleted from its medieval heyday, and its few houses are set away from the church. Lots of history has rolled by here, and in 1385 a significant chantry was founded, with a chapel in St Lawrence (known as St Andrew in those days). The chantry is gone, but St Lawrence still weaves its spell over inhabitants and visitors. The unbuttressed tower is Norman for three quarters of its height, with blocked slit and belfry windows, except for a typical Norman belfry window in the east wall. The impressive south porch is flushwork-fronted, with a niche. There are no aisles, but the nave is spacious, airy and well-lit by big Perpendicular windows. The porch cuts across one of these windows, but its glazing bars are still in place inside. A damaged pillar stoup stands to the right of the medieval south door. The chancel benefits from a magnificent, large east window, with sophisticated Perpendicular tracery. A tour of the interior shouldn't be rushed. Further evidence of Norman origins is provided by the ghost of the tower arch, just the outer moulding of the semi-circular arch is visible. Above it is an inspired George III royal arms, with faux candlesticks flanking the central achievement. There are several first-rate brasses to seek out, these all show figures and are of great interest. Most are for members of the Colby family, except for one for Thomas Glemham, who died in 1571, and a rather special early brass for the priest Edmund of Brundish (d.1360), incorrectly set into an early tomb recess near the pulpit. Don't miss the brass for John and Alice Colby (c.1560) in the nave, it shows their nine chidren and is elaborated with shields. The brasses are distributed between the nave and chancel. The font gives little away in its simplicity and plain finish, but is clearly old. Two panels saved from the C15th chancel screen are propped against the blocked north doorway. The robust pulpit is a C15th example, with traceried panels; above it is a later C17th tester and back plate. Towards the back of the nave are medieval benches with later backs, poppyheads and two damaged figures. Further east are box pews of 1826. Some C15th glass includes two fine figures of a king and ?lion. See also a very good angle piscina in the chancel, with sedilia alongside, a time-worn single misericord seat and two statue niches in the north east and south east window embrasures, denoting the former presence of chapels.

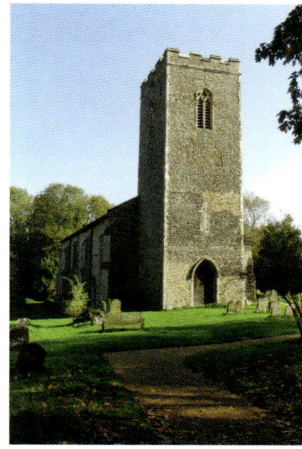

Views around St Lawrence — The porch

Interior looking north east and west — Sanctuary and east window

Pulpit and later tester — Misericord & north doorway — Medieval bench end — George III royal arms

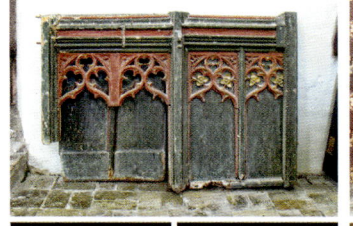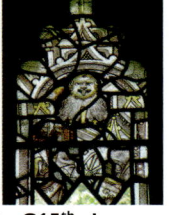

Screen panels, C15th glass — Four of St Lawrence's brasses — The font — Angle piscina, ?aumbry

BURGATE ST MARY OF PITY C2, TM 082 755

St Mary of Pity from the north west

St Mary lies deep in north Suffolk countryside that is steeped in history, with many reminders of far-off days. In woods near the church is a rare medieval ring ditch, which may have Anglo-Saxon origins; also within a mile or two are several important moated sites. Early medieval pottery from banks around the church is displayed inside. The whole atmosphere hereabouts vibrates with echoes of the past, and so it is around St Mary too, which stands alone and inscrutible in the midst of quiet lanes and footpaths. Yet this is a friendly church, keen to see visitors and to show off its merits, which are many. There are no aisles, but this is a large building, with a capacious nave and generous chancel, which are the same width. Nothing unequivocal suggests that the building was begun before the C14th, but the Decorated windows and other details might suggest slightly earlier origins. The Perpendicular makeovers that affected so many churches made little impact here beyond the provision of a south porch and a few windows. There are unusual features on the tower, small quatrefoil openings, with, above, long belfry windows, and, above these, rows of three quatrefoils on each face. The buttresses stop towards the top of the second stage. Phipson restored the church in 1865 and 1872. The configuration of the interior is interesting, with the west end being closed off by a screen. Housed here are the font, the large organ (with reredos-like panelling to its east side) and St Edmund's chapel. This western area was created by an influencial incumbent, Rev'd Appleyard, in the early C20th. He was also responsible for the 1st World War shrine in the chancel, built into and around the arch to a long-demolished chapel. This unique structure holds many items that were constructed out of shell cases, also the reverend's war helmet. It vies for attention with a remarkable tomb chest set squarely in the centre of the area before the altar rails. The tomb is for William de Burgate (d.1409) and his wife, and features on its lid arguably the finest brass in Suffolk, in wonderful, almost complete condition. On the other hand, the C15th font must be one of the worst abused examples in the county. Most of its carvings were violently hacked away, except the lions around the stem which were spared, for some reason. See also a degraded George II royal arms, a fine piscina in the chancel, a plain piscina in the nave, excellent Jacobean pulpit, some decent C19th glass, fragments of old glass, an ancient chest and other old woodwork.

The church from the west and north east — South doorway, with niche

Interior looking east — Chancel looking north east — Tomb and interior looking west — Nave looking north west

1st World War shrine — West end with font and organ — Chancel piscina — De Burgate brass

The pulpit and rood stairs — Chest, old bench and rails — George II royal arms — Victorian and medieval glass

BURGH ST BOTOLPH D3, TM 223 522

The unusually sited tower obscures the west end of the nave in this view

There is much to ponder on here at Burgh. For a start there is another very similar church just half a mile up the road at Clopton. So alike are the two that some collusion must be assumed in design and building. The site too is intriguing, St Botolph is perched on a moderate eminence in the midst of a pre-historic and Roman landscape of enclosures. St Botolph lived in the late C7th, so if the present name of the church is original, the Christians who settled here arrived very early. All that history has left a tangible mark, it can be sensed in the atmosphere, and adds considerably to the pleasure of coming here. The building itself is also rather singular, and boasts a late C14th tower off the western end of the south wall, which doubles as a porch. The rest of the church is Perpendicular, although some doorways are earlier. It seems very likely that both Saxon and Norman churches stood here, but all traces have been swept away. The greatest input into the present building came from the Victorians, who upgraded the exterior and refitted the interior, leaving only a few old items. But many of the things they retained and also some of those they introduced are of some distinction. One of the older items is met with as the church is entered through the south door, and that is a marvellous old ring handle and boss, which have somehow survived from the C13th. The gloom inside is caused by the abundance of stained glass, but this is not run-of-the-mill stained glass. Four windows are from the C19th workshop of Charles Kempe, and a splendid spectacle they make. The designer's characteristic finesse in drawing and inspired use of colour are seen to excellent effect. The other Victorian glass is also commendable. The C15th font bowl is a decent, but rather generic model, and its ornament of Evangelist's symbols and angels has been re-cut. The stem is C19th. The pulpit is a super Jacobean example, finished in characteristic C17th style. However, it had a decided list when last seen and was in need of restitution. The nave and chancel roofs are much renewed but feature an array of purposeful angels. The old sanctuary piscina has a cinquefoil head. The sanctuary was attractively refitted in the C19th with a fine set of wooden altar, reredos, panelling and rails, and an impressive mosaic floor, which extends to the chancel. Wall memorials are sparse and unremarkable, the best, of c.1850, shows a draped tablet. An old-world touch is added by C19th hanging lamps. The churchyard holds a small number of good table tombs.

St Botolph from the east and south west — Ancient ring handle and boss

The church looking east — The chancel — View west from the chancel

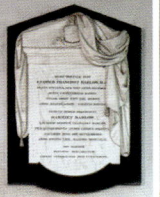

Sanctuary south east corner — Chancel piscina — The font — Vault entrance, wall tablets

C19th roof angel — Jacobean pulpit — Snapshots from the four Kempe windows

BUTLEY ST JOHN the BAPTIST D3, TM 373 501

The church from the south

Butley is located in a geographically distinctive area called the Sandlings in coastal south east Suffolk. Settlement is generally sparse and a curious, secretive ambience pervades the area. In keeping with that feel, St John stands more or less alone, some way south of its village in a large, open churchyard. An ancient church in such surroundings might be expected, and the visitor isn't disappointed, for here are clear indications of an original Norman church. The north side of the nave has no less than three narrow, round-headed windows, plus a modest, but original Norman doorway. The south side has another round-headed, slit window and a more expansive Norman south doorway. All of the old windows are blocked. It seems probable that the first church here consisted of the small nave still extant today, with perhaps an apsidal chancel, later replaced in the C13th by the one we see today. The nave is still thatched, as it must have been since its construction. The south porch is intriguing, built perhaps in the C16th in brick, but incorporating older windows. An earlier hoodmould was also emplaced over the outer arch, with lobate moulding. The unbuttressed tower was built in the C14th and is mostly of flint. Much local, brown, friable Coralline Crag stone (c.4Ma) is present in the walls of the rest of the church, adding a further distinctive aspect. Nearby Chillesford church tower is the best example of the use of Coralline Crag. C19th restorations robbed the interior of much of its character, but a few older items of interest were retained. A sanctus bell window remains above the tower arch. The C15th font stands proudly at the west end of the nave and is a typical example of its time, with lions and angels holding shields on the bowl. Perhaps its most attractive attributes are the lions *sejant* around the stem, which are full of character. The restored screen is C15th but the dado is unadorned, while above, the ogee-arched tracery is modest. North and south nave windows near the screen have medieval statue niches built into their embrasures, denoting the former presence of chapels. Stained glass in the chancel is by Lavers, Barraud and Westlake. Rood stairs in the north wall still exist behind a modern wooden door. In the south west corner of the nave is another set of ancient stairs, very akin to rood stairs; did they lead to an old gallery or into the tower? The war memorial is by Munro Cautley, whose contribution to our knowledge of East Anglian churches is inestimable.

St John from the north

Norman north doorway and window

Norman south doorway

The interior from the west end

The screen

The chancel

West through the screen

Rood stair doorway and pulpit

Mystery stairs

Window embrasure niche

The font and details of stem

War memorial

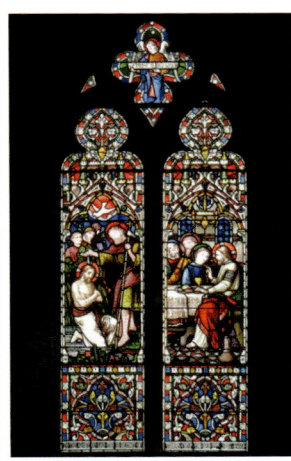
East window

BUXHALL ST MARY C3, TM 003 576

St Mary at Buxhall

For very many years, starting with an incumbent way back in the C15th, St Mary was largely the preserve of the Copinger and Hill, or on occasion, the Copinger Hill, families. They were important local landowners and had the right to appoint incumbents, and there were no less than 14 sons of the house in charge here between the C15th and mid-C20th, although the acme of their stewardship was from the C18th to the C20th. Their memorials and testimonials are found throughout the church. The Copinger Hill stronghold and sometime vicarage next door is a most imposing pile. From the outside it is clear that St Mary is a big, fairly ambitious church, despite there being no aisles, but the greyish yellow render on nave and chancel does nothing for its looks. That is somewhat compensated for by the assertive, tall, 5 stage tower, which has flushwork chequering on buttresses and basecourse. That patterning is reflected on the porch battlements. Later battlements were added to the nave and chancel walls. Most of the church is C14th and there is a fine suite of Decorated windows, the east window with its flowing tracery being a standout. By the south doorway is a renewed stoup. The north side of the church appears to be inaccessible, and is now a lawn for the big house next door. The interior is spacious and the nave is filled with an individually designed set of benches, made very competently by a lady of the Hill family in the C19th. She was also responsible for the excellent pulpit. There are many other good things to track down inside. The crenellated C14th font has crocketed arches and quatrefoils, and is delightful, but the stem is short and reduces the impact. The chancel double piscina has crocketed arches, finials and flowing tracery, and is most impressive. The continuation of this fine work over the adjoining sedilia has regrettably been lost. The latter house a C13th grave slab, with Maltese cross and double omega carving. Several windows have mosaics of C15th glass fragments, some with figures and other significant pieces. Rood stairs and doorways are still extant. Certain choir stalls incorporate old bench ends with poppyheads. The altar rails are C18th. The deteriorating George I royal arms seems to have another arms underneath. The wall tablets, many commemorating Copinger Hill family members, repay study. A nave piscina holds a lead image of the Virgin and Child, origin unknown. Recently the west end of the nave was redeveloped to accommodate modern facilities and some new fittings.

 The tower from the south
 Maltyward tomb (1796)
 The porch
 South doorway and stoup

 Looking east along the nave
 The chancel
 Nave looking west

 Rood stair doorways, pulpit
 Chancel piscina
 Nave piscina with ?lead image
 The font

 Grave slab, wall tablets
 Hill & Copinger memorials
 George I arms, Old bench ends
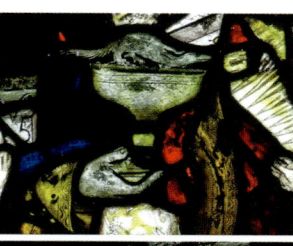
 C15th glass snapshots

CAVENHAM ST ANDREW

A/B2, TL 763 696

At St Andrew the sun gleams against a glowering sky

Make sure to have a good look at the exterior of St Andrew, for here this exercise is very rewarding. Facing the road, high on the west face of the tower, is the surviving roofline of a long-removed building. A window that must once have looked into the nave is still in place a little lower down. Speculation quickly follows as to what this building was; firstly it was notably high, which probably meant it was two storey, or, alternatively, it was the western arm of a cruciform church. The latter is unlikely as space is at a premium west of the tower. The most likely explanation is that it was a Galilee porch with a room over for ?accommodation. There is an extant one at nearby Lakenheath for comparison. The two ends of the gable between tower and nave harbour very worn blocks of carved stone that may predate the present church, which is C13th in its oldest parts. The block to the south shows two ?rabbits and to the north is a strip of dogtooth carving. There is another enigmatic block at the end of the southern arm of the gable between nave and chancel, with two carved heads. Narrow lancet windows are present in the chancel walls, with larger ones at the east end of the nave, all C13th or early C14th. Before going inside, note that the old porch leans out alarmingly. Like the exterior, the interior has many diverting features. The crackling atmosphere will immediately be appreciated, the past is very close here. But like an awful lot of the UK's rural churches, the building is little used and has become rather forsaken. The plain old font is a curious confection, whitewashed beyond appreciation. The C15th screen is modest and the later dado stencilling is very faint. Near the ricketty, panelled Jacobean pulpit is an important and rare wall painting depicting St Walstan; two figures and angels can also be seen. Opposite is a war memorial window by Jones & Willis showing St George. Much evidence remains of the structure of the rood loft. The chancel holds much of interest. The C13th angle piscina and sedilia set is attractive, the former has a crocketed arch, finial and ringed pillars. Several wall tablets line the walls, the Warrington family being prominent. A lancet in the south west corner above a blocked low-side window contains exotic medieval glass; an empty tomb recess with traces of original red colour stands nearby. Elsewhere there is an odd item, a battered, late C17th coffin plate, still attached to a section of coffin. On leaving, pause to admire the medieval closing ring on the door.

Tower west face

St Andrew from the north west

The leaning porch of Cavenham

Interior looking west

Font and tower doorway

Interior looking east

C17th pulpit

St Walstan wall painting

War memorial

Window with medieval glass

Sanctuary south east corner

Warrington tablet c.1865

Niche, coffin plate

Door ironmongery

CHARSFIELD ST PETER

D3, TM 254 565

St Peter's handsome brick tower is a fine sight

Charsfield is a very special place, it has a place in the heart of Suffolk's, and England's, story. All thanks to an author who lived in nearby Debach but based his book 'Akenfield' to a large extent on Charsfield, and the people he met and interviewed there in the late 1960's. The tale that Ronald Blythe wrote became an elegy for a disappearing world, a world where agriculture was king and events in the village revolved around the farming year, its trials and tribulations, but also its celebrations. Charsfield is not picturesque, but it still represents the soul of Suffolk, even with the gentrification brought by the inevitable influx of professional outsiders. No visit to Charsfield is complete without viewing St Peter, the central character in its story. It's a shame that the church scenes in the moving film of 'Akenfield' made in 1974 were filmed in nearby Hoo church, but that doesn't detract from St Peter's attractions. What is most striking about the church is the C16th brick tower, which looms impressively over Charsfield's main street. It contains elements retained from a forerunner, including an intriguing base course, which has a series of panels with sacred and secular monograms. A diaper pattern of diamonds enhances the tower's walls. The excellent brick porch, contemporary with the tower, has a similar base course and embellishment of diamonds, also a crow-step gable and unusual mini towers to either side. The rest of the church is of much earlier vintage, the nave north wall has a narrow, round-headed window whilst to the south is a similar blocked example, indicating C12th origin. The chancel may be of comparable age, but its narrow north window is of lancet type, indicating a C13th foundation or rebuilding. The lancet is deeply splayed inside. Later windows are Perpendicular. The interior is not grand, but is proper and harmonious, and reflects its village well. The C15th font has Evangelists symbols and other motifs around the bowl, including a representation of St Botolph. It was brutally treated by iconoclasts. The choir stalls and two nave benches were locally made, and have traceried ends and charming arm rest carvings. The roof is restored medieval and has corbels with their faces hacked away. There are two nice hatchments and two wall tablets, one of 1730 very good, the other of the late C17th more modest. Rood loft openings and stairs are still in place. Fronting the organ gallery in the tower arch are rails mounted on a beam dated 1585. Part of the old rood screen dado remains.

Views from the west and south west — The porch

View east along the church — The chancel — View west from the sanctuary

  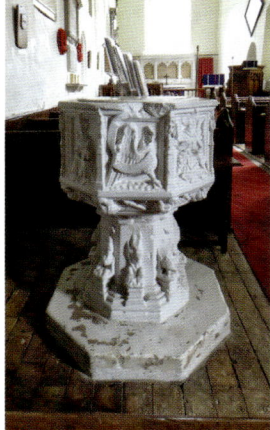 

Organ gallery and rails — Rood loft doorways and stairs — The font — Chancel window & Leman tablet (1730)

Tracery and poppyheads — Nave roof corbel — Rev'd Orgill hatchment (1837) — Norman windows

CHATTISHAM ALL SAINTS & ST MARGARET C4, TM 092 421

All Saints and St Margaret from the north east

All Saints and St Margaret may be a unique dedication, it is thought to have originated as a mix-up with names in the past, which has stuck. The building shows the scars of a long and testing life since its early days in the C14th, in particular the decay of the render does little for its looks, and many cracks and founderings run through the fabric. But All Saints bears its vicissitudes with stoic pride and its homely, rustic appearance has a melancholy appeal. The *de rigueur* tour of the exterior reveals some interesting features. The low, squat tower has clearly been reduced in height, and is very much repaired and patched, particularly with brick. Its faces are oddly featureless except for a faux-Decorated C19th west window and a brick-arched belfry window above it. The south frontage of the body of the church shows a curious configuration, apparently there are two porches. However, the one off the chancel is used as a vestry, but possibly began life as a porch, as it has a doorway opening into the churchyard. On the north side of the chancel are a sealed doorway and a bricked-up low-side window, whilst further along the nave is another blocked doorway and a turret for the rood stair. The lower of the rood stair doorways is still in place inside. The interior shows similar signs of decay to the outside, and lacks striking features, yet still emanates an enticing, antique aura. The pretty font with its bowl ornament of foliage and shields is Victorian, as is most of the rest of the furniture like the altar rails and seating, but there is a suspicion that the panels of the vestigial pulpit, oddly located in the sanctuary, may be older, perhaps C18th. The much-repaired angle piscina in the chancel and its associated drop-sill sedilia are probably C14th. On the opposite wall the embrasure of the blocked low-side window contains a superb wooden sculpture of St Margaret holding a lamb. The chancel arch was cut-down in 1770 to leave two ugly, buttress-like features. All Saints has three good post-reformation brasses, one with figures is C16th and the others are C17th inscriptions. The figurative brass shows Marie Revers and her numerous children. The inscription refers only to her, yet, strangely, the indent of her husband's missing brass is next to her. Two crude wall tablets with skulls and traces of original colour, probably C17th, can no longer tell their tale, because their painted texts have disappeared. Other features to investigate include a nice George III royal arms, a spindly C17th poor box and an attractive old chair.

All Saints porch and vestry

The church from the south east

Chancel details

East end of the church

Sanctuary furniture and fittings

Interior looking west

All Saints brasses

Slender poor box

Old chair and arm rest detail

Altar rails, pulpit

George III royal arms

The font

Low-side window and statue

CHEDISTON ST MARY   D2, TM 358 777

The church from the spacious north churchyard

St Mary is unremarkable from the outside, an impression not helped by a coating of dun render on all but the unbuttressed C13th tower (with C15th top stage), but the interior has many compelling features. Exterior features to note before seeing these gems are, firstly, a large, capped area by the nave north east wall. This is the vault of the Parkyns/Leguen de Lacroix family, originally sheltered by a mausoleum, now removed; a stone by the vault gives details of its occupants. A shallow stub of the mausoleum remains in the nave wall, and corresponding to it inside are the meagre vestiges of the local gentry's posh pew. That is now a large recess housing C18th decalogue boards and paintings of Moses and Aaron, but it retains fancy pendant ornament. The porch and southern doorways are an excellent matching C14th set, with thin, elegant attached shafts in the jambs topped by foliate capitals. By the inner doorway is an old stoup. No longer external due to being concealed by a later vestry is a lancet window with deep internal splay in the chancel north wall. It may be late C12th, but the pointed opening is not typically Norman. The interior is smart and well cared-for, and soon confounds the initial impression of having little of interest. Immediately opposite the entrance high in the nave north wall is an area of stripped back plaster which reveals, after concentrated study, a painted head which must be that of St Christopher, from the position. The C15th font is a familiar type but is a nice item, with angels and Evangelist's symbols on the bowl, and lithe woodwoses and lions around the stem. The pulpit, dated 1637, is a very fine example, with imaginative and unusual carving. It came from Cookley church when that establishment inexplicably ejected it. Some windows contain oddments of medieval, C16th and C17th armorial and other glass, some of it rather obscure, but the arms of Baxter in the east window is well preserved. A nave south window commemorating a 2nd World War pilot has delightful glass by Margaret A E Rope showing Ss Felix and George. The enchanting background work shows pastoral and rural scenes. In the chancel the singular C17th rails have pendant bulbs above alternating with sharply pointed stake-like rails below, which don't extend to the top. The angle piscina nearby is much repaired. A rare C17th volume of the Paraphrases of Erasmus, good nave roof, a window niche, two stoups, a few old bench ends with poppyheads and a super little medieval chest also reward examination.

St Mary from the east and south — South doorway

Interior looking east — Nave roof — The chancel — Sanctuary SE corner

Interior looking west — Jacobean pulpit — Old pew setting with 10 commandments — St Christopher's head

   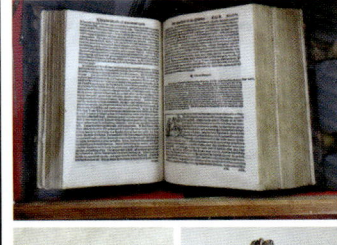 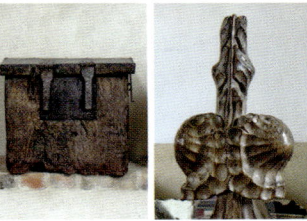

The font — Niche and stoup — Modern and C17th glass — Paraphrases of Erasmus, chest, poppyhead

COOKLEY ST MICHAEL & ALL ANGELS   D2, TM 349 753

St Michael and All Angels from the north west

The tiny hamlet of Cookley lies in lovely High Suffolk countryside. All around is deep, rural serenity, and it is hard to believe that the relative metropolis of Halesworth is only a few miles to the north east. At first sight access to the prettily sited church seems impossible without trespassing, and though the entrance is obvious enough, the necessary passage through someone's garden may deter some visitors. But that is the only way, and the gentle uphill approach is actually a very pleasant way to reach the building. St Michael's fortunes have risen in recent years thanks to remedial work in 2009, greater care being taken inside and an open door policy, so that today it presents a welcoming face to the world, very Victorian but with some interesting survivals. However, it will probably never be forgiven for unceremoniously throwing out a medieval rood screen and super Stuart pulpit during a major late C19th renovation. Fortunately the pulpit was given a new home in the nearby church of Chediston and is used to this day. Of the rood screen, a single upright was rescued from a henhouse many years ago and today offers a poignant reminder of former grandeur to the south of the chancel arch. Some other parts of the tracery are incorporated into the fronts of the choir stalls. The church building has Norman roots, there is a middle-of-the-range Romanesque north doorway which these days opens into an unsympathetic vestry of the mid-C20th; also the tower east wall contains a blocked, deeply-splayed, round-headed window, best seen internally. The lancet in the north wall indicates a C13th age for the chancel, whilst the agreeable wooden porch is modern. The interior is distinguished by fine woodwork. Towards the back of the nave are four grand old benches with poppyheads, carved ends and backs, and a few damaged arm rest figures. These include a bear and staff, a devil and, best-preserved, a languidly reclined figure. Two more plain old benches can be found in the sanctuary. The nave has a decent hammerbeam roof with wooden corbels of crowned figures holding books. Panels from box pews broken-up during the restoration were used to create the tower screen. In a frame at the back of the nave is a presentable brass of 1595 showing the Browne family. Only the well-preserved bowl of the font is medieval, it has familiar angel and lion motifs. The chancel piscina and sedilia are old but undistinguished. The handsome pulpit and flamboyant lectern are the best of the C19th fittings.

The church from the south west

The south porch

Chancel details from the south

View from the east

Interior looking east

The chancel

Sanctuary south east corner

Interior from the sanctuary

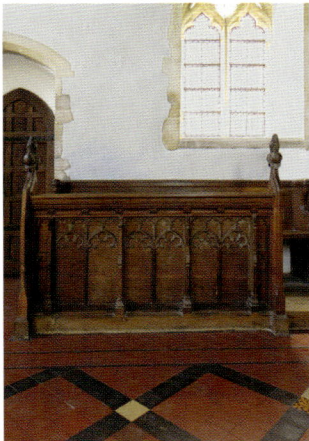
Choir stall

Norman north doorway

The font and tower screen

Browne brass (1595)

Roof corbel, nave benches

Nave bench

Pulpit and lectern

67

CRANSFORD ST PETER

D3, TM 315 647

St Peter basks in winter sunshine

Suffolk is overwhelmingly a rural county, but on a scale of rurality, Cransford is very rural. Only 160-odd people live here and even the main road through the tiny village is a narrow lane. And it is all quite lovely. As might be hoped for in such a setting, the church of St Peter is medieval and picturesquely set, but in 1848, 1864 and 1874 the church was subjected to comprehensive scourings more often imposed on urban churches. The church was apparently in a bad way in the C19th, so restoration was essential, but there are few medieval churches that contain nothing medieval inside, as appears to be the case here, except for two stone heads at the base of the tower arch. However, there are various clues externally to help establish the church's age. The C15th tower has flushwork at the base, shields set into the buttresses and C20th battlements, while the nave is probably C14th-C15th. The C14th nave south door is blocked, but curiously has a round-arched head. The chancel may be C13th or early C14th on the basis of a single lancet in the north wall, but was almost entirely rebuilt in the C19th. The north porch was rebuilt in the C19th but may retain a little older fabric. A C19th vestry stands to the south, off the chancel. There are no aisles. Despite being almost entirely post-1840 the interior is intimate, pleasantly furnished and is a good example of Victorian sensibilities, with solid work on show. There is no chancel arch or other distinction between nave and chancel. St Peter is a 'kneelers on top' church and the rows of neatly turned-out, locally-made examples make an attractive show. The dark benches have distinctive fleur-de-lys poppyheads and are probably from the 1840's, but there are two superior benches at the front with lighter colouration. One has lively carved ends, poppyheads and carvings of cranes on the arms, the latter a rebus on the village name. The reading desks and lectern are also finely worked. The stone reredos and panelling next to the altar is patterned and embattled, with IHC, pelican-in-her-piety and Agnus Dei insets. On the sanctuary side walls are Decalogue, Lord's Prayer and Creed panels. The 1848 font, in part, is a memorial to two children; the bowl is ornamented with tracery, shields, an Agnus Dei and St Peter's keys. Most of the numerous, modest wall tablets are C19th and are for members of the local Borrett clan, but on the chancel south wall is a grander memorial of 1713 for Henry and Etheldreda Dammant, in latin. An C18th chest is dated 1739.

Views from the north east and south west   The porch

Looking south east across the church   The chancel   Looking west from the chancel

Chancel south wall   Henry Dammant tablet (1713)   Borrett and Tuthill tablets (1892, 1845, 1916)

Nave benches and bench with end embellishment   The font   Candle sconce

69

CREETING ST MARY C3, TM 093 567

A Norman church once stood here, only the south door remains

The hills that rise around Creeting St Mary are not high, but nevertheless they create an attractive rolling scenery, even having their own name – the Creeting Hills. On one of them, a natural vantage point, stands the parish church. The impact St Mary makes is out of all proportion to the height of the hill, and it is immediately clear why this site was chosen for the building of a church. Indeed, pre-Christian religious groups may have used the location. Once, very close to St Mary were three other Christian churches. One, All Saints, shared St Mary's churchyard, but blew down in 1801, at which point a transept was added to St Mary to accommodate All Saints' displaced congregation. This transept was later taken down and a large north aisle under its own gable replaced it c.1884. St Olave is also long disappeared, although it was recently excavated. Creeting St Peter is still operational and stands less than 2 miles from St Mary. The south doorway, protected by a fine C15th porch with a niche and excellent flushwork to the frontage, is Norman, though restored. It has colonnettes with fluted capitals to the sides and lunettes in the arch. The stoup to the west of the doorway has fleurons in the mouldings. The tower is C14th in the lower portions, but after several vicissitudes including the collapse of a spire, the top as seen today was constructed c.1887. Substantial brick buttresses were added in the C18th to ensure that the tower did not founder downhill. The rest of the church is under one roof and may at heart be C13th, although later changes make an age assignment difficult. The late C19th saw a major overhaul throughout that largely removed the medieval elements from St Mary's interior. The restored C14th chancel piscina and the much abused C15th font were allowed to stay. The rest is mostly Victorian and little has changed since in the nave and chancel. The restorations followed Gothic Revival principles and the end result is not without appeal. Many modest memorial tablets adorn the walls and a nice brass plaque of 1908 can be seen in the chancel, but the great treasure of St Mary is a series of six stained glass windows by Kempe and Kempe & Co. These span the period 1886-1931 and contrary to the often implied loss of quality after Kempe's death in 1907, all six windows are excellent, especially the windows with King David, and SS George and Edmund. In quite another mode is a murky yet colourful Nativity of 1958 by Brian Thomas. The altar table is a super C17th example.

St Mary from the west and the north west — Norman south doorway

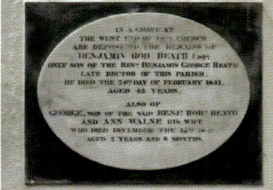

Interior looking east — Wall tablets (1851 & 1873) — The chancel — Vidal brass plaque (1908)

Chancel south east — Chancel piscina — West from the chancel — The font and cover

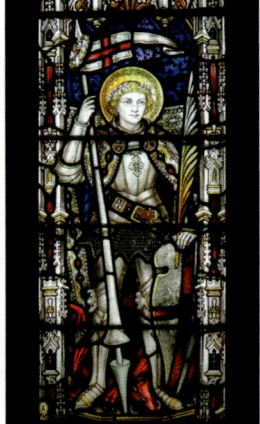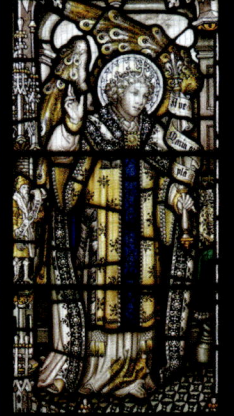

Details of four Kempe and Kempe & Co windows, and post-1907 logo

DARMSDEN ST ANDREW   C3, TM 094 529

Plain and trim, St Andrew is a classic smaller Victorian church

About 45 years ago this charming little Victorian chapel was faced with closure and selling off for, most likely, that familiar fate of other such buildings – conversion to residential use. The redundancy of 1979 was hardly surprising given that the hamlet of Darmsden shelters less than 50 persons, but those persons and their supporters were of determined brand and had no intention of losing their church. They clubbed together, bought it and brought it back into religious use. Happily, that state of affairs continues to this day and business is administered by the Darmsden St Andrew Church Trust, with one service a month. However, a recent visit suggested the church could benefit from another surge of enthusiasm, as there are signs of neglect in the interior, and it is to be hoped that the villagers and interested others will again rally round. For this, in a modest way, is an important building as it is in almost original condition and contains a characteristic Victorian ecclesiastical furnishing scheme. Architect Herbert Green designed the church in 1880 along the lines of its predecessor on the site and the overall style is Early English into Decorated. It consists of a single cell building housing nave and chancel, plus south porch and one bell, gabled bellcote. The latter contained a bell of 1710 and still may do. The setting is enviable, with views over rolling hills. An extant engraving of 1838 shows the earlier chapel and several imposing table tombs in the churchyard, but these have now gone. There would be no surprise, if, arriving on a Sunday, a visitor found the church filled with people of 120 years ago, for the building is still almost entirely of that time. For such an unpretentious building, the furnishings are aspirational and of good quality, especially the woodwork. The reredos is very fine work and shows a tryptych of St Peter, Our Lord as the Good Shepherd and St Andrew; these are flanked by panels depicting wheat and grape vines. On the east wall alongside are Victorian Lord's Prayer and Creed boards; the Decalogue boards above may be pre-Victorian. Nearby in the south wall is a simple piscina with square head and, above it, one of very few wall memorials, a brass plate for James Kemplan, who died in 1882. The openwork pulpit is small and trim and is matched by the lectern. The benches are impressive and well-built, with big poppyheads, beautifully worked. There are two war memorials, with tarnished brass plaques. The font is a big tub, somewhat Romanesque in style.

From the west and north west — West end and porch

Looking north east and south west across the church — South east corner of the sanctuary

The Creed — Altar and reredos — St Andrew — Poppyhead

1st World War memorial — The font — Piscina and Kemplan brass

DARSHAM ALL SAINTS D2, TM 420 699

All Saints' hoary walls exude antiquity

All Saints looks like it has always stood in its privileged position at the crossroads in the centre of little Darsham, and, indeed, the pointers to early foundation are clear to see. Both north and south doorways, the former crudely blocked, the latter the main entrance, are Norman. Their architecture is modest and time-worn, and detail is not easy to discern. The north doorway keystone once bore a head, but that was knocked off long ago. A coating of thick wash obscures the south doorway. To the east of the north doorway there are traces of a round-headed window, again Norman, confirming that the nave is fundamentally a C12th structure. The chancel was rebuilt in the C13th and has an original lancet window in the north wall; the three C19th east wall lancets are arranged in typical Early English style, probably following the original configuration. The C15th tower is elegant and handsome, with stepped and panelled battlements. There are no aisles, but there is a south porch, restored in 1887. The rest of the church was restored in 1879. The interior is not grand but is well cared-for and congenial. The good early C15th font has angels holding shields and lions around the bowl, lions on the stem and a rare contemporary inscription around the base. Both pulpit and holy table are Stuart, the former being a particularly refined example. A fine array of C15th or C16th benches adorns the nave, these have smart tracery and poppyheads on their ends, and the whole set is in excellent order. There is a diligently maintained brass, set between the choir stalls, for Anne Bedingfield, who died in 1641; it has impressive representations of the lady herself, plus a diverting inscription and family shields. Two other minor inscription brasses are set elsewhere. A south nave window embrasure contains a niche, denoting a former chapel in that area. The restored royal arms is for George IV. Several choice tablets beautify the church, but the pièce de résistance is a formidable memorial for Sir Thomas Bedingfield (d.1660); see also the early C19th Peyton and Purvis tablets. Members of the latter family are also the subjects of two colourful hatchments. There is much fine stained glass to admire. The oldest is a C17th Flemish roundel, but the Victorian and early C20th glass, chiefly by Cox and Buckley, is admirable. A superb figure of David with his harp is by another hand. Finally, notice a bell from HMS Darsham and the upper rood opening, the stairs up to which were found during works to harbour three skulls!

The tower from the south

All Saints from the south east

Norman south doorway

Looking south east across the church

The chancel

From the sanctuary looking west

Nave benches

Jacobean pulpit

George IV arms, Purvis hatchment (1816)

C17th Flemish roundel

King David and his harp

Anne Bedingfield brass (1641)

Thomas Bedingfield memorial (1662)

The font

DEBENHAM ST MARY MAGDALENE   C3, TM 174 632

St Mary Magdalene from the spacious south churchyard

Extensive recent housebuilding to the west of St Mary has done Debenham no favours, but the ancient centre of the village retains echoes of its medieval heyday, and St Mary is central to that feeling. Comparable old market towns Lavenham and Long Melford have grander churches, but they are also tourist hotspots, with all the pressures that entails, whilst Debenham still offers the visitor the time and space to pause and take in the atmosphere. St Mary is a large church with bags of character and some splendid survivals. Its roots are planted far in the past, the lower part of the tower is Saxon or, at latest, Saxo-Norman, and its western quoins exhibit some of the finest long and short work in East Anglia. The north face has some herringbone coursing. The lower of two slit windows in the south face of the tower may also be Saxo-Norman, and the one above, Norman. The top part is C14th and somewhat truncated following partial collapse. Running west from the tower is a spectacular C14th 'Galilee' porch; the embellished west frontage has big (restored) niches and an impressive doorway with Jacobean gates running across. There is an upper room reached by a wooden Jacobean stair. The excellent inner doorway has recessed mouldings. The arch into the nave from the tower is probably Norman. The C13th chancel has both lancet and plate tracery windows, but was restored in the C19th, whilst the nave with its big Perpendicular windows and imposing arcades was largely configured in the C15th. There are a lot of things to see and admire inside. A considerable late C16th tomb chest in the chancel is for Sir Charles Framlingham and his wife, and another in the south aisle, equally impressive, is late C17th and for John Symson. The Jacobean pulpit is the last vestige of a triple-decker. The C15th font is badly damaged and somewhat overshadowed by its large C19th cover. The C14th chancel piscina is a fine item, but the one in the north aisle is an ugly melange of parts salvaged from elsewhere, including a bishop's head. Two C17th hatchments hang on the chancel south wall. C15th glass fragments are mounted in a north aisle window, and there is good C19th and C20th glass elsewhere. John Framlingham and his wife are commemorated on a floor brass of the early C15th, whilst the plate from Charles Gawdy's coffin from 1650 is also preserved. The lower rood loft doorway is still extant. See also the fine capitals of the nave arcades and a medieval chest in the south aisle.

Tower and Galilee porch

Tower long and short work

From High Street

Interior looking east

The chancel

Chancel piscina

Framlingham tomb

Symson tomb

North aisle piscina

Font and cover

The pulpit

Interior from the chancel

Tower arch, capital, old chest

C15th, C19th and C20th glass

Processional cross (1980)

EARL SOHAM ST MARY

D3, TM 236 632

St Mary is an impressive sight from The Street in Earl Soham

St Mary exhibits its impressive west tower to passers-by on the A1120, inviting them to pause and investigate this imposing church, and indeed the pretty village of Earl Soham itself. The only approach to the church is past the tower to the south porch, and the other oddity is that the north side of the church forms the grounds of the big old rectory, except for a small area retained by the church. Couple this with the fact that the south side is thick with trees and vegetation, and the prospects for external photography are considerably circumscribed. The view from the west is the only clear and available one. All the attention externally is therefore focused on the tower, a tall 4-stage construction with a lovely west frontage. Here is a fine doorway with fleurons and crowns in the mouldings and roses in the spandrels, flanked by flushwork arcading. Above is a good Perpendicular window with ornate niches either side and another, even richer, above, with a handsome canopy. All three have plinths for statues. There follows a much smaller window with a shield above it. The stepped battlements also display flushwork. The south porch is C15th and has a worn statue on the gable and an even more decayed carving below it. The inner doorway is distinguished by paterae in the mouldings and shields in the spandrels bearing the instruments of the Passion and the Trinity. Inside, attention is drawn to the impressive set of nave benches with bold tracery, buttresses, figures and upmarket poppyheads on their ends. Despite looking initially like an authentic C15th set, the benches comprise originals removed and stored in the 1880's, which were restored, re-fabricated, augmented with new materials and re-fitted between 1928-40. It is a pleasant exercise to spot the original parts. The font is a typical, though much abused, 'East Anglian' example with the usual Evangelists symbols and angels holding shields around the bowl and lions sejant around the stem. It is topped by a handsome C17th cover. The pulpit is a superior C17th piece, with tester. The attractive altar rails are in the Jacobean style but may be C19th. The medieval roof is a robust example of king-post type with carvings in the spandrels and headless wall-post figures under canopies. King-post angels may have been sawn off. Excellent glass is by M.E.A. Rope and Burlison & Grylls. The splendid royal arms is for Charles II. There are modest piscinas in the chancel and nave south east and north east. See also a good old chest and some decent wall tablets.

Priest's door

The trees close in, from the south east

South doorway

The church looking east

The chancel

Altar and altar rails

Chancel south east corner

Nave looking west

Nave roof

The pulpit

Nave seating & details

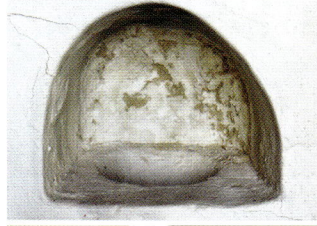

Nave south & chancel piscinas, font

Charles II arms, Abbay tablet

Rev'd Groome tablet

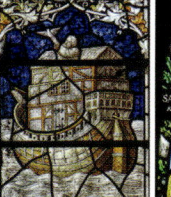
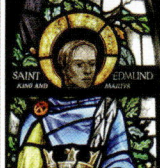
Old chest, west window & Rope glass

EASTON ALL SAINTS

D3, TM 283 587

All Saints remarkable south front

Easton lies in an attractive area of south east Suffolk, with many fine villages and sites of historical interest close by. The village can hold its head high in such company, not least for its distinctive church of All Saints. The tower changes morphology as it rises, using broaches usually seen on spired churches to translate the C13th square bottom section into an octagonal top stage. The lower stage of the tower is uncoated, while the C15th upper stages are rendered. Another unusual feature is the C19th porch cum vestry off the chancel, complete with gable cross, side windows and niche. It was designed to match the C15th south porch. The wave-like west wall of the churchyard is of 'crinkle-crankle' type, a local speciality. It is part of a considerable wall of that kind which encompasses Easton Park. To the north many years ago occupants of Easton Hall walled off the north porch for their sole use. A diverse set of windows enlivens the nave and chancel. Inside, an emotive atmosphere embraces the visitor, despite the usual Victorian makeover. Fortunately, that renewal did not result in the wholesale loss of older features and fittings. The plain C15th font stands in front of a dais at the west end which supports a considerable C19th organ, whose pipes almost reach the roof. Rood stairs are set into a nave north window embrasure and emerge higher up. They mark an early division of nave and chancel, which has now moved eastwards. The largest of three formidable wall memorials has black marble columns, pediment and cartouche; it is for Lady Mary Wingfield (d.1675). The two others are much alike, for brothers George Nassau and the 5th Earl of Rochford, and feature weeping ladies draped over urns. There are three excellent memorial brasses too, the oldest of the early C15th shows a knight in armour; the other two are for members of the Wingfield family and date from 1584 and 1601. Much attractive woodwork adorns the church. The nave box pews are early C19th, and are a handsome and harmonious set, whilst the modest pulpit is C17th. But the most extraordinary woodwork is in the chancel, where, in the sanctuary, are two prominent and exotic C17th family pews, either side of the altar. More restrained late C17th altar rails complement them. The nice piscina and sedilia are partly obscured by the south pew. The rare wooden royal arms are Hanoverian, pre-1801, and there are several hatchments. An obscure C14th figure and C15th canopy work occur in the tracery of certain nave windows.

All Saints from the north east

Tower and south porch

Chancel porch/vestry

Looking north west

The chancel

Wingfield pew, altar rails

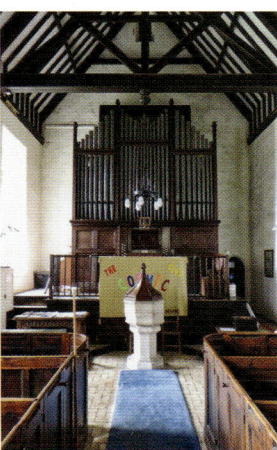
West end, font, organ

The pulpit

Pre-1801 Hanoverian royal arms

Rood stairs and doorway

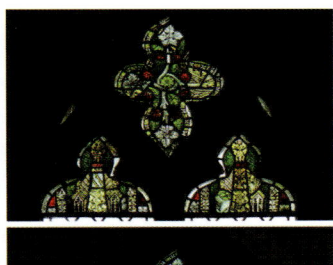
C15th canopy glass

A knight, early C15th

Radcliff Wingfield, d.1601

Mary Wingfield memorial, c.1675

George Nassau memorial, c.1823

FALKENHAM ST ETHELBERT   D4, TM 293 390

St Ethelbert's tower stands well in its fine graveyard

Falkenham is sited on the Felixstowe peninsula, which is defined by the River Deben to the north east and the River Orwell to the south west. Ipswich and its satellite villages do their best to seal off the peninsula but there is still a gap to the east and once through that a secretive and insular landscape reveals itself, its villages self-contained and independent, like Falkenham. Felixstowe and its suburbs intervene to the south and the special aura disappears. Even St Ethelbert is hidden away, its presence largely unsuspected from the road, but its discovery is rewarding. It lies in a fine arboreal churchyard with the bonus of a terrific view from its eastern edge across the Deben to the low hills beyond. The church has seen its share of tribulations and ruination has threatened at times, resulting in the loss of the original chancel and a wholesale makeover in Victorian times. A tiny brick apse was substituted for the chancel in the mid-C19th. The grand tower has passed through all of that unscathed and has stood proud since the early C15th. It has a very good west doorway with lion headstops and three shields as a lintel. The spandrels house two more shields and paterae line the inner moulding of the doorway. Unusually, the belfry windows are paired. A panelled flushwork parapet completes the attractive picture. The C14th porch was converted to a vestry at the end of the C19th. The interior lost most of its medieval features during the restoration campaigns, but the nave retains a C15th hammerbeam roof, which is complemented by a C19th set of angels on the hammers and as corbels. The C15th font of local design is in excellent order as a result of being plastered over when danger threatened. Revealed in full glory today is the familiar embellishment of lions, Evangelists symbols and angels holding shields. There was previously a gallery across the tower arch and its doorway remains at the west end of the nave. Only a thin scattering of tablets adorn the walls, the most prominent are for George and Mary Boddam, who died in 1838 and 1884 respectively. An early C20th brass records that Catherine Eaton was instrumental in a restoration undertaken in 1903. The miniature chancel has little room for enhancement but behind the altar is a decorous wooden reredos made in part, it is said, from the panels of a C14th Flemish chest. Charming patterned glass fills the small apse windows. A rather appealing chamber organ of c.1760 stands close to the chancel step.

Tower and porch/vestry

From the east

West doorway headstop

Interior looking east

Apse and arch

Altar and reredos

Interior looking north west and south west

Hammerbeam roof and angels

For Catherine Eaton

Roddam tablets (1838, 1884)

The font

Apse stained glass

Organ of c.1760

83

FARNHAM ST MARY

D3, TM 362 599

Windows are at a premium on the north side of St Mary

All churches have their own distinctive atmosphere, but sometimes the intensity of that atmosphere is more pronounced, as here at Farnham. The hilltop setting, up a steep lane that sneaks its way off the dreaded A12, begins things well. Here the Romans had a base and later the Normans built this gem of a church. A strong tang of antiquity envelopes the site, both externally and internally. Two Norman slit windows, one each side of the nave, have deep splays inside, while both tower arch and north doorway retain their semi-circular heads. The chancel is Early English and has two big, wide lancet windows and a blocked doorway on the south side, whilst the north side is windowless, although there might be traces externally of one towards the junction with the nave. The original south doorway into the nave has been converted into a window and retains a stoup to the east. Such is the instability of the footings that the nave south wall leans significantly outwards and has had to be shored up with three substantial buttresses, perhaps in the C19th. Partly obscured by the middle one of these is a blocked lancet window. That the nave roof was lowered at some stage is demonstrated by the earlier roofline on the tower and free gable to the east. The lower part of the C15th tower is formed mostly of white bricks, whilst the later top stage and battlements are of red brick. The 'feel' inside is to be savoured. It begins with the delightful brick floors. There was some restoration here in the C19th, but the ambience is firmly of the distant past. The first impression of the font is that it is a Purbeck Marble type in remarkably fine order, but closer examination reveals it to be a recent model, possibly made in the C19th to replace an original of the same form. Both rood openings are still in place, with agéd stairs ascending between them. Late C18th/early C19th box pews fill the nave, still in original condition, complete with brass handles (kept lovingly bright) and distinctive latches; the simple pulpit is a matching piece. The chancel screen has gone, but a section of its tracery was salvaged, and these days is mounted on the west wall. The chancel piscina has an interesting design, Romanesque in appearance with a semi-circular head and possibly C12th, while the drop-sill sedilia alongside, in contrast, are very basic. The chancel itself is the most restored part of the church and lacks character. Apart from the piscina, only the Victorian Decalogue boards on the east wall merit attention.

The chancel

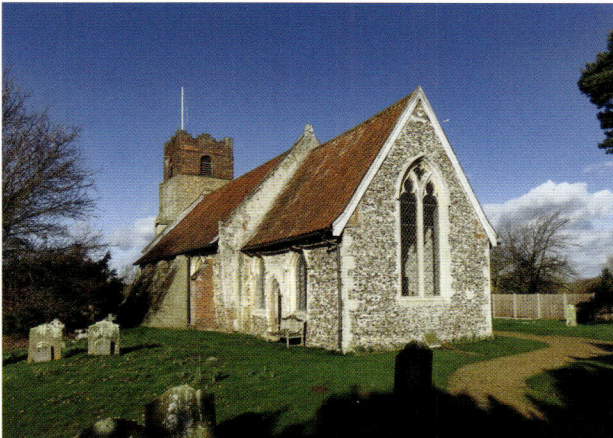
St Mary from the south east

Norman nave window

Interior looking east

The chancel

Chancel south east

Chancel piscina

Interior looking west

Rood loft doorways and stairs

North doorway

The font

The pulpit

Portion of screen, pew detail

FELSHAM ST PETER   B3, TL 946 570

Pride of Felsham – St Peter

Felsham is set in a deliciously rural area in mid Suffolk, where winding lanes eventually find their way to charming villages or hamlets. The time-honoured association of church and pub is also demonstrated perfectly here, as they face each other across Church Road. The mostly C14th–C15th St Peter is a jewel in this scene and is a lovely church to behold. The north side faces the street; thus the main entrance is here, and, fittingly, entry is made through a very fine porch, embellished with much impressive flushwork, lion stops, niches, windows with transoms and handsome buttresses. Paterae beautify the mouldings of the outer entrance doorway. To the south there is another porch, but its secondary function is reflected in its modest design and size. The tower, dated accurately to the early C15th, is another great asset, with its wide double-doored west doorway and Decorated-inspired window above. To the south is a grand stair turret. The nave is battlemented and in its north wall retains the rood stair turret, although no trace of rood stairs or doorways exists inside. Most windows have attractive Decorated designs. The chancel was rebuilt in 1873. The interior was subjected to extensive restoration in the late C19th, to designs by Herbert Green, who did much work in East Anglia. Unfortunately, his scheme resulted in the removal of almost all medieval items and the installation of a perfectly seemly and harmonious furnishing scheme, but one which, sadly, lacks character. Recent efforts have resulted in great improvements in the layout and amenities, which include a new ringing platform, kitchen, toilet and carpets. The one outstanding survival from medieval days is the C15th font, which, it is safe to say, is unique. The deep bowl at the top is handsome and unusual enough, with its tracery and shields, but the base is formed of another very distinctive C14th font bowl with green men, strange beasts, standing men and other rare motifs on its panels. A distressed medieval piscina remains in the nave at the site of a chapel. The excellent royal arms for George IV was originally for his predecessor and acquired an extra 'I' when George III died. The war memorial is otherwise unexceptional but is notable for the inclusion of a woman on the short list of 2nd World War deaths. A large organ case looms in the chancel and there is also a distinctive chair, which looks older than the 2000 inscribed on it. The oldest of the sparse wall tablets is from the late C18th and the old parish bier stands ready for the call.

The north porch

St Peter from the north west

Rood stair turret

Interior looking east

The chancel

Interior looking west

The pulpit

Sanctuary chair

George IV royal arms

Parish bier

The font

Nave piscina

For John Dalton d.1788

War memorial

FRAMSDEN ST MARY   C3, TM 200 597

St Mary from the south

First impressions of St Mary are good, it is a nicely balanced church with a fine tower and a row of pretty C16th clerestory windows to the south, with brick frames and tracery. The south porch is excellent, beautifully designed and decorated with flushwork panelling, three niches and gabled battlements. The tower is also admirably embellished with flushwork panelling at the base and flushwork quatrefoils on the parapet. Its west frontage is particularly impressive, with a wide doorway with double doors and large fleurons and other paterae around the inner moulding, and smaller versions on the outer. Above the doorway is a frieze of two shields (originally three) alternating with flushwork panels, flanked by very smart niches. More shields occupy the spandrels. Porch and tower are both C15th, while the rest of the church is largely early C14th. The dull render on the walls of the south aisle and chancel do detract a little, but the real surprise comes when the visitor walks around to the north side, to find that the nave and chancel walls are whitewashed, in marked contrast to the appearance of the south front. There is no north aisle, but a clerestory of sorts has been effected by inserting three windows in the heightened nave wall. These days the nave is rarely used, perhaps only for christenings, marriages and funerals, and services take place in the chancel. However, the nave is kept up and houses items of interest. The arcade points to the early C14th. The lower rood loft doorway is still open, and the ancient stairs still ascend, but to nowhere. The typical C15th East Anglian font is much damaged, this may have happened in the years following the Reformation, but most probably in the C17th. Even the lions on the stem lost much of their anatomy. In the aisle is a stylish, partly restored C14th piscina, with trefoil arch and pillars to the side. Also, in the aisle is the church's only wall tablet of note, early C18th and in good order, with the text on black marble. Several Victorian banners bearing improving texts can be seen above doorways and arches. In the chancel is another good piscina, of angle type, also a set of fine misericords, not original to the church, their vibrant carvings only lightly abused. There is also a handsome C17th table and old bench ends on choir stalls. Easily missed is an intriguing small Saxon figure, incorporated, on its side, into the frame of a window. Another more obscure Saxon fragment is said to exist in the aisle, hinting at the presence of a Saxon building on this site almost a thousand years ago.

 Lych gate
 Tower west front
 South porch
 Scratch (Mass) dial

 Interior looking east
 Chancel looking east
 Chancel looking west

 Nave looking west

 Misericords
 Rood loft stairs
 Chancel angle piscina

 Aisle piscina
 The font
 Saxon figure

 Around the church

FRECKENHAM ST ANDREW A2, TL 665 717

A grand statement in stone

Freckenham in the extreme west of Suffolk is a village of contrasts, on one hand the main road through it is busy, and imposes a semi-urban feel, yet the narrow lane that winds to St Andrew is quietly rural. The church is a curious mixture, there are clearly ancient factors here but also a Victorian crispness brought about by extensive renovation in the late C19th. This can be seen both inside and outside. The oval site itself is the oldest feature on view and may have been formalised as a religious site in pre-Christian times. To the north long roofs sweep down to cover the north aisle and vestry. The tower was completely rebuilt in 1884 after collapsing in 1882, but in the same form as the C14th precursor, and most, if not all, of St Andrew's windows were renewed, again probably following the original designs. The pretty porch is finished in C13th style but is C19th. There was clearly a desire to maintain continuity with the past and carry on the story that began so early. The present building was founded in the C13th, evidence for which is in the chancel, where the windows have slim internal shafts and the east window is in triple lancet form. The restored double piscina is also a sure sign of C13th work, as that particular configuration was only employed in that century. The church was extensively renewed by George Street in 1867-8. In many instances medieval and Victorian work was integrated, making discrimination of old and new difficult. Street's work included raising the chancel by seven steps and the installation of dormer windows which look down to where a rood loft may once have stood. Of the older features, the font has an inscrutable plain octagonal bowl, but the sites of the medieval locking mechanism, now plugged with stone infills, indicate its age. The C15th nave benches are one of the church's highlights but are extensively restored. Several have bold, lively poppyhead carvings, made whole with much Victorian work. One vivid poppyhead depicts a demon forcing a figure into the jaws of hell, while others show a woman at her rosary and a priest in the pulpit. On the aisle north wall is a C15th alabaster tablet, salvaged during restorations and perhaps from a reredos, showing the legend of St Eligius shoeing a horse. The barrel roofs of nave and chancel are possibly medieval, but the aisle roof is perhaps older and has angel bosses and beast corbels. An old altar table, C19th Decalogue, Creed and Lord's Prayer boards, wall tablets and good stained glass by Hardman and Lonsdale are all worthy of attention.

The porch | St Andrew from the north east | Southern aspect details

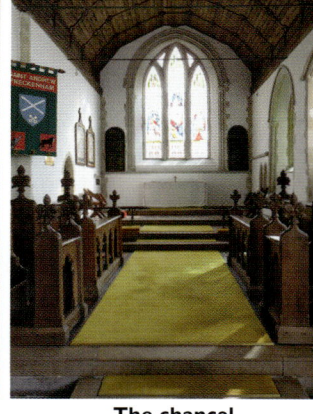

Interior looking east | The chancel | Sanctuary piscina and sedilia | The font

Interior looking west | Pulpit, woodwork | Vestry piscina, tablet, Annunciation (part) 1899

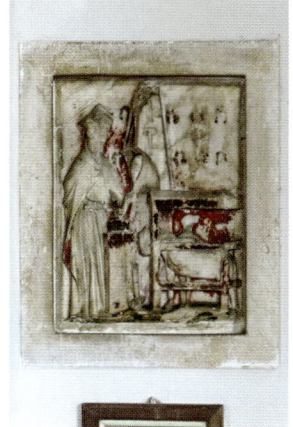

Poppyheads, benches, Lord's Prayer and Creed boards | The legend of St Eligius | Aisle roof angels & corbel, table

91

FRISTON ST MARY MAGDALENE D3, TM 413 604

A gloomy March day sees the daffodils in bloom at Friston

The small village of Friston, population c.350, lies astride the B1121 road to the south east of Saxmundham and is split into two parts, a smaller part to the east of the road around the church of St Mary Magdalene and a larger area to the south west which includes some modern housing. Between the two parts is a strip of fields. St Mary enjoys an attractive setting on a small rise and consists of west tower, nave and chancel in one, and a south porch. The antiquity of the building is confirmed by the simple, plain north doorway, now blocked, which has a semi-circular head and is Norman or perhaps earlier. The south doorway may also be Norman in the portion below the arch, but the heavy arch itself is sharply pointed and may be later. The long, low shape of the single cell housing nave and chancel is also indicative of early foundation, although the latter is usually dated as C13th and may be an extension of an C11th or C12th church. The tower was originally C14th, but was rebuilt using the original materials in 1900-1, and authorities differ on the fidelity of the reconstruction. Nevertheless, the distinctive niches, one in each buttress and three towards the top of the west face, appear to be authentic, and may or may not be in their original positions. The interior is delightful, due to a large extent to the charming early C20th decorative scheme in the chancel, which uses stylised foliate stencilling and monograms on pastel walls and ceiling to create elegant patterns, which include worthy texts. At the entrance to the chancel stands a fine Jacobean pulpit. There is no chancel arch. At the west end is a C19th balcony with seating and an organ. Very apparent is the C15th nave roof, like the skeleton of a whale thorax, with much of the structure plastered over, leaving only the dark principals and wall plates showing starkly against the white plaster. On the north wall opposite the entrance are a set of large, and very rare, wooden James I royal arms, found under the tower in pieces these were reassembled in the 1930's. The font is very odd, bowl and stem are quite plain and rather crudely fashioned but are mounted on an inverted, much older font. Near the entrance is a nice C17th table, previously used as the altar. Above the pretty reredos, the east window contains excellent glass of 1906 by Powell and Sons. There are few memorial tablets, but the one for Rev'd Baker of 1877 in the chancel is typical of its time. See also the cased cover of an early bible, an 1811 charity board and consecration crosses on the south doorway.

St Mary from the west and north west — South and north doorways

Interior looking east — The east end — Looking west across the church

West end with balcony — The roof from the balcony — The pulpit — A section of chancel wall

East window glass — C17th table, ex-altar — James I wooden royal arms — The font

GISLEHAM HOLY TRINITY E1, TM 514 885

'All things bright and beautiful'

Gisleham village is tranquil, and the countryside around gentle and mellow. The presence of a lovely round-towered church is entirely appropriate, and it is good to be here, especially on a sparkling Spring day. The simple round-headed tower arch and therefore the lower part of the tower could be late Saxon or early Norman. The topmost octagon is C14th. The blocked north doorway has lost its arch, only the jambs remain, but the capitals of these are Norman and thus date the nave. The chancel may also be Norman at heart, but the windows are C14th Decorated, as are those of the nave. However, many of Holy Trinity's windows, which form a uniform set, are Victorian replacements and therefore may be unreliable. The C15th porch has a good frontage, embellished with a curving parapet bearing shields, a niche and flushwork arcading at the base. A stoup is set by the south doorway. The thin internal shafts of the south windows could indicate an Early English element in the chancel, but the butchered angle piscina is C14th. The contiguous drop-sill sedilia alongside utilise a C13th tomb lid as a seat. In the northern corner of the chancel east wall is a large niche, the left side missing, which is hard to explain, unless the north wall was rebuilt further south at some time. The Victorians were busy inside and the red and black C19th tiling running along the church's central walkway, and the dull seating, may not be to everyone's taste. As so often, the C15th font was retained, it has quatrefoils and shields around the bowl with the unusual feature of small heads within the quatrefoils, similar heads encircle the bowl base, interspersed with vines and grapes; lions guard the stem. Of great interest are two C15th wall paintings, in the splays of two nave north windows. The Annunciation painting is in very good order, while St Walstan in the other window is somewhat less well preserved. Both subjects are attended by prominent angels. The old, arch-braced nave roof is mostly plastered. The rood beam remains in place. The church has one brass, consisting of a shield and inscription, for Adam Bland who died in 1593. Of the Victorian features, the east window stained glass of 1896 is notable. Although not signed, the style, colouration and dedicatory panel suggest it is by the Kempe workshop. There are a few panels of C15th glass in a nave north window. The Napier wall tablet of 1848 tells a sad tale, while the Bucke tablet is from the 1920's. The church is enhanced by old hanging lamps, now converted to electricity.

From the approach path | The church from the south east | Blocked doorway, porch, stoup

Looking east along the church | The chancel | Interior looking west | Piscina and sedilia

Tower arch and font | The font | Bucke tablet | Bland brass (1593)

Paintings in the reveals of two north windows | East window, St Andrew | Hanging lamp

GLEMSFORD ST MARY the VIRGIN   B3, TL 834 483

A welcome awaits at St Mary the Virgin

Glemsford lies amid fine countryside studded with grand and renowned churches, and while not quite in the same league as Lavenham, Long Melford, Cavendish etc, St Mary is a large and ambitious church, with two aisles and two substantial porches. If the hordes are too much at the famous churches, the visitor can take refuge at Glemsford and enjoy the excellent features of this likeable church. The likelihood is that they won't be disturbed. There's plenty to see from the outside of this predominantly Perpendicular building before the pleasures of the interior are sampled. The south frontage is lovely, with a tall, handsome porch covered everywhere with flushwork; three niches are set above the doorway and there is striking parapet. The porch roof is impressive, and the inner doorway has tiny fleurons and niches in the mouldings. The door itself is splendid, very old and ornamented with narrow panels with tracery. Superb flushwork embellishes both the south aisle and chancel, and bold battlements almost obscure the clerestory behind. There are chancel chapels to north and south, both with donor's dedications. The north side of the church is more subdued, with flushwork only on the chancel chapel, and the porch is a modest affair. The tower is C14th and the core of the church is also of that age, but the porches and aisles are characteristic C15th work. The chancel chapels are early C16th. Victorian restorations diminished the interior but didn't rob it of all interest. The C15th font, especially the stem, bears the scars of age and iconoclasm, but the bowl is intriguing, with a curious mixture of images, including Evangelists symbols, an angel, and bishop's and king's heads. There are three wall memorials that are worthy of attention, from the late C17th, late C18th and early C19th; the late C17th Kerrington and Knight memorial is particularly showy. Also, on the wall is a stylish and unusual war memorial. The pulpit is a gracious Jacobean model with typical panelling, whilst the carved supports of its book ledge are more imaginative than is normally seen. Nave and south aisle roofs are modern, but the north aisle has a very fine late C15th/early C16th tie beam example, with carved beams and wall posts, a few of the latter retain mutilated figures. An extraordinary C14th chest, with stout iron bands and mellowed wood resides in the north aisle, below a set of early C19th Lord's Prayer, Decalogue and Creed boards. Both rood stair doorways can still be seen, now blocked.

South porch

St Mary the Virgin from the east

Tower gargoyle

Looking east

The chancel

Looking west from the chancel

View across nave to south aisle

Around the rood stair doorways

The pulpit

North aisle roof

Old chest

The font

Kerrington & Knight tablet, late C17th

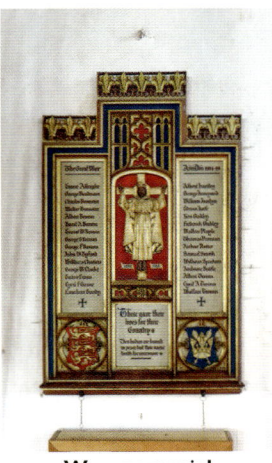
War memorial

GOSBECK ST MARY

C3, TM 150 556

St Mary's south west tower/porch looms large over the small church

Isolated churches are a feature of East Anglia and St Mary at Gosbeck is a notable member of that group. The tiny straggle of houses in the main area of population is some way off and St Mary has only one building nearby. The charged atmosphere created by the remote setting is quite tangible, especially as the churchyard is completely enclosed by a tight ring of trees. The bold C14th tower with its later Perpendicular parapet with flushwork and pinnacles seemingly strayed here from a much bigger building, and it dominates the small church beneath it. The tower's setting at the south west corner is unusual, and as with so many others in that position, the base is both a porch and the main entrance. Above the outer doorway is a delightful niche, with an ornate square head and stool for an image. Victorian restoration imparted a freshness to the stonework of the nave and chancel that belies the church's antiquity, but St Mary's true origin is suggested by the quoins in the nave's north wall, which feature 'long and short work', that totem of Saxon building. Doubt has been cast on the authenticity of this work, and the quoins may have been reconstructed, but it is probable that they reflect the form of the original corners of a late Saxon or early Norman nave. Further evidence for this age assignment is provided by the simple, unmoulded, round-headed north doorway, and a slit window near to it, with wide internal splay. A small Victorian vestry, with brick quoins, abuts the chancel north wall. Inside all is compact and well-maintained, with a strong tang of the Victorian age. The nave has an old but extensively restored hammerbeam roof. The chancel roof was made to match in the late C19th. Various wooden bosses are mounted on the hammer ends of both roofs, and there are angels too at their intersection. The octagonal font is a generic Victorian example with quatrefoils on the bowl, having flowers and leaves at their centres. The rim is crenellated. The pulpit is Jacobean with a recent stone base, but appears to have been reconstructed at some point, although it retains its characteristic central arches. There is no chancel arch or screen, but part of an old screen dado survives and is mounted on the chancel wall; it bears intricate tracery. A screen of 1909 divides off the west end of the nave. The window glass is quite smart and is the work of Heaton, Butler & Bayne, and Worrall. The parish bier is dedicated to the fallen of World War 1. The reredos is C20th and has panels painted in the medieval style.

St Mary from the east and north east   **Norman door, 'long and short work'**

Interior looking east   **The sanctuary**   **Interior looking west**

Norman window   **Roof looking west**   **The pulpit**   **Section of rood screen**

The parish bier   **The font**   **Glass by Heaton, Butler & Bayne**

99

GREAT ASHFIELD ALL SAINTS C2, TL 995 677

All Saints red porch offers a splash of colour on a dull day

Great Ashfield comprises a straggling patchwork of houses spread over a wide area, the remnants of a larger medieval settlement. All Saints, located in one of several small groups of houses and farms in the parish, has just a few houses for company, but not far away is the degraded motte and bailey of a Norman castle and to the south east is the skeleton of a once important 2nd World War airfield, which began life in the earlier C20th global conflict. All Saints itself is not a grand church, but the presence of a north aisle and moderately ambitious brick built C16th south porch speak of prosperous days in the past. Today it is a well-maintained, cherished church with keen echoes of its medieval and pre-Victorian past. Though restored in Victorian times, including a part rebuilding of the chancel and south wall, and extending the Perpendicular north aisle, many important earlier features were retained inside. Most of the basic fabric is C14th and C15th, but the south doorway and a chancel lancet date from an earlier church. The tower is C14th, with a perky mini-spire, west doorway, stair turret to the second stage and some flushwork at the base. The porch frontage is ornamented with narrow flint flushwork panels, a niche, stepped parapet and crumbling sundial. The bold north doorway is blocked. The short nave is filled with benches and other fittings, which creates a slightly claustrophobic feel. The arcade is mounted on stubs of the old nave north wall, as is the font. The latter is a solid, plain example of indeterminate age, but clearly old and possibly pre-Decorated in origin. The undoubted highlight of the interior is the woodwork. The Jacobean pulpit is a marvellous piece of 1619, with a splendid tester and panelled box, with arcading and diamond ornament. The legs are bulbous and finely chiselled. Next to the pulpit is an excellent little prayer desk built using C15th materials, on the desk end are a winged beast and carvings of blacksmith's tools. The reredos and altar may be contemporary with the pulpit and the reredos features similar panelling. In the east wall is a C14th ogee headed niche and the north wall lancet nearby has a deep splay. The altar rails are a fine C17th set. There are many C15th benches in the nave, one with tracery and other motifs on the ends; most have posh poppyheads and damaged bench end figures. Vibrant glass by A.K. Nicholson adorns the east window. Rood stairs are in place and both doorways open. On the walls are four hatchments. There is lots more to discover in this first-class church.

Porch and tower | From the north west and west

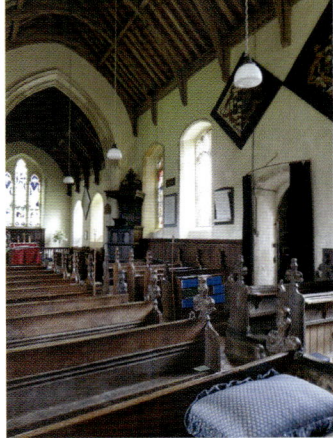

Interior looking south east | The chancel | Interior looking west | The font

The east end | Rood stair doorways | USAF memorial chapel | Sanctuary north

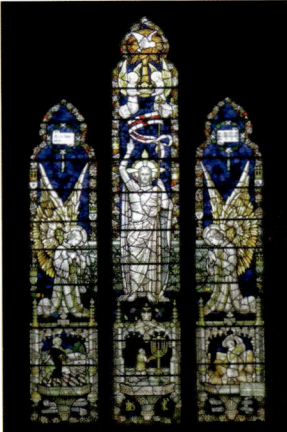

The pulpit | Old benches | Reading desk near the pulpit | East window

GREAT BARTON HOLY INNOCENTS   B2, TL 889 660

A tall tower and a fine setting – Holy Innocents at Great Barton

Holy Innocents is a big, appealing church, one of only five with this dedication in the country. The standout feature is the C15th tower with chequerboard pattern flushwork at the base and a particularly attractive frieze and parapet. The latter has stylish flushwork panelling, shields and stepped battlements. The frieze consists of skilfully worked patterned roundels. The layout of the church is C15th aisled nave with grand 16-window clerestory, C13th chancel and south porch. A tall stair turret in the north east corner of the nave projects beyond the clerestory roof. The chancel has a priest's doorway to the south with nook shafts, next to it a tomb recess with substantial arch, plate tracery windows and east buttresses with pinnacles. The C15th porch boasts a sundial, brick parapet and brick and flint arcading at the base; the front is rendered. The size of the interior is impressive and fine features can be found amongst what is a dominantly Victorian (1850's) furnishing scheme. The arcades are markedly different, that to the south is early C14th and has one octagonal and two round piers, and capitals with fleurons, whilst that to the north has composite late C15th piers that flow into the arches. The medieval font has a deep, plain octagonal bowl on a stem and four pillars, but it is the tall, finely worked cover that draws the eye. It is modern but finished in the Gothic style and is an admirable piece. The nave benches form a marvellous set and were constructed in the mid-C19th, some have C15th bench ends. The ends of the central two ranks of benches are enriched with neat and varied tracery, and all have poppyheads. The front two benches have dogs on the arms. The nave roof is C15th, with headless angels. In the sanctuary is a super C13th piscina with ogee arch, trefoil, crocketed gable and pinnacles with heads at their base; drop-sill sedilia are alongside. A plain, C14th, kennel-shaped piscina resides in the south aisle. An impressive memorial for Sir Henry Bunbury (d.1860) is set on the north wall of the chancel, and other Bunbury memorials form part of a small but diverse range of wall tablets in the church. An array of high-class C19th and C20th stained glass beautifies the building, by such as Heaton, Butler & Bayne, and the Morris workshop. Exceptional windows can be seen in the south aisle, and in the north aisle are fragments of C15th glass. The entrance to the rood stair turret is behind a curtain in the chancel. Part of an old rood screen closes off a vestry at the west end of the south aisle.

Tower and porch | From the south | Chancel doorway and tomb recess

Interior looking east | The chancel | The interior from the sanctuary

South and north arcades, benches | Font and cover | Bunbury memorial (1860)

  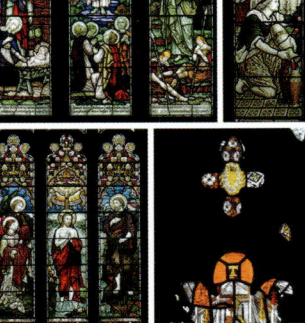 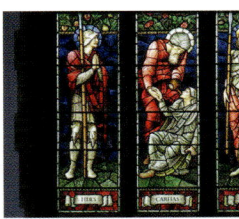 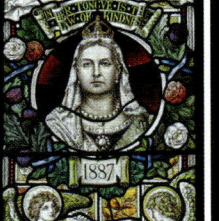 

Chancel piscina | Aisle piscina, wall tablets | Highlights of Holy Innocents superb stained glass

GREAT BRADLEY ST MARY the VIRGIN   A3, TL 674 531

St Mary's evolution is reflected in its varied appearance

St Mary the Virgin at Great Bradley, in the far west of Suffolk, may not win too many prizes for beauty, but it lacks nothing in individuality and character, and the setting on a quiet lane away from the village is very congenial. A coating of weathered render does nothing for the tower, but the lighter coloured variety on the chancel is rather more cheerful. To complete the patchwork effect, the south wall of the nave is uncoated flint- and stonework and the south porch red brick. There are ancient roots here, the church has two fine Norman doorways into the nave, a rather unusual and impressive south doorway and, as is so often the case, a more modest north doorway. The southern one is protected by a slightly odd, but appealing, C16th brick porch with a frontage pockmarked with niches, a high, stepped gable and square-headed doorway. The C14th tower has a battlemented stair turret that projects above the parapet, and lions and shields on the buttress setoffs; internally there is a fireplace for baking communion wafers and bread that vents through a flue set low on the north face of the tower. The chancel is from around the end of the C13th, it has a priest's doorway and was shortened from the east in the C18th, the east wall being reconstructed in brick, brown ferruginous stone, flint and limestone blocks (?quoins). Much of this material was probably recycled. Two apertures below the east window have been infilled with bricks. The interior is clean and uncluttered, and all the features are easily seen and appreciated; an air of antiquity prevails. The chancel arch has Norman jambs, but the original arch has been replaced by a later pointed one. To the north of the arch is a substantial Jacobean pulpit, looking all the bigger for being in a small church. It has a sunburst tester. In the south nave wall, adjacent to the chancel arch, the site of the old rood stairs is outlined as indents in the walls. The remains of a piscina can still be seen. Another gouge is located in a corresponding position in the north wall, also with traces of a piscina. The C14th font bowl has quatrefoils centred with fleurons, and shows substantial damage sustained when the medieval locking mechanism was removed. A very fine set of sedilia which probably included a piscina was truncated when the chancel was shortened; a single sedile remains. Four simple tablets in the chancel record 74 years service as rectors by members of the Wilder family. The east window glass movingly commemorates a Wilder killed in the 1st World War. A parish bier survives.

From the west and north east — Norman south doorway

The interior from the west — The chancel — The nave looking east

Site of rood stairs — Font, organ, tower arch — Truncated sedilia — Nave south piscina, aumbry

    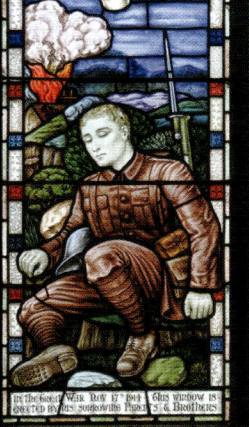

The Wilder dynasty of rectors — The pulpit — Bier — In memoriam, Reginald Wilder

GREAT GLEMHAM ALL SAINTS   D3, TM 339 616

All Saints on a fine Spring evening

Great Glemham has no great claims to fame but here is the essence of England, a pretty (but not 'chocolate box') village in mellow countryside, home to 200-odd souls, which retains a venerable pub, a red telephone box utilised now for community purposes, and of course a fine medieval church in All Saints. The mainly C14th building stands on the edge of the village, with attractive open vistas beyond. The setting could hardly be better. The tower is a familiar type, four-square and four-staged, with flushwork parapet and battlements, the string course below set with small heads, gargoyles and other motifs. It looks higher than it really is due to the low stature of the rest of the church. The northern buttress carries a niche, with another one set above the west window. The south aisle is associated with C13th arcade piers within. The north porch is constructed of split black flints, with a pretty niche with shields above the outer doorway (matching the one on the tower west face), and flushwork panelling at the base. The inner doorway has a flattened 'Tudor' head and small head stops, with a stoup to the east. Another 'Tudor' doorway, made of moulded brick, once opened into the chancel, but is now blocked. The chancel has a broad lancet window which suggests a mid to late C13th date. A special treasure is the focal point of the interior. This is a C15th Seven Sacrament font, in remarkable order. The eighth panel of the bowl depicts the Crucifixion. These East Anglian specialities are all defaced to a lesser or greater degree, but the Great Glemham example is amongst the best preserved. There are missing heads, but the carving remains strong and detailed. A lily crucifix can be seen on the stem. Traces of colour are present, also on the blocked rood stair doorway in the nave north east corner and the basic C13th piscina in the chancel, which has drop-sill sedilia alongside. The rood stair doorway is especially interesting on account of its embellished head, which features carved, coloured blocks with a floriate design. The sturdy, arch-braced nave roof is restored medieval, with much original work, including wall plates and some bosses. The Victorian angel corbels bear very melancholy expressions. Excellent early C20th glass can be seen in the east window and elsewhere, by Powell and Sons, and there is C15th glass in the chancel, including Eucharist and Passion emblems, and a cage-like structure of uncertain affinity. The few wall tablets are plain, but interesting. George Crabbe the poet ministered here in the late C18th.

All Saints from the west and east   **The north porch**   **North, chancel & south doorways**

Interior looking east   **The chancel**   **Interior from the chancel**   **Wall tablets**

Sanctuary south east corner   **Sanctuary piscina**   **Seven Sacrament font and close-up**

Rood stairs doorway   **C15th and early C20th stained glass; latter by Powell & Sons**   **Solemn roof angel**

GREAT SAXHAM ST ANDREW B3, TL 788 628

Crisp winter sunshine bathes St Andrew

Few settings in East Anglia are more atmospheric and drenched in the past than that of St Andrew at Great Saxham. A sequestered lane leads to a rich post-feudal landscape, with the big house nearby, for here is a classic hall/church association. There was a Norman church here, and maybe one before that, established when the manor came into being. The Norman evidence is the Romanesque north and south doorways, with, oddly, the north being the more imposing; maybe that was once the main entrance. The short, high nave retains typically Norman dimensions, despite later rebuilding. The south doorway is protected by a modest C15th porch, which retains original elements, like the roof. St Andrew was subjected to three periods of renovation and reconfiguration, in 1798 by the patron William Mills, again in 1820 when new windows and other changes were wrought, and finally in 1869 there were 'major alterations' which included adding an organ chamber and a vestry butted up against the south wall of the C15th tower. The 1869 campaign left a superficially Victorian interior, but there are many interesting older items here. The font is in very good condition for a C15th model and appears to be recut. There are quatrefoils with central floriate bosses on the bowl. Nearby above the north doorway are good, if dark, royal arms for Queen Anne and above the south doorway is a hatchment for Thomas Mills. Also, at the west end are a number of medieval benches of three different designs, charmingly rustic and time-worn, with thin poppyheads. The west window contains a mosaic of outstanding Swiss and German C16th and C17th glass, largely miniature pieces but a very important collection. The east window also contains post-medieval foreign glass of significant quality and completeness, the pieces and scenes here on a larger scale than those of the west window. C19th glass includes settings by Lavers & Barraud, Ward & Hughes and Heaton, Butler & Bayne, some of high standard. The brass eagle is dated 1818, the pulpit to the south of it is Stuart, with typically carved panelling. In the chancel floor is a tomb lid in which are set John Eldred's brass effigy and a complete set of inscriptions and shields. On the wall nearby is another memorial for the man, with bust; he was a famous merchant and traveller of his time and died in 1632. Other wall tablets are of moderate quality. Chancel stalls and the Mills family pew incorporate carved C18th panels. Some of the old tiling in the chancel is patterned.

The tower

St Andrew from the north east

Porch, north and south doorways

Interior looking east

The pulpit

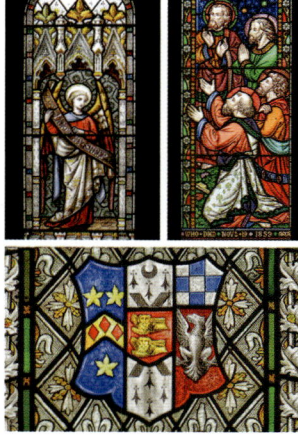
Ward & Hughes, Lavers & Barraud glass

The chancel

John Eldred (d.1632) brass and wall memorial

East and West window glass

Stall, chair, Anne royal arms

Mills, Magnay, Dawson tablets

West from the sanctuary

Nave benches and detail

The font

109

HAUGHLEY THE ASSUMPTION of the BLESSED VIRGIN MARY C3, TM 026 623

The church from Duke Street

St Mary stands in an area steeped in history. Apart from the church itself, which is mainly C14th and C15th, there is a wonderfully preserved site of a Norman castle just to the north, with motte and bailey clearly delineated, and an intact moat around both. An outer bailey enclosed the whole site and extended south. The present church stands in this extended area; perhaps a Norman forerunner was also sited here. Haughley itself is a fine old village and retains many of the amenities once common to many villages. St Mary has great character, much of it attributable to the south west tower, which has a grand outer doorway and may be C13th in its lower portions (see the original east and west windows, with Y-tracery). There is a lean-to south aisle with imaginative Decorated windows and bold gargoyles. The chancel was revamped in the C15th with posh Perpendicular windows. There is an eight-window clerestory. A C19th vestry off the north west wall of the nave was joined in recent years by the 'Castle Room', constructed sensitively to blend in with the existing church fabric; these two buildings house modern amenities. The interior is extensively Victorianised, and most furnishings are of that period, but hints of St Mary's medieval past peep through here and there. The font is a lovely example of C15th craftsmanship, with bold carvings on the bowl of Evangelists symbols and angels holding shields. The stem is also worth close examination, here are proud lions and mysterious men of the woods. Two excellent, though quite different, C14th piscinas can be seen in the chancel and aisle. The chancel example has a delicately worked ornate head with ogee arch and trefoils, while the one in the aisle has a cusped arch. There are many wall tablets, the older and more elaborately worked C18th tablets are for members of the Smyth family, while the more numerous and simpler C19th sarcophagus type are for Crawfords or Wards. The Crawford tablets are grouped together on the aisle south wall. The nave and aisle roofs are outstanding, and very different. The restored nave roof is probably C15th and has substantial, castellated tie beams and arch braces; also large floriate bosses. In contrast, the C16th lean-to aisle roof has crested major timbers founded on C19th angel supporters, with bosses and spandrel ornament. The chancel barrel roof is C19th. There are five hatchments, ranging in age from 1758 to 1835. The distinctive, delicate glass of 1860 in the aisle east window is by Kings of Norwich.

| The south west tower | St Mary from the north west | Main entrance through the tower |

| Looking east along the church | The chancel | Interior looking west | Aisle piscina |

| Chancel piscina | The font | Wall tablets |

   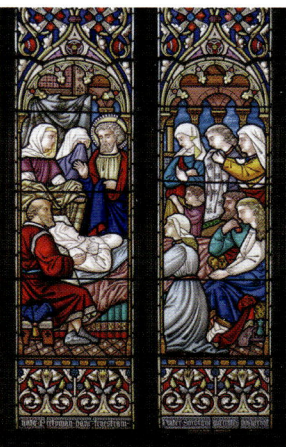

Aisle and nave roofs, boss and aisle roof angles   Hatchments   South aisle east window

HAWSTEAD ALL SAINTS

B3, TL 855 592

Hawstead church from the south east

All Saints is quite simply a terrific church, there isn't nearly enough room here for the photographs and text needed to do it justice; a visit is essential. Even without its crowning glory, the monuments and memorials in stone, wood and brass, this would be an outstanding church. To begin with, the setting is pleasing and there is plenty of appeal in the exterior. Admire the two very similar middle-of-the-range Norman doorways to north and south with their chevron adorned heads. Also the fine early C16th tower with exquisite flushwork, ornamental and heraldic panels at the base and on the parapet, and prominent stair turret extending beyond the stepped battlements. The west face is a grand composition with large Perpendicular window and embellished doorway. The interior is a treasure house of commemorative art, packed with tombs, vast monuments and beautiful wall tablets. Many are in the opulent chancel, but they are distributed around the whole church. This exhibition of the sculptor's and stonemason's craft is so overwhelming that it is easy to overlook the brasses, woodwork, stained glass and other super items here, but that would be a mistake. Of the monuments, there are three vast and extravagant examples in the chancel by the cream of C17th sculptors. The one for Sir Robert Drury from the early C17th against the north wall is by Nicholas Stone. Opposite is an exquisite monument by Gerard Christmas for 14 year old Elizabeth Drury, who died in 1609. The figure of the reclining girl is wonderfully realised. The final mega-monument is for Sir Thomas Cullum, an enormous and lavish late C17th piece whose full description would take several pages. Surrounding these three monsters are smaller but no less impressive memorials for Drury's, Cullum's and others. The oldest memorial is a remarkably preserved tomb and effigy of 1271 for Sir Eustace Fitz-Eustace; near the pulpit stands the mid-C16th tomb of Sir William Drury, it has fine brasses on the lid. More resited brasses are on the wall nearby. The copious C19th and C20th glass is exceptional, by designers like A.K. Nicholson and Henry Holiday. There is some fragmentary older glass but several apparently old roundels and panels are clever reproductions. On top of the restored screen is a Sacring Bell. There is splendid woodwork of various ages; see the nave roof, pulpit, lectern, communion rails, cherubs above the hymn board, choir stalls, old benches and reset poppyheads; also an old wall painting and hatchments.

| All Saints tower | The church from the north west | Norman doorways |

| The interior from the west | The chancel and monuments | The interior from the east | Pulpit and Wm Drury tomb |

| Wm Drury brasses | Nave & chancel roofs, chest | Hymn board cherubs, old poppyheads | Elizabeth Drury tomb |

  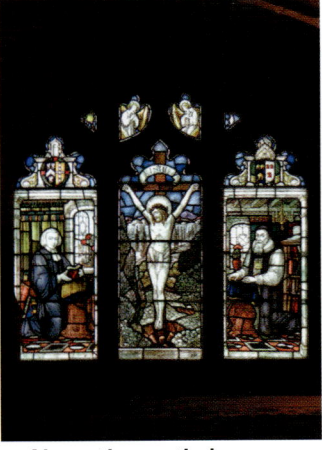  

| Eustace tomb and 2 Drury monuments | Above the north doorway | Examples of modern & ancient glass | The ?Norman font |

113

HELMINGHAM ST MARY C3, TM 190 576

Long winter shadows creep over St Mary

It is curious that the alphabet should throw up two of the best Suffolk 'monuments churches' in succession, for here at Helmingham is another wonderful display of great memorials and the skill of sculptors and stonemasons. The church is literally filled with memorials and monuments to members of the Tollemache dynasty, who still reside in the impressive Helmingham Hall nearby, and have done for over five centuries. St Mary itself must take some share in the limelight, for it is a fine building, with an especially good tower. The roots of the church go back to the C13th, although only the south doorway provides evidence of that. Most of what we can see externally is C14th and C15th, with a considerable Victorian overprint which included refacing the exterior and renewing windows, thus creating a deceptively crisp sheen. The Victorians were also very busy inside and almost all the opulent fittings are from that era. The tower is tall and assertive and detailed records tell us it was begun in the late C15th. The strongly Catholic tone of the carved inscription at the base confirms the pre-Reformation date. Intricate flushwork enlivens the stepped and pinnacled parapet (dated 1543) which is further enhanced by shields and secular and religious monograms. The west doorway is impressive and is flanked by two niches. Just above it is a frieze with an arcade interspersed with more monograms. A dormer in the nave roof was inserted to accommodate the height of an immense monument. The smart porch is C15th, with flushwork at the base, flushwork gable, niche and shield. The interior is a riot of monumental art, most of exquisite quality. The only medieval items are the nice early C16th nave roof and the superb C15th font, in such undamaged order that recutting must be suspected. There are lions and shield-holding angels on the bowl and superior lions around the stem, very unusually perched on stone heads. Victorian mural texts are everywhere. There are too many memorials to detail fully in the little space available, so the following are highlights only. The most awe-inspiring is on the south nave wall and is for a line of Tollemache's, dated 1615; the dormer window was inserted to accommodate it. Opposite is the opulent monument for one of several Lionel Tollemache's, dated 1640. Two lovely mid-C18th Classical memorials reside on the chancel north wall, a similar example is in the nave. A fine tablet bristles with weaponry, and many of the rest are superb examples of memorial art. Try and see them all.

The top of the tower   From the west   Porch and dormer window

Interior looking east   The chancel   The nave from the chancel steps   West end, tower arch

Fabulous monuments and memorials, all for Tollemache's and dated 1615, 1640, c.1804, 1810 and mid-C18th

For Sir Lionel Tollemache, 1729   Early C18th tablet; 2 Tollemache memorials   The font   Glass of c.1845

115

HEMLEY ALL SAINTS

D4, TM 285 423

Trim and prettily set, Hemley All Saints

Poised at the edge of marshes bordering the River Deben, on a lonely lane that leads through them to the river, the setting is everything at Hemley All Saints. The area around is empty and evocative, yet the immediate vicinity of the church is verdant and intimate. The building is not grand, but is nevertheless nicely balanced and possesses a mellow brick tower of around 1500 that looks well in sunshine. It is ornamented by diamond diapering in dark brick, and has a prominent stair turret to the south. The rest of the church represents a rebuilding of a dilapidated C14th original in 1889, but it seems that much of the earlier fabric was reused. Thus, to all intents and purposes, All Saints is a Victorian church with a medieval tower. However, the C14th south and blocked north doorways were retained for the 1889 church. The C19th windows follow Decorated patterns and the mixed fabric was finished in crazy-paving style. The porch with its intricately carved barge boards, steep roof and open wooden windows is an attractive feature. The area is popular with walkers, so All Saints benefits from some 'passing trade'. Inside, all is neat and well-maintained, and services are held every week. Very little is of any age, but the big square Purbeck Marble font bowl has primitive arcading that suggests it is older than the classic C13th examples of that type common throughout East Anglia; it may be C12th. The plain legs and thick stem appear to be younger. Unfortunately, repairs to the bowl were clumsily effected using unsuitable cement or filler and this detracts significantly from the font's appearance. The design of the benches was based on that of the C15th set that preceded them, which were past saving. The dark wood reredos is intriguing, and at first sight resembles a large, ornate C18th sideboard. It has languid putti either side and in the middle, a lamb lying on a cross on a book sealed with the Seven Seals. This latter may indicate a religious, rather than secular, origin for the piece. In front of the reredos is a nice Jacobean altar table. The George III royal arms is of standard type and was possibly moved to its present position over the south doorway from above the tower arch. The nave and chancel roofs are of markedly different designs, the former is of king post and tie beam construction while the latter is a handsome example of a wagon roof type. At their junction is a rudimentary wooden chancel arch. The south frontage of All Saints is happily clear of obstructions and presents a welcoming face to the world.

All Saints tower

From the north

Tower and porch

Interior looking east

Altar and reredos

Looking north east

Looking west along the church

South west from the lectern

The font

In the chancel

George III royal arms

Wall tablets

The organ

Flowers

HENLEY ST PETER

C3, TM 158 513

St Peter from the south

Henley is within the orbit of Ipswich and as such is a desirable base for commuters, but despite its largely modern housing, the village has not become over-developed. The best part, unsurprisingly, is around St Peter. The exterior has several interesting points. On the south side one window stands out, and a very unusual one it is to find in a parish church. It is flat-headed with three lights and is thought to have come from nearby Shrubland Old Hall when that was rebuilt; it dates from c.1520. The frame and two panels above and below are terracotta and these elements are closely decorated with a variety of motifs, including urns, shields interspersed with animals, swags, dolphins, facial masks and foliate embellishments. To the west of the window is an old grotesque head embedded in the fabric, salvaged from a rebuilding at some stage. To the east is a shallow turret for the rood stairs. The tower has a dedication above the west doorway asking for prayers for the souls of Thomas Seckford (who paid for most of the tower) and his wife; he died in 1505, which gives a broad date for the tower. The buttresses have attractive flushwork panelling and there is more flushwork at the base of the tower. The doorway has spandrels with emblems of St Peter and St Paul. To the north is a large, rather extraordinary composite building in the area where a north porch would be expected. This comprises the old village school of 1838, which has gabled transepts and a porch, plus a tall chimney. It was rebuilt in 1904 and these days serves as a church room and vestry. Entry to the church is via a modest south porch, but the doorway within is more noteworthy. Once entirely Norman, it was subsequently modified to have a pointed head. There is chevron and billet ornament in the head and, peeping out of the west jamb, the head of a nook shaft. The door itself is probably C14th and has original ironwork. Inside, C19th refurbishment was extensive, but a few old items remain. The C13th chancel has a good piscina and sedilia set, the latter with squinch arches. In the opposite wall is an aumbry and nearby is a highly worked lectern with exuberant carving, probably C19th. Most of the wall tablets are unexceptional, but the one of 1717 for Elizabeth Vere is excellent. At the west end are three C19th hatchments, also the nondescript font of c.1845. Both rood stair doorways are in place but long since sealed. The C19th balcony at the west end once extended around the adjacent walls. Mid-C19th stained glass featuring St Peter is of good quality.

St Peter from the west and north — C16th terracotta window

Interior looking east and west — Chancel, north side

Piscina and drop-sill sedilia — Rood stair doorways, pulpit — The font — Eliz. Vere Tablet 1717

Mural tablets — Mary Medows hatchment (1809) — Elaborate lectern and aumbry — South doorway

HERRINGSWELL ST ETHELBERT A2, TL 718 699

Sunlight highlights St Ethelbert's south frontage

The extreme west of Suffolk around Mildenhall is not generally renowned for its beauty, but Herringswell is a little-known gem. Literally on a road to nowhere, it is the perfect small village, if the lack of amenities is overlooked. Unsurprisingly, pride of place goes to St Ethelbert, which is set prettily on the western edge of the village. It is diverting to ponder what the church would look like today if fire hadn't intervened in 1869 and gutted the interior. Architect Arthur Blomfield was called in to restore what was left, and did a good job, saving what he could of the old fittings. Norman quoins, some coursing and a nook shaft survive in the church walls, but the building is basically C14th. The C14th tower survived the conflagration and is somewhat unusual in morphology. The eastern half is founded within the church, necessitating the provision of supporting pillars and flying buttresses inside. The western portion has a considerable stepped buttress cum stair turret to the south and a shallower buttress to the north. Another striking buttress runs up the middle of the western wall, as far as the start of the top stage. Either side of it lower down are two niches, others can be found in chancel buttresses, above the south doorway and above the transept south window. The transept springs off the nave to the south and once housed a chapel. The porch is C14th, and has a reset ?Norman stoup by the inner doorway. Inside, almost all is Victorian, but some features survive from the old church and there are notable and important contributions from the C20th. The old features may include the font, which equally could be C19th, but details below the bowl are Early English in form. In the transept is a blocked entrance to the rood stair, also a large aumbry and small piscina, which were associated with the chapel that once existed here. In the chancel is a fine, large C14th double piscina, its arches, finials and pinnacles heavily restored. In the east wall are two probably contemporary niches. The vestry doorway is also C14th. If that was all there was at St Ethelbert, the church would still be worth a visit, but there is something else that sets the church apart. This is the C20th stained glass, which fills almost all the windows and forms a stunning collection. Most was designed by Christopher Whall and members of his circle Paul Woodroffe, Jasper Brett and James Clark, and all are magnificent. Intensity, vivacity and powerful modelling are common to all. Two later windows of 1954 and 1992 are not quite on a par, but are still admirable.

St Ethelbert from the east

View from the north

South doorway

Looking east

Chancel arch and chancel

Looking west

The west end

The font

Double piscina and niche

Rood stair door, aumbry, piscina

For the fallen

Details from three windows

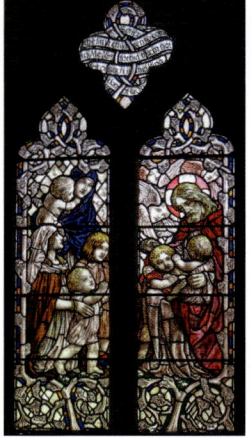
'Suffer the little children'

By Dean Cullum 1992

HINDERCLAY ST MARY   C2, TM 027 768

St Mary's fine tower dominates the scene from the north west

St Mary's attractions are hidden away off the beaten track behind a screen of trees. The air of seclusion adds to the excitement of exploring this intriguing church, which has many fine features. The C15th tower is tall and imposing, and has large, bold belfry windows that boast excellent Perpendicular tracery and unusual chequerboard flushwork panelling beneath. There is more flushwork at the base of the tower and on the stepped battlements. On the south face is a formidable stair turret. The C14th porch is full of character and only lightly restored. It retains most of the original outer wood doorway, fashioned almost entirely from one length of timber. The sides are wooden post and slat construction with brick bases. Many of the windows are Decorated, especially in the chancel, but earlier still is the blocked north doorway which has the merest suggestion of a point at the apex, dating it perhaps from around 1200. The interior is a most pleasing space, with artifacts and features from many centuries forming an absorbing ensemble. The oldest thing on view is the arcade to the south aisle; the piers are round and low in the Norman style, but the pointed arches indicate a Transitional or Early English date. The octagonal font is plain and may be C14th. The choice angle piscina in the chancel is early C14th and was later restored; beside it are drop-sill sedilia. The screen is rebuilt, but contains some C15th parts and panels. Above it on the north side of the chancel arch is the stump of the rood beam. Slots cut in the arcade piers indicate that the south aisle was originally enclosed as a chapel. The narrow tower arch is C15th, and is closed by an C18th screen, which is matched by another enclosing the vestry to the south. The church's seating is diverse and interesting. In the south aisle are C18th box pews, some family-sized, while in the nave benches with rectangular ends at the front are succeeded westwards by a set of smaller, early C17th benches with shaped ends and diamond poppyheads. The latter are carved with a variety of motifs, including plants, flowers, churchwardens initials and the dates 1617 and 1849 (when some restoration was undertaken). The pulpit is fairly plain but has prominent bannistered steps; it may be late C18th or early C19th. Four windows contain first rate, colourful modern glass designed by Rosemary Rutherford, sister of John Rutherford, rector here from 1975-86. Old graffitti carved on benches includes the game Fox and Geese. See also George III arms and an excellent wall memorial in the chancel of 1711.

C14th porch

St Mary from the south west

North doorway

Interior looking east

Rood screen

The chancel

Angle piscina

Thompson tablet (1711)

Box pews, pulpit, Geo. III arms

'Fox & Geese', poppyheads

C17th benches, poppyheads

Nave looking west

The font

Fragments of old glass

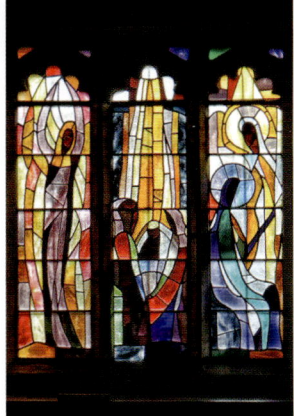
Rosemary Rutherford window

HOMERSFIELD ST MARY

D2, TM 285 853

Serene in the sunshine, St Mary at Homersfield

Homersfield enjoys a close affinity with neighbouring villages of the Elmham group, and was commonly known as St Mary, South Elmham in the past. The county boundary with Norfolk lies very close and the northern county can be seen from the churchyard. St Mary is an unassuming, modest church with no great treasures or architectural high points, but it is well-ordered and welcoming, and is everything a small village church should be. The lack of historically important features and fittings is mostly due to all-pervasive Victorian renovations and refits, the main one in 1866. It seems that the church was in a delapidated state by the middle of the C19th and that was the driving force behind the restorations, which resulted in the interior being thoroughly scoured of old things. Despite all that the church retains a venerable atmosphere. As to age, there are two pointers to a Norman church standing here nine centuries ago. One slit window survives in the nave and in the west face of the tower a long slit may also be Norman. Higher up in the tower the belfry windows are Y-shaped from around a century later. Windows in the rest of the church span the C13th (two lancets in the chancel) to C15th (east window), with much Victorian renewal. There is a good south porch, at heart C14th, but like everything else, it has been restored. In the chancel south wall is an impressive C13th priest's doorway, with a recessed surround of many orders. With nothing of any age within, a study of the Victorian fittings is recommended. These are not ambitious or of superlative quality, but they are instructive of the workings of the Victorian ecclesiastical mind, for little has changed here since that age. Both the font and the double piscina in the chancel are copies of medieval predecessors. The former is a reproduction of the familiar Purbeck Marble type, with a square bowl and 4-bay arcades on each face. This type first appeared in late Norman times. The double piscina mimics an Early English forerunner, and very well done it is too. By the wooden reredos with its three arches are two boards for the Commandments. The wooden eagle lectern is a memorial of the 1st World War. The rest of the furnishings are modest, standard issue pieces. The organ in the chancel is also of a common Victorian type and is overlarge for the area in which it is placed. Two paintings can be seen on the nave walls, the larger is Italian and depicts the Nativity, the smaller, the Virgin Mary.

The church from the east and north east — Tower and porch

Norman window — Interior looking east — The chancel

The interior from the sanctuary — The pulpit — Double piscina

The font — The organ — Eagle lectern — Madonna and Child

HORHAM ST MARY

D2, TM 210 724

St Mary is a church of three distinct components

Horham lies to the west of Eye in the midst of mellow countryside populated by many fine churches, such as Fressingfield, Laxfield and Wingfield. St Mary cannot quite equal those well-known edifices, but it has much to recommend it, not least the atmospheric interior and grand tower. There is great antiquity here too, two Norman doorways survive, the southern one is the showier, with typical chevron ornament in the head and two attached shafts each side, bearing fluted capitals. The sealed northern example also has fluted capitals, but only on one set of shafts, and a modest roll-headed arch. The nave into which these doorways open is short and low, despite later heightening, and clearly retains its Norman dimensions. The chancel is probably C14th, but was much rebuilt in Victorian times and given a new east window. Documentary evidence points to the tower being late C15th to early C16th. It is an imposing structure, with much flushwork. That at the base is much degraded but the stepped battlements have a marvellous scheme of panelling, shields and monograms. A bold stair turret ascends dramatically at the south east corner of the tower, and the west doorway has delicate attached shafts and crumbling spandrel carvings. Unusually, there are two belfry windows on all sides except the south, where the stair turret leaves room for only one. The highlight of the interior is undoubtedly the woodwork, much of which dates from the early C17th, with some very fine and elaborate pieces. The impressive pulpit may be the cut-down remains of a double or triple decker, with some of the removed pieces reused in other furniture, e.g. the reading desk nearby. Also close to the pulpit is a finely-worked panel dated November 29th 1631. In the chancel are two rather spectacular, elaborately carved chairs, one fronted by an exotic reading desk. They are probably C17th, but may be hybrid pieces. The fascinating nave seating comprises a varied mixture of C15th and later benches. Some have genuine poppyheads, others are replacements. Several have fleurons on the ends and a few have linenfold backs. There are two old chests, one medieval and ironbound, the other Jacobean. Other items of note are the original rood beam, rood stair doorways (the higher blocked), a robust C15th font of characteristic form with angels, lions and a contemporary cover, angle piscina, old heraldic and fragmentary glass, Morris & Co war memorial, Decalogue boards and consecration crosses.

Tower from the north west

From the north

C15th and C12th doorways

Looking east from the nave

The chancel

Sanctuary south east corner

The nave looking west

Seating and poppyhead

Pulpit & rood stair doorway

Chest, chair, C17th panel

Font & cover

Angle piscina

War memorial

Armorial glass & fragments

127

ICKLINGHAM ST JAMES　　　　B2, TL 770 730

Looking across the busy A1101

Icklingham used to have two working churches and two active pubs. Sadly, reflecting modern realities, the pubs have closed (one may be reopened) and one church is redundant. The latter, All Saints, lost the vote when the village was obliged to choose between it and St James for closure. However, All Saints is looked after these days by the Churches Conservation Trust, and probably sees more visitors than St James. That is not to say that St James lacks all interest, but sweeping Victorian restoration removed most medieval fittings and imposed a rather heavy atmosphere, which the villagers do their best to overcome. The building is basically C13th and C14th, with C15th additions and alterations, but so much was done in the C19th that interpreting its evolution is not easy. Records tell us that the aisles and the panelled parapets on them, also the nave, were faced with split flints at that time, and that the tower collapsed in the late C18th and was rebuilt in 1808. Oddly, apart from a west window and a single belfry window to the east, there are no other openings in the tower. Both aisles have original doorways and doors. A square outline on the chancel north wall and evidence of infilling indicates that a building (?chapel) once ran off the chancel at that point. It seems that the clerestory was fabricated in the C14th, as the windows are Decorated. The Perpendicular arcades inside have attractive piers with capitals confined to the inner shafts, and the arcades lead the eye nicely along the nave to the related chancel arch. South of the tower arch is the C15th font, of familiar form, with quatrefoils on the bowl and tracery on the stem. Nearby is the church's outstanding feature, a substantial chest of the early 1300's, originally in All Saints. It has beautiful iron scrollwork throughout and three hasps, and is of national importance. Though rather neglected, a number of wall tablets tell the tale of the local Gwilt family. The oldest tablet on view is for John Talbot and his daughter, who died in 1689 and 1704 respectively. It is in poor condition, but the one recording the gifts of east window glass and reredos in 1866 by Gwilt and Gibbs family members is exquisitely lettered. Each aisle has a medieval piscina, indicating the past presence of chapels; the chancel has a double-arched example. In the north aisle is a niche by the east window, and an aumbry with original doors. Several windows have stained glass of moderate quality, but the window of 1880 by Mayer & Co in the south aisle is worth a look.

St James from the west and north west　　　Gargoyle

Interior looking east　　　The chancel　　　Chancel south east corner

Nave looking west　　　The font　　　Chest, rood stair doorway, piscina　　　Aumbry with original door

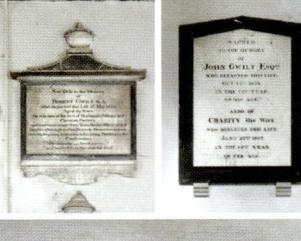

Glass by Mayer & Co (1880)　　　Gwilt family wall tablets　　　Benefaction boards　　　Milners safe

IKEN ST BOTOLPH

D3, TM 412 566

Magical and spiritual places, Iken and St Botolph Church

Anywhere else, the church of St Botolph would attract little attention or celebration, but it is where it is situated that sets it apart. For here, it is strongly suspected, is where the pioneering Christian missionary St Botolph founded a monastery around the middle of the C7th, and here a church has stood (when not being pillaged and razed by marauding Vikings) ever since. The foundations of a very early timber church were discovered beneath the present one during excavations in 1977. And it is not just the story of St Botolph that grips the imagination, for the area around Iken in which it unfolded is wonderfully atmospheric and beautiful, sitting as it does on a bluff above the broad River Alde in a sequestered landscape. No wonder pilgrims and visitors find their way here in some numbers. The present church was begun in Norman times, the nave was built then, and two blocked Norman windows survive in the north wall. The tower is C15th and the chancel completely of 1853, when it was built to replace a derelict predecessor. The south porch is C15th or C16th, with its gable infilled much later with brick. Both the tower and porch have neat flushwork. The stepped tower parapet, with flushwork panelling, is particularly attractive. A stair turret ascends to halfway on the southern face of the tower. The future of the church was put in serious jeopardy in 1968 when sparks from a churchyard bonfire ignited the thatched roof of the nave and a major conflagration ensued. The nave was completely gutted and the roof destroyed, although the tower and chancel escaped relatively lightly. For many years the nave stood open to the elements, but an admirable campaign by the small local community and other agencies to rehabilitate the church began in 1984, and by 1995 the nave had a new roof and was partially refitted and restored inside. The fire exposed the rubble walls of the nave and these were left largely unrestored. Much other work was done elsewhere in the building and the end result was a wonderfully evocative church in full empathy with the illustrious history of the site. The features inside are few but significant, led by a substantial piece of the carved shaft of a C9th Anglo-Saxon cross, found in the infill of a tower wall. The nave also retains the bottom entrance to the rood stairs, an attractive medieval niche with piscina nearby and a very fine C15th font with Evangelist's symbols and angels carrying instruments of the passion around the bowl. The chancel fittings of 1853 are seemly and of good quality.

The porch

St Botolph from the south

West doorway and window

The church looking east

The chancel

Altar and reredos

Nave looking west

The font

Norman window

Rood stair doorway

Credence shelf, two piscinas

Niche

Saxon cross shaft, east window, Agnus Dei

131

ILKETSHALL ST ANDREW   D1, TM 379 872

St Andrew stretches out in its wild graveyard

St Andrew is a super round tower church in an enviable setting, on a quiet lane away from it all. The building is full of interest, inside and out. The tower is rather enigmatic, by comparison with other round towers it could be late Saxon or Norman in the lower half, with a later C14th or C15th octagonal top, a familiar configuration in East Anglia, but it has also been suggested that it may be all of one build, the octagonal top two stages included, constructed in the C13th or C14th. The tower arch inside is pointed and C13th/C14th in aspect, which might support the late tower speculation. Also, the fabrics of the lower half and the octagon appear to be similar. However, the local guide states that 'Saxon material' was found in the structure of the tower. There is no doubt about the age of the nave however, it has good Norman doorways north and south, the former less ornate, as is usual. A Norman window survives in the nave north wall. A Norman chancel may once have existed, as there are carved Norman stones worked into the base of a south buttress, but the present structure is late C13th or early C14th on the evidence of a broad lancet in the north wall. The south porch is impressive, with a parvise, built of flint but with much repair and rebuilding in brick. The narrowness of the nave and its leaning walls add to the sense of antiquity inside. Early in the C21st a series of very rare and diverse medieval wall paintings were discovered. Subjects include a clear Wheel of Fortune, a church or cathedral, angels and other figures in arcades, and other indistinct subjects. Some of the benches are C16th and possess fine and varied poppyheads. At the back on the south side, the back of one bench is enlivened with uninhibited rustic carving of cherubs, swags and curlicues. The north set of benches includes a bench end with similar, but not exactly comparable, carving. The nave roof wall plates are medieval with handsome carved spandrels. The chancel roof is a good copy of the older nave roof, with the addition of a suite of pretty angels. The pulpit has Jacobean elements, and its original tester stands nearby, in use as a table. There is much else to see before leaving. A wooden Charles II arms and two garter shields on the west wall, octagonal early C15th font with shields in quatrefoils on the bowl, medieval niches in the nave north and south walls, skeleton of a tomb recess in the chancel, a brass of 1624 in the nave floor, C17th altar rails and C14th piscina in the chancel.

The south porch, with parvise

St Andrew from the south west

Doorways and windows

Interior looking east

The east end

Looking west from the sanctuary

Tomb recess

Font, window & niche, ledger slab

Wall paintings

John Verdon brass (1624)

Pulpit and tester table

Roofs

Roof angel, spandrels & poppyhead

Carved bench & detail, bench end

Charles II royal arms, garter shields

133

KENTON ALL SAINTS C2, TM 191 659

Distinctive and attractive, Kenton All Saints from the south

The area around the delectable little town of Debenham, which includes the hamlet of Kenton, is a tranquil refuge from life's trials and tribulations. A day exploring the many lovely churches hereabouts is balm for the soul indeed. One might tire of repeating 'charming', 'attractive', 'beautifully set' and other enhancing adjectives, but here again is a church that deserves all of these. Not for great treasures, for there are none, but for the sheer delight of being here. The highlight on the outside is the charming little C16[th] south aisle, which was commissioned by the local Garneys family around 1524 as their chapel. It is all of warm red brick with blue brick diapering. Even the super windows are of brick, with flattened 'Tudor' tops. An age-worn doorway opens into the chapel from inside the C15[th] porch, which itself previously had an upper room. The outer doorway of the porch has pretty paterae in the arch mouldings. The nave is Transitional based on the two round-headed doorways into it, the southern one is the more intricate of the two and has roll mouldings in the arch and leaf capitals, the latter a sure sign of late Norman/Early English work. The chancel was heavily reconstituted by E. Hakewill in 1871, but he partly restored and reused the round-headed priest's doorway. The lancets on both sides of the chancel indicate work of around 1300, but the impressive, though rather overwrought, east window in Early English style is Hakewill's. The tower is Decorated, with neat west doorway with window above, and belfry windows with Decorated tracery. The parapet features a most unusual flushwork design of linked roundels. The interior is well-maintained and appealing, and has enough features to satisfy the enthusiast. The chancel arch will attract attention, with its clustered marble shafts and flamboyant capitals, a real Victorian confection. The rest of the chancel fittings are more or less all Victorian too, except for a fine Elizabethan bench of 1595. The nave houses the rest of the old survivals, including a C13[th] Purbeck Marble font bowl which stands on a much later stem; an earlier stem can be found in the chapel, alongside a plain C16[th] piscina. There are three old niches, one of them in the chapel. The remade pulpit has Jacobean elements; behind it are both rood stair doorways, the upper blocked, whilst the lower is open and occupies most of a window embrasure. See also an old bench, consecration crosses and early C18[th] lead tablets bearing the names of church worthies.

The church from the east and north east — Garneys Chapel, porch and tower

Interior looking east — The east end — The church from the chancel

Looking across to the Garneys Chapel — Rood stair openings, niche, pulpit — The font — In the Garneys Chapel

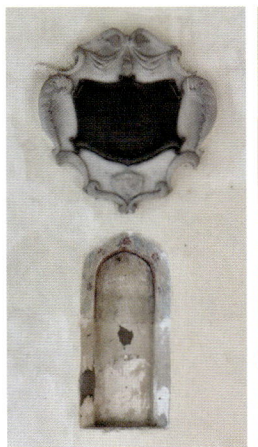

Consecration cross, lead tablets, old bench — Elizabethan bench (1595) — Wall tablet, niche — South doorway

KNODISHALL ST LAWRENCE D3, TM 425 619

St Lawrence from the south west

Just off a sylvan country lane, surrounded by mature trees, lies the church of St Lawrence, slumbering comfortably in its capacious churchyard. All is peace and serenity. The original village of Knodishall has largely disappeared and the main area of settlement is now at Coldfair Green and Knodishall Common, some distance from the church. One of the meanings suggested for the name Knodishall, Cnott's remote valley, seems to encapsulate the situation of this likeable church. Although the exterior is largely that of a classic medieval building (but see Tudor brick windows in the south nave wall), once within it is clear that the interior was thoroughly scoured and reinvented by the Victorians. A single feature externally remains from the church's early days, a plain Norman doorway to the north. Fragmentary Norman stones were also recorded from the nave north wall. Most of the rest is C14th. The effect of the bold C15th tower is dramatic when approached from the path off Church Road, and the west front is elaborated in its lower part with a handsome doorway embellished with a square head with shields in the spandrels, and headstops. Above the doorway is a splendid Perpendicular window and the parapet has flushwork panelling, shields and gargoyles. The south nave wall was shored up with a row of beefy brick buttresses in 1843. Here also a blocked south doorway with the top half converted to a window. The vestry off the north chancel wall dates from 1838 and the organ chamber to the north from 1907. Excavations for this chamber revealed a piece of a piscina, which was installed in the historically correct place in the chancel. The Victorian interior initially promises little of historical interest, but there are intriguing items to be found. The Purbeck Marble font, with typical arching, appears to be the oldest feature, and may be C13th, but the relative freshness of the carving suggests that it has been recut. Above the entrance to the tower are tracery panels from the old rood screen, surmounted by an unusual gilt Hanoverian royal arms. The pulpit is a deep Jacobean model with finely carved panelling, while opposite is an ornate, but later, reading desk. To the right of the vestry door is a holy water stoup. Nearby on the wall is a nice remounted late C15th brass for John Jenney and wife. The east window glass is by Nicholson Studios (1935) and nave south is by Simpson & Sons (1910). There is also an older roundel and a shield. The hanging brass corona lamp holder is attractive.

Tower west front

St Lawrence from the north

Norman doorway

Interior looking east and west

Reading desk

Screen tracery, Hanoverian arms

The pulpit

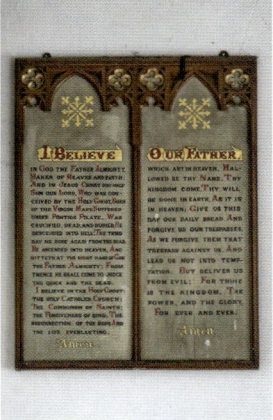
Creed & Lord's Prayer

Vertue shield (mid-C20th), piscina, stoup

The font

Glass by Simpson & Sons

Old roundel, shield and Virgin Mary

Jenney brass (c. 1460)

LACKFORD ST LAWRENCE B2, TL 797 702

St Lawrence enjoys a sumptuous rural location

Lackford St Lawrence enjoys a superb, sequestered setting in a beautiful churchyard, serene and alone. In an area stiff with churches, this is one of the best. Nearby is the excellent nature reserve of Lackford Lakes, making a visit to this part of the world even more alluring. It is not immediately obvious, but at its heart St Lawrence is a Norman church. The evidence is subtle and can only be appreciated inside, where the most obvious clue is a round-arch above the south doorway. But even more tantalising is a thickening of the walls towards the east end of the nave. The easternmost pier also incorporates a stretch of wall. These may be seen as strengthening measures for the support of a central tower; the easternmost bay in an earlier configuration may have opened into a north transept. However, many changes were wrought over the centuries since the putative tower stood, and much evidence has been swept away. A C15th tower now stands in the more accustomed position at the west end, with a bold stair turret and, always distinctive, crow-step battlements. The Victorians built a new north aisle and heavily reconfigured the rest of the church. A long, sweeping roof was fitted over the nave and the aisle. Yet the restorers retained much of interest from earlier days, and the interior of St Lawrence rewards study. The south porch is C14th and harbours Victorian banners above the inner doorway, while the north vestry was part of a big restoration in 1868-70. Inside, there are some mysteries. For example, in the chancel is an intriguing setting for the stepped sedilia, which seemingly were accommodated by slicing away much of a window. A trefoil-headed opening was cut in the window embrasure, and a characterful head stop set next to it. A blocked opening in the window's west embrasure may once have led to the rood stairs. A corresponding opening is set opposite, to the east of the chancel arch. Also in the chancel are a simple trefoil-headed piscina, a tomb recess and a long niche in the east wall. An ornate squint looks from what was once a north chapel into the chancel, and incorporates a piscina. Another open piscina is cut into the step of the dropped sill of a south nave window. The pulpit is a plain C17th example, but the splendid C14th font is ebulliently carved with foliage trails. A C13th coffin lid, old bench ends and poppyheads, and a little old glass also number amongst St Lawrence's many attractive features. Recently installed modern facilities are a welcome addition.

St Lawrence from the east and north west   **In the south porch**

Interior looking east   **Chancel arch and chancel**   **Interior looking west**

Piscina and sedilia   **East wall niche, coffin lid**   **Tomb recess, old chair**   Squint/piscina, head stop, Greaves tablet

The font   **The pulpit**   **Bench details**   **Glass of various ages**

LAWSHALL ALL SAINTS   B3, TL 864 542

Grey clouds scud past All Saints on a typical English summer's day

Nowhere in East Anglia is particularly elevated, although the tiresome tag of being flat is not justified. Around Lawshall the contour lines record 100m or more. And that, for this region, is high. In the little village itself the reading is 103m or 338'. However, there is little sculpture to the land and no sensation of height. All Saints looks, and is, a church rebuilt in the C15th, a fact confirmed by bequests made at that time. Only the bold C14th tower avoided extensive reconfiguration. A clerestory was added and the handsome Perpendicular arcades inside suggest that the aisles were also constructed then, perhaps replacing earlier ones. The south porch and its inner doorway are Perpendicular too, the latter with a conspicuous surround with square head and spandrels. The chancel is C19th, rebuilt by Butterworth in 1857-8 in Early English style, including a typical group of three lancets in the east wall. Butterworth also remade the porch and effected other restorations. The north aisle east window is partly obscured by his chancel roof which sweeps down to cover chancel, vestry and organ chamber. The interior has little old work, probably as a result of Victorian and later re-ordering. The idiosyncratic font is medieval, with quatrefoils and tracery on the bowl, defaced heads on the underside and more tracery around the stem. It is painted in lively style in red, blue and a little green. The colouration is medieval in inspiration, but the date of painting may be much later. Probably painted at the same time are a suite of stone angels and the string course on which they are mounted, located on the nave walls. The angels are a little difficult to date but may be C15th. There are some quality items in wood to admire, especially two excellent chests, both post-medieval but 3-400 years old. One has intricately worked locks and hinges, including a representation of the ancient symbol of the double eagle, whilst the other is impressively carved, with three diamonds on the panels. A C17th or C18th chair in the sanctuary is highly ornate, with flowing carving. The furnishings of the chancel are restrained, but include a lot of Minton tiling, including the reredos. There are a handful of wall tablets, the most distinctive being for a Dutch pilot who crashed in World War 2, designed by the renowned Dutch typographer Jan Van Krimpen. The Baillie floor slab and Butterworth's piscina and sedilia in the sanctuary are worth a look, as is the east window glass by students working at Horwood Brothers of Mells.

| Tower and porch | All Saints from the south east | South doorway |

| Interior looking east | The chancel | Interior looking west |

| Piscina and sedilia | The font | Nave angels | Three wall tablets |

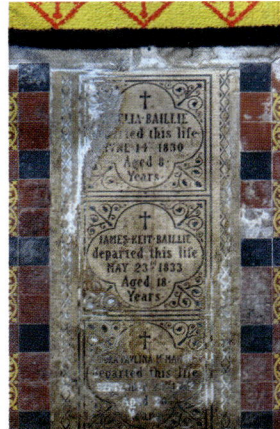   

| Baillie floor memorial | Two venerable chests | Fine old chair | Two panels from the east window |

LEAVENHEATH ST MATTHEW B4, TL 954 372

St Matthew from the west

Leavenheath St Matthew is a notable church in several ways. For a start it is one of the few parish churches in Suffolk that is not a listed building. That is rather odd, given that the history and evolution of the building are of some interest. It is set away from the village, barely a few metres away from the very busy A134. Because of the fast road and a shielding of trees it is very easy to flash past the church, yet it is worth finding, for it is a rare church building begun in 1835 in the reign of William IV, before the ecclesiological and neo-Gothic revolution of the 1840's and thereafter. It remained a single cell building much in the mould of a non-conformist chapel until later in the C19th when a tower, chancel and south aisle were added by Satchell and Edwards, completing the slightly offbeat construction we see today. Quite why a tower was erected to the south west instead of being added to the west end is unknown but perhaps it was desired to preserve the frontage of the west wall with its pretty porch and square-headed lancet above. The east end of the south aisle was configured as a chapel or private area and still has an altar today. Architectural details are very underplayed but mild Early English and late Perpendicular themes can be noted. The church is almost entirely built of brick, which was left uncovered in much of the interior except for the nave walls, which are plastered. The effect of the open brickwork inside is by no means unattractive, especially the arcades, which are enhanced by contrasting limestone for the arches. Unsurprisingly there is nothing of any great age inside, but the simple and dignified fittings create a quietly engaging atmosphere, one that is helped considerably by the degree of care that clearly goes into the church's upkeep. The early pre-Victorian church was very largely overprinted by later changes, but the dainty font may be from those days. Attention is centred on a most unusual war memorial, which features seven battlefield crosses grouped below the memorial tablets. All but one of these has a photograph of the named soldier. Yet, the crosses are not from the battlefields, they were clearly fabricated later, for they are identical, with the same lettering and IHS headings, finished with the same paint. However, the sentiments they embody are clearly genuine and as valid as ever. Three brass tablets for church worthies are beautifully maintained. For the bulk of its history St Matthew stood as a chapel-at-ease to Stoke by Nayland St Mary but was later raised to the rank of parish church.

| Chancel east wall | From the north east | West porch | South west tower |

| Interior looking east | The chancel | Interior from the sanctuary |

| The south aisle | Chapel altar | A corner of the sanctuary | The pulpit |

The font — Three brass plaques — The war memorial and one of its soldiers

LIDGATE ST MARY

A3, TL 720 581

St Mary from the south west

Lidgate church is remarkable, both the building and its setting, and a visit is an absorbing experience. Many churches have lost their links with the past over time and getting the 'feel' of such places can be an elusive business, but not here. On a hill above the village in the tranquil acres around the church a great motte and bailey castle once stood, with three baileys. Much of the castle site north of the church is wooded today and investigation is frowned upon, but enough remains accessible to provoke a frisson or two. There are ditches to the north and west, and the 'Bailey Pond' lies to the south, but the most tangible remains are in the churchyard, and consist of a portion of wall lying to the east of the church. The position of St Mary within one of the baileys suggests that in its earliest form it was the C12th castle's single cell chapel. The present nave may retain that Norman ground plan. Evidence of Norman foundation can be seen in the south doorway, which though reset and modified when the C14th aisles were built, retains Norman stylings and tympanum. Significant portions of the church are C13th, including the chancel, which stands a little higher than the nave. The tower was probably begun in the C13th and finished in the C14th, the top stage is unbuttressed and lacks battlements. There were upgrades in the C15th, C19th and C20th, but successive restorers treated the church kindly and a strong tang of early days was retained, helped by much old woodwork. The nave and aisle benches are a varied set of C16th types, mostly simple and sturdy; some have linenfold carving and one has tracery on its end. The pulpit is an attractive Jacobean model on a broad base with finials. Both aisles have east chapels, enclosed by good screens, to the north medieval and to the south early C20th. The octagonal medieval font is plain and appears to be entirely original, even the base, which was often replaced. Both rood loft openings and associated stair turret survive. Chancel and south aisle have piscinas, the first is C13th with chunky pillars. The small recess next to it is piscina-like but enigmatic, while the south aisle piscina is C14th, with a cusped head. The chancel also contains a double aumbry. A C14th brass is set before the communion rails, the figure wears priestly robes, but his identity is uncertain. St Mary contains an exceptional array of graffiti, mostly on the piers, some showing great flair. Look too at the fancy nave chandelier, C15th chancel screen and some excellent C19th stained glass by Clayton & Bell.

Castle wall in the churchyard

Another view of the castle remains, St Mary beyond

South doorway

Interior looking east

Chancel screen, chancel behind

The chancel

Interior looking west

Interior looking north east

Rood stair doorways

The pulpit

Benches

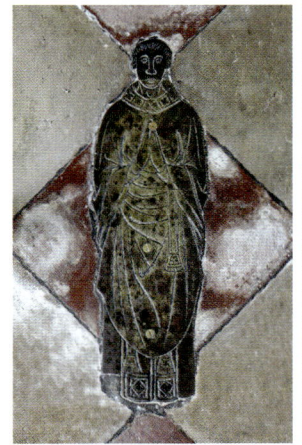
C14th brass

The font

Chancel piscina and aumbry

Graffiti

145

LINDSEY ST PETER

B3, TL 977 449

Centre stage is St Peter's remarkable south porch

The area in south Suffolk around villages such as Lindsey and its neighbours Whatfield, Semer, Chelsworth and others, is particularly special. There is something in the air hereabouts, in the sparsely populated, deeply rural landscape that can promote an inner serenity that is seldom equalled anywhere else in these crowded islands. The scenery is not breathtaking, there is a modest beauty certainly, but more than that is an atmosphere, a profound resonance and connection with the past. All that can be felt intensely in and around the churches, and particularly gems like St Peter. Nearly all are very ancient, and were probably preceded by others, right back to Anglo Saxon days. There is no evidence at St Peter of anything structural much older than 1300, because, even in rural backwaters, the churches were at intervals renewed and reconfigured, but internally there are reminders of what stood here before. Twice towers have collapsed and probably no money was available to rebuild again, so today a simple wooden bellcote built around 1836 suffices at the west end. The south porch is the highlight of the exterior, its openwork wooden structure founded on stone walls is large and rustic, the bony roof timbers pale with age. It was constructed in the C14th, and then sensitively restored in the C19th, with many timbers being retained. The south doorway is a hoary, antique structure, but both priest's and north doorways are blocked. The interior has a powerful, ancient feel and many compelling features and fittings. The font is the best indicator of an earlier church, it is early C13th and still bears Norman stylings in its rugged bulk and square form, but the arches on the bowl panels are pointed, indicating its true age; on top is an unusual C17th cover. Only the dado of a C14th chancel screen remains, it has two painted panels to the north and six to the south, erased of all decoration. The stalls on the south side of the chancel are formed from screen panels too, with old bench ends. The pulpit incorporates C16th panels. Nearby are both rood stair doorways and the large, elaborate window next to them has heavily damaged, once extravagant niches in its embrasures. An important chapel must once have stood here. The box pews to the north are C18th and the lovely three-sided altar rails are C17th. See also the early C19th chamber organ, nave roof, chancel piscina, George I royal arms, Hobart wall memorial of 1611, remarkable graffiti on the arcade piers, wooden corbels and a small area of wall painting.

The west end

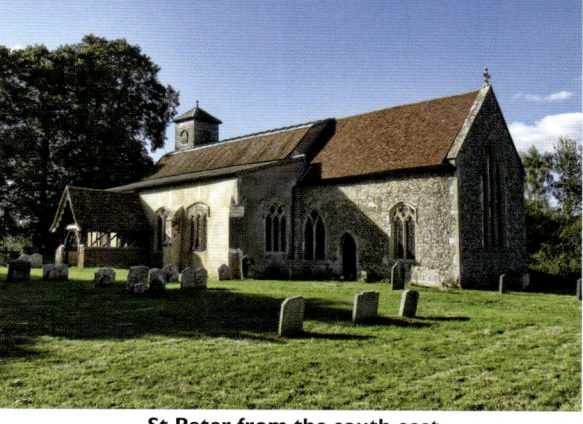
St Peter from the south east

Inside the porch

Looking north east

Screen, northern section

Screen, southern section

Niche, rood stair doorways, pulpit

The sanctuary

Sanctuary south east

Piscina, poppyhead, royal arms

Box pews, bench end arms

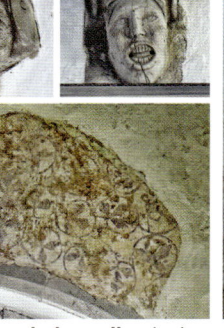
Wooden corbels, wall painting

The font

Hobart memorial, early C17th

North west from the chancel

147

LITTLE BEALINGS ALL SAINTS D3, TM 229 479

All Saints stands proudly on its little hill

The suburbs of Ipswich and urban Woodbridge lie quite close to Little Bealings, but as is the way in East Anglia one very soon enters deep countryside after leaving the conurbations, and all around the village is woodland and pleasant vistas. The setting of All Saints is very picturesque, on a slope above most of the village houses, with trees and cover all around. In truth the surroundings and setting are arguably the best of All Saints attributes. That's not to say that the church building has little merit, it is trim, well-loved and maintained, with a relaxing and welcoming ambience. However, in terms of interesting historical or architectural fittings, it has very few. Enthusiastic scourings during successive restorations and upgrades resulted in the removal of almost everything from before the C19th. And there must once have been a lot of ancient things within these walls, for there is some suspicion that the south nave wall contains Norman work. The dimensions of the small nave would also not be inconsistent with Norman origins. The chancel is C13th, the tower/porch C14th and the north aisle was constructed in 1851. The curious tower is set to the south west, maybe due to uneven, sloping ground to the west of the nave or perhaps lack of space. The thickness of its walls can be appreciated when passing through into the church. Vestiges of the Decorated tracery that once adorned all the belfry windows can be seen in the western one. A rather unfortunate wooden shed is sited west of the tower. The north aisle, which has its own gable, looks much bigger than it is because of the very small original nave and chancel. The aisle must have been very much needed in the days of big church attendances in the C19th and early C20th. The area of C16th brick walling and window to the south may be repair following removal of the rood stairs. The interior is an agreeable space. The arcade to the north aisle is a bold feature and is finished in Decorated style. The ceilings are plastered, but cornices are still visible, those of the chancel are C15th, the ones elsewhere are later copies. The only medieval fitting left in the church is the C15th font. This is a typical East Anglian type, with lions and angels holding shields around the bowl, but brutal treatment, probably in the C17th, destroyed all but two panels; all the lions around the stem were chamfered flat. The pulpit is C17th with C20th base and steps, a set of Lord's Prayer, Decalogue and Creed boards are C18th and the good east window glass of 1899 is by A. L. Moore.

The south west tower

All Saints from the north east and from the east

Interior looking east

The east end

Colvin tablet, mid-19th

Interior looking west

Looking south from the north aisle

The pulpit

East window, A. L. Moore

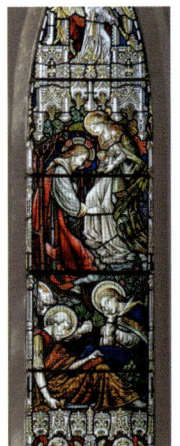

East window

The font

Lord's Prayer, Decalogue, Creed boards

A church well loved

LITTLE CORNARD ALL SAINTS   B4, TL 901 390

All Saints from the south

Little Cornard may shelter just 290 inhabitants or so, but the interest in and around the village is considerable. Saxons and Danes fought here, and the mid-C14th Black Death was first reported in Suffolk in Little Cornard. About a century later, in 1449, according to legend, two dragons, one from Suffolk and one from Essex, fought on nearby Kedington Hill, watched by frightened villagers. The well-known hymn *Hills of the north rejoice* by Charles Oakley was given the tune *Little Cornard* by Martin Shaw in 1915. The village lies in gentle, rolling countryside and the church of All Saints is beautifully positioned on a low hill away from the village. The church is almost hidden from sight by trees and missing it is almost inevitable without a map, or insider knowledge. The approach is over rough tracks through a farmyard and the revealing of the church when the churchyard is reached is delightful. The presence nearby of big brother Great Cornard and even larger Sudbury is unsuspected. The church is modest but full of charm and is clearly cherished by the villagers. The tower is C14th and is topped by brick battlements and an endearing early C19th cupola, inscribed at the base with the names of vicar and churchwardens of the time. There are no aisles, but an unusual C17th two storey vestry stands next to the chancel to the north. The nave may be early, perhaps C12th; its walls contain a liberal proportion of old ?Roman tiles and have some herringbone coursing. Its quoins are also formed with tiles. The rest of the church is C14th, the crenellated south porch a century or so later. The frame of the blocked north doorway is riddled with graffiti. The interior holds no great treasures, except a calm and restful atmosphere. The octagonal C15th font is located under the tower, and, while it is not a striking example, it is unusual, having panels with traceried double openings alternating with quatrefoils containing shields. The stem also has traceried panels. The C14th piscina in the chancel has a cinquefoil head and a C19th bas-relief of Christ at the Last Supper at the back. Next to it are drop-sill sedilia. In the east wall is a tall niche. Other drop-sill sedilia in the nave indicate the former presence of chapels. Several windows have stained glass of varying quality by artists such as Charles Clutterbuck, Clayton & Bell and Tim Armstrong. The window of 2008 by the last named incorporates a C15th roundel. There is a late C19th wall tablet and another more exotic tablet with four carved tiles that has a Middle Eastern look.

From the south east

Tower from the west

North doorway

South doorway

Interior looking east

The chancel

Chancel south east

The piscina

Looking west from the chancel

The pulpit

The font

Clutterbuck glass

Details of other glass in the church

Sidney tablet, Deeks plaque

Mystery tablets

Nave roof, oil lamp, Roll call

151

LITTLE WALDINGFIELD ST LAWRENCE   B3, TL 924 451

St Lawrence's stair turrets add a touch of distinction

St Lawrence stands in an area well-endowed with some of the finest parish churches in the country, but like a pocket battleship in a flotilla of its bigger brothers, it refuses to be overlooked, despite being less ambitious than the great ships of Long Melford, Lavenham, Clare and their like. The success of the late C15th wool trade allowed money to be poured into these churches, and so it was with St Lawrence. The C14th Decorated church that stood here was transformed at that time by Perpendicular opulence, with two aisles, grand windows, porches, clerestory and battlements being added. One of the church's most prominent features was also installed in the C15th, the two stair turrets that rise majestically at the east end of the nave, with their later mini spires. In the body of the church these stairs, which served the rood loft and then the roof, were reached through doorways in the nave and chancel, some of which still exist. On the chancel external north wall are the scars left by the removal of a chantry chapel, with ghostly echoes of the doorway, piscina and aumbry. Piscinas elsewhere in St Lawrence mark the sites of Guild Chapels. Both porches are fine edifices, the north one entirely of Tudor brick, with a curious stepped facia into which is set the doorway and a niche, ending in a central turret-like pinnacle, flanked by two others. The capacious interior houses many gems, including three medieval roofs beneath which are stately arcades with battlemented capitals and elaborate hood moulds with head stops, crockets and finials. The same hood mould design is repeated elsewhere in the church. A string course in the nave is enhanced by paterae, as is the surround of the south doorway. Local magnates of the woollen cloth trade, members of the Appleton, Wincoll and Colman families, are commemorated in a set of incomplete, but otherwise well-preserved C16th brasses. The C14th font has rare carvings on the bowl of monks at their devotions, alternating with Evangelists emblems. The pulpit is a superb Jacobean example with impressive carvings, reading shelf, scroll brackets and acorn bulbs, all supported by a single column. The nearby reading desk and chair are contemporary. The chancel floor was raised in Victorian days, shown by the present very low position of the piscina and sedilia. The pleasing altar rails are C17th. See also a number of old benefaction boards in excellent order, two magnificent chests, one C14th and the other C15th, good Clayton & Bell glass of 1897 and a panel of C15th glass fragments.

St Lawrence from the south west and north east | The south doorway

Looking east | The chancel | Chancel south east | Looking west

Roof boss, nave roof, reading desk | The pulpit | Clayton & Bell stained glass | Medieval glass fragments

C18th tablet, Benefaction boards | The font | Appleton, Colman, Wincoll brasses | C15th and C14th chests

METFIELD ST JOHN the BAPTIST — D2, TM 294 803

A hoary old boundary wall sets off St John very nicely

Metfield lies in border country, a little over 2 miles from the boundary with Norfolk; to the north east lie the South Elmham group of villages. Metfield is a small village, and at its heart lies St John the Baptist. It is not a large church and lacks aisles, but a handsome C15th south porch, stately Perpendicular windows and a nicely proportioned C14th tower add distinction. The rest of the building is C13th and C14th, heavily overprinted by a C15th rebuilding. Further restoration followed in Victorian times. The two-storey porch is the star of the show, the front elevation is embellished with fine flushwork, battlements (continued on the sides), niches and a splendid doorway, with lion faces, crowns, fleurons and a bishop around the mouldings of the arch. A single lugubrious headstop survives and the spandrels enclose big Tudor roses. The roof is vaulted with rare timber ribs and a wealth of lively and characterful bosses (and Swallow's nests!). The inner doorway is contemporary and has lions couchant for headstops. The C14th priest's doorway into the chancel is suitably proportioned for the stature of the people of those days. Three very worn C18th figures take the place of pinnacles on the corners of the tower battlements, the north west figure is lost. Immediately obvious on entering is the substantial balcony, which appears to be of late date, perhaps mid-late C19th. It holds an equally imposing organ. Beneath it resides a C15th font, not of the first rank, but in very good order, with lions and angels holding shields of the Jermy family around the bowl and lions sejant against the stem. Leaning against the west wall are two portions of the old medieval rood screen, one of them fairly well-preserved. The church has two modest medieval piscinas, one in the chancel and one in the nave south east corner, partly hidden by the rotund Victorian pulpit. The royal arms for George IV have been well restored. Stairs to the vanished rood loft are set in the embrasure of the nave north east window, and above the site of the loft is an excellent example of a Canopy of Honour. Both nave and chancel roofs are C15th, the latter particularly attractive. Either side of the chancel arch in the chancel are the only two wall tablets of note, for members of the Banks (late C18th) and Hunter (early C19th) families. Of special interest is the mechanism for the C17th tower clock, housed beneath the tower. C18th Lord's Prayer and Creed boards are set either side of the east window.

St John the Baptist from the north west | Porch and details | Porch roof bosses

Interior looking east, Canopy of Honour | Canopy of Honour detail | Interior looking west, west balcony | Rood stairs

Old screen, George IV arms | The font | Banks and Hunter tablets, late C18th and early C19th

Chancel piscina | Early C17th clock mechanism | South doorway and vaulted roof

METTINGHAM ALL SAINTS C1, TM 362 899

The leaning round tower of All Saints is clear in this view from the south

Only a few metres away from All Saints traffic rushes by on the busy B1062, but a screen of trees filters out the worst of the noise. The churchyard is nicely enclosed and is a good place to restore equilibrium after a spell on said road. Further refreshment is available at the tearooms just down the road. Mettingham is in the north east of Suffolk, very close to the border with Norfolk. All Saints boasts a fine round tower with a decidedly woozy outline, and some authorities claim Anglo-Saxon origins for it, using evidence from the deep window splays within. Ragged quoins at the west end of the nave consist of stone blocks and flints and are also taken to indicate pre-Norman origins. That the Normans themselves left their mark here is clear from the excellent north doorway, with three orders of decoration in the semi-circular arch and thin columns with scalloped capitals to the side. A strange animal head is set at the top of the arch. Unprotected by a porch, the doorway has resisted weathering well, helped by restoration. The rest of the church is C13th-C15th. The south porch is repaired in brick, the façade being all of that material. The south aisle east wall butts up tightly to the blocked priest's doorway in the chancel, showing that it post-dates the latter. Inside there are lots of nooks and crannies to investigate. Whilst nothing is exceptional, there are many excellent features and fittings. At first glance the font is a typical C15th 'East Anglian' model with lions and angels around the bowl and lions around the stem, but there are several variations, like human heads and paterae instead of angels beneath the bowl, and the lion's feet around the stem (where present) rest on large human heads. Nearby is an extremely obscure painting of the Crucifixion, of uncertain date. Above the tower arch is a doorway. Lead roof plates bearing the imprints of worker's boots, removed during restoration, are displayed. In the aisle south wall is a tomb recess, with ogee arch and finial, but much of it is obscured behind the organ, as is a sizeable wall tablet. Other wall memorials include an art deco style bronze plaque of c.1900 and two fairly ambitious, but degraded, tablets of the late C17th and mid-C18th. The royal arms for George III are in need of restoration. There is an old roundel, and very good recent glass by the likes of Christopher Webb and Jones & Willis. Old bench ends reside in the chancel, and, unusually, two piscinas. A fine eagle lectern stands proudly. The rood beam and one rood loft entrance are still in place.

All Saints from the west and the east — **Norman north doorway**

Interior looking east — **Fine eagle lectern** — **The chancel** — **Two chancel piscinas**

Interior looking west — **Glass new and old** — **Faded George III royal arms** — **Nave west end**

The font — **Wall plaque and tablets** — **Old poppyhead, lamp** — **Boot prints in old roof lead**

NACTON ST MARTIN   C/D4, TM 217 396

St Martin is completely rendered, as can be seen in this view from the south

St Martin enjoys a sequestered setting with the added tang of the sea, close to the shores of the Orwell river estuary; the pleasant village of Nacton is further inland. In many ways the church is unusual and that is quickly appreciated when the visitor takes stock from the churchyard. There's a distinctly arts and crafts look to several details, including a dormer window and the south porch, which have plenty of rustic woodwork on show. The sweeping nave roof that encompasses the south chapel is also characteristic of that movement. Yet the squat tower has clearly stood for many centuries, notwithstanding its belfry stage, removed in the C18th or C19th. Clearly great changes were wrought to the building, while the medieval tower, as so often, was left alone. Two all-encompassing restorations were undertaken in 1859 (R.M. Phipson) and 1906-8 (C.H. Fowler), whilst the south chapel was built in 1870. The early C20th changes overprinted much of the earlier work and included the addition of the porch, organ chamber, vestry, north aisle and new roofs, whilst the interior was overhauled and refitted, so that what we see today is a Victorian/Edwardian furnishing scheme, installed with little regard to cost, and an informative example of the religious mores of those times. Older items do survive. Externally some of the windows are original and place the building of the church in the interval of C13th–C15th. One window in the north sanctuary wall is now marooned inside after the building of the north aisle enclosed it in the late C19th, but its morphology dates it around 1200, and it is the clearest indication of the church's, otherwise unsuspected, early origins. The south doorway is medieval, as is its door. A nice C15th 'East Anglian' font is prominent inside, but even that didn't escape restoration, and the stem lions and wildmen have a rather gaunt look due to loss during re-cutting. A C14th piscina survives in the nave south east corner, with niches in the embrasure of the neighbouring window, confirming the former presence of a chapel there. The influence and patronage of the rich local families of Vernon and Broke is demonstrated by the plethora of wall tablets for various family members, but only the older C18th and early C19th tablets are of any distinction. The best of St Martin's features are stained glass windows by Kempe & Tower, Clayton & Bell, C. C. Powell, Burlison & Grylls and Wm Wailes. A medieval shield survives in a chancel window. The nave roof is impressive.

Tower and porch — St Martin from the north east — South doorway

The church looking east — Niches and C14th piscina — The chancel — Late C12th lancet

  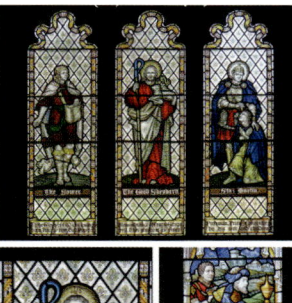 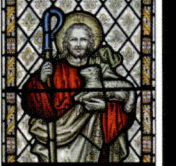   

Interior from the sanctuary — The west end and font — Glass by CC Powell, Burlison & Grylls and Kempe & Tower

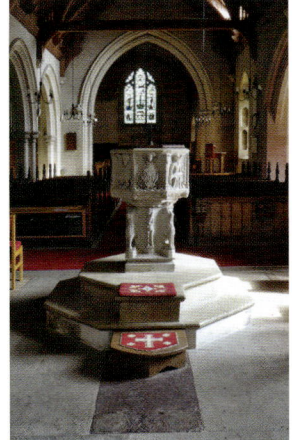  

The font — Nave roof — C18th and C19th wall tablets, mostly for Broke family members

NAUGHTON ST MARY

C3, TL 998 482

Crystal clear winter sunshine bathes St Mary

George H. Rose is little remembered these days, but in the early to mid-C20th he was a prominent Suffolk artist, specialising in traditional landscape and country scenes. His work still comes up occasionally in fine art sales, but he was perhaps better known for his regular features in the East Anglian Magazine, of happy memory, that centred on one or more of his sketches with appropriate notes or connected story. Like much else in the Magazine, the mood evoked in his articles was one of wistful and evocative nostalgia. George Rose also loved churches, they feature often in his paintings and sketches, particularly the one he looked after here at Naughton as churchwarden until his death in 1955. At least two of his pieces were about Naughton St Mary, one a particularly dreamy and meditative essay about the play of sunlight around the chancel arch and walls, with suitable sketch. He would instantly recognise his church today, it cannot have changed much, or its surroundings. The atmosphere he clearly recognised and loved is still there, this is a rustic, mellow church to savour. Not a grand church, there are no aisles, extensions or great artefacts, but one to linger in as a living testament to an England passing into memory. St Mary is an ancient church, the presence of a much mistreated Norman font and a blocked, round-headed, slit window in the middle reaches of the south side of the unbuttressed tower testify to that. A C13th plate tracery window survives in the chancel south wall and the nave north doorway, now blocked and with a window in the top half, is of the same age. The cramped but charming south porch is C14th. The interior is seemly and beautifully kept. The C14th roofs are mostly ceiled but sticking out like black fossil bones are tie and ridge beams, wall plates and king posts. The aforementioned font was once square, but the bowl was later mutilated into an octagonal shape and its arcades partly erased. The font resides in the north doorway recess, whilst nearby are a set of crude but appealing C17th benches. On the nave north wall are two medieval paintings, neither very clear, but St Christopher and the Christ-child can be discerned in one; the other, much deteriorated, may be the perils of gossip or a more obscure subject. There is a plain C14th chancel piscina and another, with cusped, trefoil head, in the nave. The top half of the lower rood stair doorway, with traces of steps and newel, is still in place. In the chancel is an elegant chamber organ of 1777.

St Mary from the north east

Chancel north, nave north and south doorways

Interior looking east

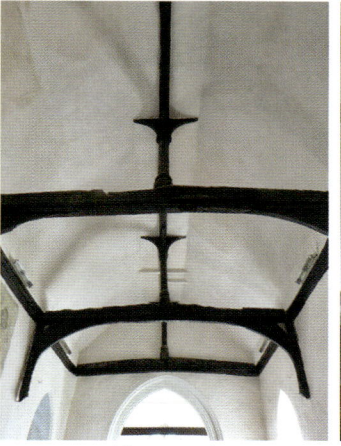
Nave roof

The chancel

Chancel south east

The nave looking west

Nave north wall painting

Painting, tablet, nave piscina

Chancel piscina

Lower rood stair doorway

North doorway and font

C17th benches in the nave

1777 organ

NAYLAND ST JAMES　　　B4, TL 975 342

St James is hemmed in on three sides by neighbouring houses

St James is a real enthusiasts church, there is something here for everyone, a lot of it of exceptional interest. Much of the building is C15th, but the chancel and unbuttressed tower are C14th, also a north aisle window. Land was obviously at a premium in Nayland in the Middle Ages, because St James is hemmed in by houses and streets on every side but the north. Those hoping to get a clear view for a photograph from this one more generous vantage point will be disappointed, however, as the church is partially masked by trees and bushes. The building is large and imposing, of a type common in south Suffolk, built on money from the wool industry. The exterior rewards careful study, for example, there is a spire, quite a rarity in East Anglia, rebuilt in 1963. The south aisle has a spectacular porch at its west end which, unusually, has a west frontage and doorway. It was built in 1525 by a local wealthy merchant. Unfortunately, the ornate front with its three niches, panelled battlements and pinnacles is now rather eroded. Further east is a prominent external rood stair turret, indicating that the rood loft would have extended across both aisles. The north aisle has a niche in an angle buttress and impressive Perpendicular windows. The battlemented north porch, which houses the main entrance, opens into the north aisle. Before going inside, see the west doorway in the tower, which has four steps up to it, and the priest's doorway into the chancel, sheltering under a miniature porch. The well-maintained interior is spacious and light, thanks to a clerestory that extends along the chancel, and has fine, sweeping arcades without capitals. There is much excellent work by the Victorians, but recent generations have also played their part in creating a lovely setting. Of the older features, the nave roof is restored medieval, with nice bosses, including a Green Man. The font has a C19th look, but may be recut and therefore older. There are several good brasses, although most figures are heavily worn. Two royal arms are for William IV and one of the other Hanoverian kings. Figures from the old rood screen dado have a new home on the south aisle south wall, where both rood stair doorways are still in place. The C19th and C20th glass by Kempe & Co, Baillie & Mayer, R.A. Bell and others, is excellent. A medieval chest is in very good order. Both aisles and the chancel retain old piscinas. The west gallery is C18th. A Constable painting of 1809 forms the altar reredos. There is much more to discover in this grand church.

From the north churchyard

Porch into south aisle

Priest's doorway and porch

North doorway

North aisle west end

East along the nave

Aumbry, piscina; chancel south east; memorial

Piscina, rood loft doorway, headstop

Pigott? brass, c.1528

Glass by Bell, Baillie & Mayer and Kempe & Co

Interior looking west

Rood screen, Green Man boss

William IV & Hanoverian royal arms

Medieval chest

The font

163

NETTLESTEAD ST MARY   C3, TM 088 494

St Mary from the south

There is almost nothing to Nettlestead, just a few houses and a lot of space, but a more glorious past is testified to by The Chace and High Hall, which were previously the headquarters of two important medieval manors. From the Hall came the influential Wentworth family, who played a part in the accession of Mary Tudor to the English throne. The church of St Mary slumbers alone in its churchyard and all around is silence and serenity, unlike the time during the 2nd World War when it was damaged by a stray bomb. The layout is simple, just west tower, nave, chancel and south porch, and St Mary's roots go back deeply into time. A Norman slit window in the nave north wall has a rare, ornate arch with three orders of decoration, and the nave is short and relatively high, a configuration typical of that period. The chancel is quite long, and may be C13th, whilst the unbuttressed tower is C14th. The latter has a prominent stair turret to the south whose fabric contains four fragments of Norman arcading, possibly from window arches. The Tudor brick porch is an interesting design, the half-round gable seems to be influenced by Dutch architecture. It encloses the C17th arms of Sir Thomas Wingfield and his wife Alice. Most windows are Perpendicular, later restored, but the east window is a late C19th Decorated design. Close to the nave south east window is a small, round-headed half window, which may have been a squint. The interior is marvellously atmospheric. Up above, the nave shows the black bones of an old roof, the rest mostly ceiled. The tall pulpit is a typical Jacobean example but the panelling and decoration are more enterprising than many. Above the pulpit is a large royal arms for George IV, most attractive after restoration. In the nave floor nearby is an early C16th brass of an armoured knight, which remarkably is little worn after centuries of footfall. The inscription is missing, but given the local connections, it may be one of the Wentworths. The east window has two flanking arches and in the sanctuary south wall an elaborate C15th piscina has drop-sill sedilia alongside. On the sanctuary north wall is the C17th Sayer memorial; only the figures and inscription of the original monument remain. The C19th choir stalls have some medieval parts, but the arm rest figures are Victorian. The C14th font, reconstructed after bomb damage, has Evangelist's symbols and curious, intense figures around the bowl, and strange, emaciated lions around the stem. The doorway and stairs to the rood are still in situ.

The porch   **Norman window**   **From the north east**   Norman fragments in the tower turret

Interior looking east   **The pulpit**   **George IV royal arms**   Brass of unknown knight, c.1500

The chancel   **Chancel south east**   **Chancel piscina**   **Mid-C17th Sayer memorial**

Interior looking west   **Rood stairs**   Woodwork, poppyhead, bench end figure   **Font and bowl panels**

165

NEWTON (NEWTON GREEN) ALL SAINTS　　B4, TL 919 412

All Saints from the north west

Newton village stands astride the busy A143 road near Sudbury, but All Saints is located in the little outpost of Newton Green to the north. All Saints is a singular church, because when in 1975 funds were not forthcoming locally to fully fund essential repairs, the parish was only able to renovate the chancel. It then turned to the Redundant Churches Fund, now Churches Conservation Trust, for help with the rest. The Trust agreed to do so, and at the same time took over responsibility for the tower, nave and porch. Thus, today the parish worships in the beautifully appointed chancel and the Trust looks after everything else. When space is needed for large events, the Trust generously makes the nave available. Apart from the glass and wood screen that seals off the chancel from the nave, the visitor could be unaware of the division and the church still be considered as a whole. Externally, the tower is a good C14th example, with diagonal buttresses, an intersecting west window and brick parapet. The C14th timber-framed porch is restored but the roof retains old king post and tie-beam elements. Many interesting C14th headstops can be seen associated with the windows. The nave and chancel are early C14th but the blocked Norman north doorway, with chevrons and roll moulding in the head and fluted capitals on the thin piers, demonstrates that a C12th church once stood here. Inside all is clean and seemly, the nave a little bare following renovations and clearing carried out by the CCT. However, there are a number of fine items to admire. The C15th font has a shallow bowl with double quatrefoils on the panels, fleurons beneath and thin panelling around the stem. The tall Perpendicular pulpit stands on a wine-glass stem and the panelling has intricately worked tracery. A Latin inscription runs around the panelling, requesting prayers for the donors. Nearby is a plain, ogee-headed piscina. An identical piscina is set in the south wall opposite. A large C14th wall painting runs along the north nave wall, depicting the Annunciation, Visitation and Nativity, but only the western section is distinct. In the opposite wall is a tomb niche containing the effigy of a lady, her face hammered away. On the chancel north wall is a superb C15th tomb, in wonderful condition, probably for Margaret Botelier. Opposite are handsome sedilia and a double piscina, in fine order. The east and other windows contain armorial and other C15th glass. The chancel also houses a distinctive C17th lectern.

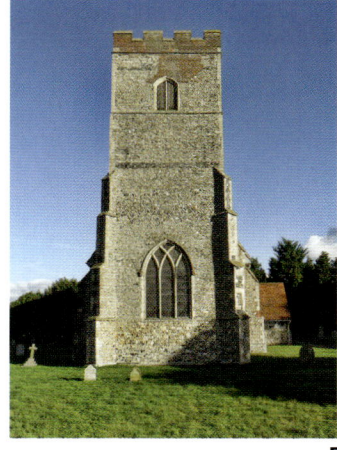

From the west and south west | Norman north doorway

Nave looking east | The font | Wall painting

The pulpit | Nave south wall piscina | Niche and effigy of a lady | The nave looking west

The chancel looking east | Chancel C15th glass | Chancel north wall tomb | Chancel piscina and sedilia

167

OLD NEWTON ST MARY   C3, TM 059 624

St Mary from the south

Old Newton has a population of around 830, which reflects the proximity of Stowmarket and the A14, so the environment verges on the urban, with much modern dormitory housing. But things are different around St Mary, which stands some way to the east away from the main village in a quiet, secluded churchyard. The peace and seclusion creates an appropriate atmosphere for exploring this attractive and diverting building. Unlike so many East Anglian churches, St Mary did not undergo major reconfiguration in the C15th, and retains its Decorated nave and chancel north windows and C14th layout. These windows feature superb Reticulated and Curvilinear tracery, but the south chancel wall has curious C19th iron-framed windows to the south and an east window consisting of simple vertical mullions. Nave and heavily buttressed chancel seem badly matched, the latter's roof apex stands higher and the pitch is more acute than the low angle nave roof. But the position of an earlier nave roofline on the east face of the tower makes it clear that the early roof was higher and steeper than the present one, and would have integrated neatly with the chancel roof. The C14th tower has smart flushwork on the parapet, Y-shaped belfry openings and lancets lower down. The neat porch has blocked side windows and a small niche below a parapet topped with a pinnacle. The interior is congenial and harmonious. The space below the C19th steeply inclined balcony has been enclosed by a glass and wood screen to make a useful area. Just in front of it are two old benches with rather flamboyant poppyheads; more can be seen in the balcony. The C15th font stands in front of the screen and has lost its base. The decoration of lions and shield-bearing angels on the bowl, and lions and wildmen around the stem, has been roughly treated in the past. A large George II royal arms is mounted on the nave north wall, and beneath the thick patina is of fine workmanship. The pulpit is C17th and pleasantly aged but unlike many Jacobean pulpits it is quite plain. Nave north windows contain some old glass, including canopy work and two savage beasts. The war memorial, in the form of a fretwork mosque, is very odd, not to say unique. A lead plate from an old roof has been preserved, complete with inscription and churchwarden's names. The chancel arch is tall and imposing. A fine C14th piscina and sedilia set resides in the chancel, also two ornate C14th niches either side of the east window. Two lovely old chairs are worth finding.

The church from the east and south east — Windows and priest's doorway

 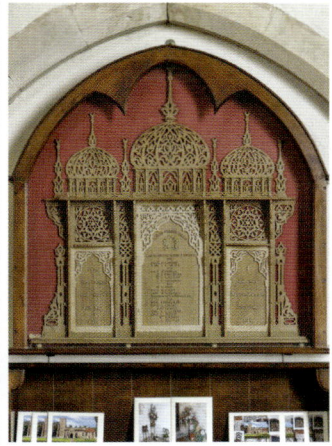   

Looking east from the balcony — Eastern inspired war memorial — George II royal arms — Old glass in the nave

The chancel — East wall niche — Chancel window, piscina and sedilia — West from the sanctuary

The pulpit — Roof lead, two fine chairs — The font — Benefaction board, old benches

OUSDEN ST PETER C3, TL 735 595

An enticing prospect – Ousden St Peter

St Peter is a remarkable and alluring church, from the uncommon layout to the features and fittings inside. It should be on all enthusiasts' lists for visiting. A central tower always stimulates interest, and while many of them have been restructured since being built in (usually) Norman times, the one here has been little altered beyond receiving a later parapet. It is a very rare survival. The belfry windows have typical Norman imposts and round heads, there are characteristic slit windows lower down and two niches on the east face. The chancel is C18th and may be at least the third rebuilding; bold traces of one of the earlier rooflines can be seen on the east face of the tower. Somewhat unusually a north transept springs off the east end of the nave, this too is C18th, with a nice Decorated-style north window with old armorial glass in the tracery. It was built to accommodate the local gentry. Next to it is a pretty, partly openwork porch of 1909. The nave is also Norman and its north doorway, part of which is now a window, is an odd confection, with a strong lintel carved with nailhead ornament and an arch of Roman tiles enclosing a tympanum with an overlapping tile pattern. A nave lancet is Norman too. An exploration of the interior is a diverting, not to say exciting, exercise. A walk around is accompanied by a sense of mystery as the visitor processes from one area to another, the view to the next veiled by walls pierced by low Norman arches. The latter are hoary with age, their capital carvings eroded, but enough remains to see that these are strange and arcane. The nave has many good things. The stylish C18th pulpit has marquetry on the panels, while behind it is a large C13th niche. On the eastern wall of the nave, above the arch, is a bold royal arms, now Hanoverian, but likely to have originally been for Charles I. On the same wall is a superb wall monument for Leticia Moseley, who died in 1619; the grisly skeleton at the bottom should not be missed. The C14th font has quatrefoils and other motifs on the bowl and stem columns that sweep outwards to engage the bowl. On the nave walls are two hatchments, of 1803 and 1863. The old roof is partly ceiled, with paterae on the wall plates. The north chapel contains a large C19th wall memorial for members of the Ireland family, featuring a grandiose, High Victorian Gothic design. The chancel has little of note, but the altar rails are a good C17th set, and there are ?early C19th Commandment, Creed and Lord's Prayer boards.

From the north and south east — North doorway and tower window

From the nave looking east — The pulpit — Hanoverian royal arms — Moseley memorial (1619)

The nave looking west — Hatchment, old glass, font — Under the tower looking east — The chancel

Lord's Prayer, Commandments — View west from the chancel — Arch details — C19th Ireland memorial

PETTISTREE ST PETER & ST PAUL   D3, TM 298 549

St Peter & St Paul from the south

St Peter & St Paul's is a stately, C13th-C15th church. Its impressive C15th tower is a landmark for miles around, with attractive chequerwork at the base, extending onto the buttresses and reappearing in two tiers at the top. The base of the nave south wall and its two buttresses have similar work, with an isolated patch on a north buttress. A little under halfway up the tower is an unusual single-light window, with a cinquefoil arch and square head, the latter formed by a stringcourse diverted from its horizontal course. Within this head is worn stone tracery. This was probably once a niche for a statue. Projecting from the tower south face is a stair turret. Above the west doorway arch is a head composed of alternating light and dark stone, a pattern that complements the flushwork. The south and blocked north doorways have the same feature and general design. The nave walls were raised at some time to accommodate very small quatrefoil clerestory windows. These cannot have admitted much light and are now blocked. The chancel is C13th on the evidence of Y-shaped and lancet windows. There are no porches, so entry is directly through the south doorway, into a capacious interior. The nave is filled with monotonous Victorian seating, but that is offset by some enticing objects. There are three decent C18th and C19th wall tablets around the pulpit, all sharing the same formal design. Similar ones reside in the chancel. Below the tablets is a cinquefoil-arched piscina, whilst the sill of the nearby window has been dropped to form sedilia, completing a suite of features that confirm that a guild chapel was once established here. Above the tablets is the higher of the rood doorways, now blocked. The lower doorway is not preserved. Across the nave the former presence of another guild chapel is confirmed by a similar piscina and a recently exposed niche, plus another in the window jamb. The recently revealed niche contains a stone infill that includes a large block with inscribed crosses, possibly part of an ancient mensa. Further exploratory excavation in the south wall revealed a stoup near the south doorway. The font is plain and nondescript. On the east nave wall is a nice C18th benefactions board. A few old benches have been retained, with poppyheads, some of which are beautifully carved. In the chancel see a restored angle piscina, a little C13th and C14th glass, Clayton & Bell east window glass, a plain old chest and a fine, wall mounted C16th brass for the Bacon family.

From the west and north east — **West, south and north doorways**

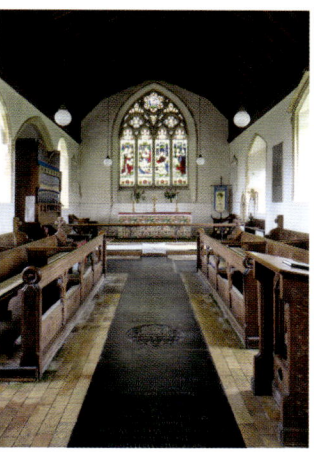

Interior looking east — **Tablets, rood doorway, pulpit** — **Piscina, niche, ?mensa stone, stoup** — **The chancel**

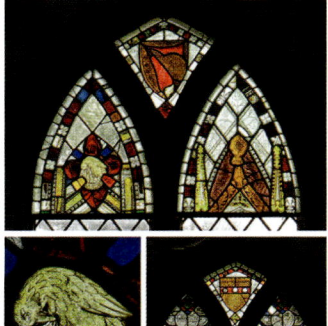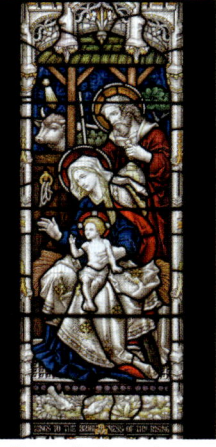

Medieval glass — **Bacon brass, late C16th** — **East window glass** — **Chancel angle piscina**

The church from the sanctuary — **Bench ends, benefaction board** — **The font** — **Chest, Whitbread tablet, organ**

PRESTON ST MARY

B3, TL 946 502

Evening shadows lengthen at St Mary

The main approach to St Mary is from the west, and from that viewpoint the church is seen to be a fine edifice, but it is not until the magnificent C15th north porch is encountered that the church demands a higher assessment. Entirely covered with exquisite flushwork, the porch also boasts grand Perpendicular side windows, pinnacles, battlements, clasping buttresses with niches and a handsome gable with niche beneath. Many other external features combine to complement the porch, such as the bold west front of the tower (rebuilt in the late C19th, re-using the old features), which has a super doorway flanked by two niches, with another above, all surmounted by a big Perpendicular window. The nave has a neat clerestory and battlements. Aisles, tower and porch are also battlemented, while the aisles have a suite of impressive C15th windows. The interior has many choice features, not least the font, which is a first rate Norman example, heavily carved on all four faces of the bowl with interlace and other twining designs, interlinked arcading, a Tree of Life and ranks of star-like motifs enclosing a florid cross. There are engaged colonnettes at the corners. The supporting columns have Norman designs, but are more recent. Both rood stair doorways are in place and nearby above the chancel arch is a typical Victorian banner. The C19th stained glass is of mixed quality, but some of the Clayton & Bell work is good, and a fascinating collection of medieval to C16th armorial glass appears in several windows. The chancel sanctuary is beautifully appointed, with extensive use of twinkling mosaic in the reredos and large flanking panels. There is more mosaic in a south aisle tablet for J.E. Wright of 1908. The C14th angle piscina in the sanctuary is in good restored order, with drop-sill sedilia alongside. On the south chancel wall is a plain black-letter tablet of 1729 for Nicholas Colman, also a faded late C18th marble tablet for two babies of the Cooke family, complete with an affecting verse. On the opposite wall are an early C19th tablet and an early C20th brass plaque. The chancel floor is handsomely tiled. Reset across the tower arch is the heavily restored dado of the old chancel screen. The church has two remarkable survivals, a wooden Elizabeth 1st royal arms and a Decalogue board, very similar in design, which opens in triptych fashion. The two outer boards have bible quotations. Though C17th or earlier, they are in excellent condition. In the north aisle is a tomb niche. Two brasses are recorded in the chancel floor.

The north porch

St Mary from the south west

Tower west doorway

Window

Interior looking east

Rood stair doorways, pulpit

C16th and Clayton & Bell glass

Through the chancel arch

The chancel

Colman tablet 1729

C19th wall memorials

Sanctuary south east

Interior looking west

Elizabeth 1st arms, Decalogue board

Restored screen dado

The font

RAYDON ST MARY

C4, TM 049 386

St Mary is both quirky and likeable

In the middle of the C18th Raydon's west tower collapsed, damaging the nave and leaving only one intact bell. The tower was not rebuilt, instead a mini-belfry was erected in its place to house the remaining bell. At the opposite east end of the church two buttresses are extended skywards to create two distinctive super-pinnacles, with fluted columns topped with an extravaganza of heads and crockets. Between the two a clock is mounted on the chancel gable, another unusual feature. Two chancel south side buttresses also have crocketted gables. The entire building is a rare survival of a Decorated church of the late C13th-early C14th, the Perpendicular overhauls so common elsewhere by-passed Raydon, or else there was no money for upgrading. The windows and doorways are especially rewarding of study, even the C19th east window is finished in admirable Decorated style. The south doorway has a battered stoup to its right, a niche above and worn headstops, and is sheltered by a curious wooden openwork porch, whose timbers, in part, may be old. The chancel has tall and slim low-side windows to both north and south, with transoms, below which the aperture is filled in. The north side vestry extension is C19th. The interior, despite the Victorian seating, retains an antique atmosphere and several features date from St Mary's early days. The lower rood stair doorway is open to reveal age-old steps winding upwards. Opposite in the south wall is a C14th piscina, indicating that a chapel once operated there. But that one does not bear comparison with the superb C14th double piscina in the chancel, which is designed to resemble a Decorated window. On the nave south wall is a lovely little Victorian Gothic tablet for Mary Hopes. Two late C15th brasses could easily escape notice, they are for Reydon husband and wife; one is an inscription for Thomas and the other is the figure of Elizabeth, unfortunately she has lost her top half. The chancel has much of interest. Apart from the piscina, already mentioned, there is a good medieval tomb niche in the north wall, with a cusped arch and headstops. Two excellent tablets grace the walls, one of 1663 for John Mayer is elaborate, while the other of 1907 for Eliza Coyle, of granite with white stone carving, is dignified and tasteful. Several chancel windows have fragments of medieval glass in their tracery and the low-side windows have distinctive arches and headstops. The economy-sized font is C19th, and rather odd, but it possesses a neat C18th cover.

| The west end | St Mary from the north east | Low-side window, pinnacle |

| Interior looking east | Lower rood stair doorway | Nave piscina | Nave tablet (1870) |

| The chancel | Chancel tablets | Tomb niche, piscina, old glass | Low-side window and headstops |

| Interior looking west | Reydon brasses, late C15th | The font | South doorway |

177

REDE ALL SAINTS B3, TL 804 559

All Saints from the south

The small village of Rede (pop. c.135) is a working and a workaday village, and probably always has been, traditionally providing a workforce for the needs of the land. There are a few attractive older properties, but no-one could call Rede 'chocolate-box'. Yet the name has some resonance beyond the village boundaries, and that is because of topography. Just to the west of the village is Great Wood, wherein is set a radio mast. Near to it is the highest point in Suffolk, a dizzying 136m (a little over 446 feet). There is no sense of height, the area around is basically a plateau with a few rolling slopes. All Saints church would win no prizes for historical or architectural grandeur, but it is exactly the sort of solid, decent church on which to base the spiritual life of the inhabitants, and there are also a few intriguing features to pique the visitor's interest. Externally the church was heavily restored by the Victorians in at least three phases, which included rebuilding the chancel and south porch. The tower of around 1300 was rebuilt too in its upper stages, but lower down the fabric is fascinating, showing several phases of building and repair. The nave was also restored, but its groundplan and a round-headed window point to a Norman origin. On the north side externally the Norman window has a brick surround and nearby is an odd square window with curious tracery of cusped cross bars that meet a quatrefoil in the middle. It is C19th but may have replaced a window that lit the rood; if not, its purpose is mysterious. The C14th porch was so thoroughly overhauled as to appear C19th, but the niche above the doorway is original (with a modern statue), also probably the fancy gable cross. Inside, most of the seating is C19th, but some older woodwork was retained, including bench ends and poppyheads. Some chancel stalls have the unusual addition of misericord-type seats on their ends, with good quality carving beneath. Discarded older misericords can also be seen. The C17th pulpit is treated with a dark stain and is plain except for nice fans at the top of the panelling. The book rest has scrolled brackets. The plain font is crude and inscrutable, and defies accurate dating, but is clearly old. The roofs are ceiled but a single, large tie-bar with carved spandrels stretches across the nave. The reredos is a lovely item, of white and lilac marble with inset polished stone spheres. The east window glass is by Clayton & Bell, and the piscina nearby is possibly the restored medieval original.

From the west and the north **The porch, north side details**

Interior looking east **Altar and reredos** **Chancel piscina** **Chancel woodwork**

The organ **View west from the sanctuary** **The pulpit** **Nave woodwork**

The nave looking west **The font** **Tie-beam bracket** **A look back before leaving**

REDISHAM ST PETER

D2, TM 408 843

From the south west

St Peter is one of Suffolk's lovely smaller churches, tucked away in a tiny village and full of charm. It once had a tower, but that fell in the C19th. Being on sloping ground probably didn't help, and there was no move to replace it. These days a simple wooden bellcote sits on the nave west gable. There are no aisles, but a brick porch stands to the south. More brick was used to raise the nave walls and heighten the west wall, probably in the wake of the tower collapse. The chancel is early C14th on the evidence of the cusped lancets to the south. The west window lancets are Victorian. The partly C12th fabric is coarse and varied, with field stones and other re-worked materials such as limestone blocks forming a significant proportion. Quoins at the nave north east corner consist of stones and flints, a very early indicator. For such a small, minor church, the nave doorways are a surprise, for they are Norman, and in the case of the southern one, very ornate. The latter has three main orders in the arch, of decorated wheels in the label, chevron in the middle and most prominent order, and a smaller band of chevrons forms the inner order. One set of the engaged shafts in the jambs has fluted spiral ornament, while the outer frame is formed of semi-circular billet ornament. This doorway alone is a good reason for a visit, but also see the blocked north doorway, which is less ornate, but still impressive. The wooden shed that obscures it is unfortunate. The interior is small and homely, with evidence of Victorian restoration. But enough was left to make a survey rewarding. At the west end is a good C15th font, with large Tudor roses and shields on the bowl, and delightful and well-preserved angels with outstretched wings beneath. By the south door is a plain stoup. The crude George I royal arms on the nave south wall are very dark, but try to see the seriously underfed lion and unicorn, with gaunt ribs showing. The pulpit is an excellent James 1st model, full of character, with unusual cross-hatched carving at the base and splendid book rest brackets. Stained glass behind it may be by Christopher Webb. Tucked into the corner of a nave bench is an alms box of unusual design. The chancel is simply appointed, but quietly attractive. Some of its stalls are partly old, with good poppyheads and unlikely bench end carvings, including a house and animals eating from bowls. The plain C14th piscina tapers towards the base.

From the south and east, weathercock

St Peter from the north west

North doorway

South doorway

Interior looking east

The pulpit

The chancel

Chancel south east

Piscina

Bench end carvings

The church from the sanctuary

George I royal arms

Font and organ

Alms box

Holy water stoup

REDLINGFIELD ST ANDREW C2, TM 186 707

St Andrew from the south west

There are few more curious churches in Suffolk than St Andrew at Redlingfield. That is not to say it doesn't have considerable character and charm, and many unusual facets. For a start, there is no road to it, and the congregation and visitors must walk from the village to a little bridge and then take a field path to the building. However, it may be that arrangements are made to park at the adjoining Hall Farm at service times. A few years ago St Andrew was in a fairly parlous state, with incursions from the weather causing growing concern, indeed it was placed on the Buildings at Risk register, but a splendid effort from church stalwarts and villagers to source grants and raise money resulted in the roofs being repaired, and other repairs and maintenance being undertaken. The effort is apparently continuing, to turn St Andrew into a community resource with the provision of modern facilities. A visit these days is a real pleasure. The church was once part of a priory estate and the area still hints at the layout of a religious foundation, with one significant priory building remaining standing in a neighbouring field. As for the church building, it is full of interest and mystery. The mystery centres on the strange 'tower' at the west end which has a Tudor? brick base to a third of the height, with buttresses and the remnants of a stair turret, and is completed by a decidedly odd lath and plaster construction resembling a little house, with pantiled roof. How that configuration came about is still largely unknown. The nave is clearly ancient (the north side wall leans rather precariously) and the ghost of a narrow window to the north and the fabric suggests a Norman origin. It was raised with brick at some point. The chancel of c.1820 is also of brick but with the original C14th east and south windows and priest's doorway refitted. The interior has a lovely ambience, but contains little of significance. The much-abused C15th 'East Anglian' font has typical Evangelists' symbols and angels on the bowl and mutilated wildmen and lions around the stem. The hefty cover is C17th. A large C14th piscina in the nave south east wall indicates that a chapel once functioned there. The royal arms is for George IV, but the escutcheon indicates that it was originally for a Hanoverian monarch of pre-1801. There is a nice benefactions board of 1828. The old tower arch, now blocked and seen only as a trace in the wall in its lower half, can be seen to the west. See also a few pieces of old glass and the double arch of the blocked north doorway.

The way in | From the west and north east

Garneys tablet, chancel doorway | In the porch | South doorway | Interior looking east

Nave piscina | The chancel | West from the sanctuary | Old glass fragments

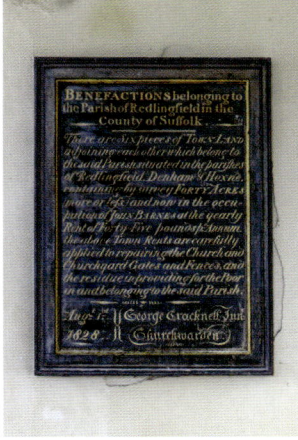

The font | Blocked north doorway | George IV royal arms | Benefactions board

REYDON ST MARGARET

E2, TM 491 782

St Margaret from the north east

Reydon is one of Suffolk's boom settlements, as both its size and population continue to expand. Highly desirable neighbour Southwold is too expensive for many buyers, thus their attention is often directed to nearby Reydon, which already comfortably exceeds Southwold in the number of permanent residents. To that extent it has lost much of its small village feel, but St Margaret stands aloof from the real estate mania in its considerable churchyard in a quiet rural setting about three quarters of a mile north west of the main village. The church is mostly C14th and C15th, with the chancel being rebuilt in the latter century. The fabric of the chancel is mixed and irregular and includes many recycled blocks of roughly dressed yellowish limestone. The origin of these blocks is unknown, it is unlikely that they came from an earlier church, unless a significant part of it was built of limestone, again improbable. The fabric of the tall, early C14th tower also contains large stone inclusions, though few of the yellow limestone type. There is evidence that a building once stood off the chancel north wall, probably a chapel, an area of infill is visible with a doorway and vestiges of a pillar piscina. An ornate boot scraper is dated 1793. Though no doubt a huge boon to the congregation and others, a sprawling 1988 extension to the north is jarringly incompatible with the main church architecture. As is usual, the interior was reconfigured in the C19th and the result was not unsuccessful, but it is the present-day re-ordering which has really transformed St Margaret for the better. There are few wall tablets but look out for the typically Victorian example for Mary Wilmer, also a few ledger slabs. Medieval St Margaret must have been a very pious place, almost every Perpendicular window in the nave and chancel has a figure niche, those in the chancel more ornate. Both nave and chancel have modest medieval piscinas, the latter accompanied by drop-sill sedilia. There is a nice show of C19th and early C20th glass by H. Hughes and A.L. Moore, but the east window figures by Ward & Hughes are reset in plain glass, to their detriment. The 'Woman at the Well' by Moore is especially striking. The Queen Anne arms is excellent. Rood loft stairs and doorways remain in place. The C14th font is not of the first rank and is outshone by its cover of 1920. Admire too the rustic tiled floors. The superb C17th chest must be seen, also the wooden corbels in the porch and a dramatic monument of 1921 in the churchyard for Fanny Watts.

The porch

The church from the south east

North chancel wall, chapel site

Interior looking east

Tablet, ledger, niche

Niches

West from the sanctuary

Chancel and nave piscinas

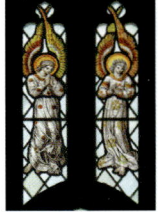
Glass by Hughes, Ward & Hughes and Moore

Nave looking west

Queen Anne royal arms

The font

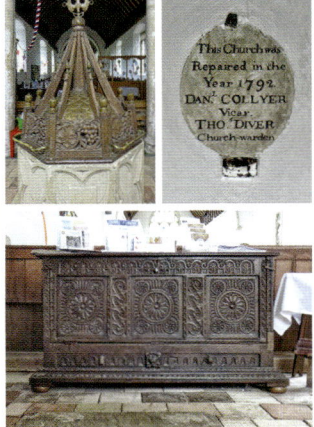
Font cover, tablet, chest

Porch corbels

Watts monument

RINGSFIELD ALL SAINTS   E2, TM 403 884

All Saints peeps out from behind a screen of trees

Most Ringsfield inhabitants live in Ringsfield Corner, about a mile south of the tiny village of Ringsfield proper, where stands All Saints church. This rural setting creates a beguiling atmosphere around the church, but, unfortunately, from most angles All Saints is obscured by intrusive trees. The narrow, unbuttressed C15th tower displays entasis; the quoins describe a gentle convexity as they ascend, and pinch in at the final C17th brick and flint stage. The chunky open pinnacles and low stepped battlements are a distinctive touch at the top. The thatched body of the church is low and long, with a gabled transept off the chancel north wall. Eminent Victorian architect William Butterfield gave All Saints a thorough overhaul in 1883-4, including rebuilding the chancel and constructing the transept, and establishing the origin of nave and chancel is not easy, but is probably pre-15th. Butterfield also resited a considerable monument of c.1599 for Nicholas Garneys on the outside south wall of the chancel, in its correct historical position. The edifice is mostly in brick, with a rare outside brass and a carved mermaid. Another funerary monument stands in the angle of the north transept and nave, a large, eccentric C19th extravaganza featuring angels, for Caroline Murat, a relative of both Napoleon and the King of Naples, and the wife of the owner of Redisham Hall. Most of Butterfield's attention inside was directed towards his new chancel, but elsewhere there is still much of antiquarian interest. The pulpit is fundamentally Jacobean, but other parts have been incorporated in the box; the tester is most impressive. The Jacobean theme is continued with a wonderful set of seating in the nave, beautifully and tastefully carved, some benches with finials. One older bench survives under the tower. Odd Jacobean panels appear in the chancel and elsewhere, some of which may be from the pulpit. Other contemporary panels carry biblical texts. The two short sections forming the chancel screen are also C17th and are very striking, with balusters, obelisks and texts. One of two continental glass roundels is in excellent order, and the later glass by Clayton & Bell and Bell & Beckham is of high quality. The latter firm are often associated with the work of Butterfield, but Ringsfield houses their only glass in Suffolk. The C15th 'East Anglian' font is in good shape despite some damage and has the usual angels, lions and Tudor roses around the bowl and superior lions on the stem. Two good wall tablets are set on the north nave wall.

Nave, C16th porch and tower

Garneys monument

Murat monument

All Saints from the west

Interior looking east

Pulpit and north chancel

The screen to the north and south

Chancel woodwork

Chancel piscina

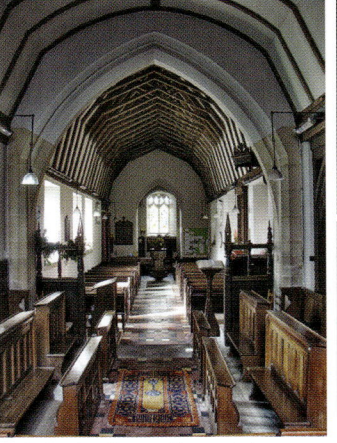
Interior from the sanctuary

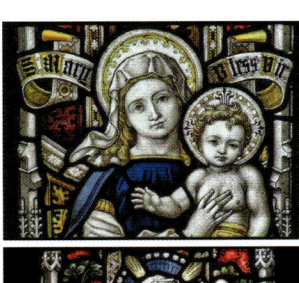

Clayton & Bell glass

Christ in the temple (C16th)

Nave benches and text

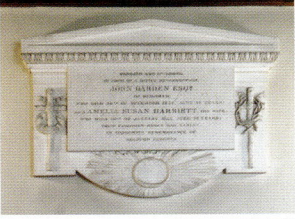

Garden tablets, C19th

The font

RINGSHALL ST CATHERINE   C3, TM 042 528

Deep in the heart of Suffolk countryside, Ringshall St Catherine

Ringshall St Catherine stands in a deeply rural situation some way north of the main village. The nearest settlement of any size is Needham Market, a little over five miles away to the east. In complete contrast to St Catherine's setting, nearby is Wattisham Flying Station, the biggest British military base of its kind in the country. Looking at the church it is remarkable that it is still standing. The Norman nave in particular was at one point so precarious that huge tie-beams were emplaced to prevent structural failure; these were carried through the walls and secured externally by substantial wooden pegs, a most unusual occurrence. Also, to the north one of the widest buttresses of any parish church prevents that wall from collapse. It is to everyone's benefit that these measures worked, for this is a fascinating building, not only is the nave Norman (there are three deeply splayed slit windows, two blocked, and the jambs of the south doorway to confirm that assignment), but the low tower is a rare, almost complete C12th construction, its outline resembling a wedding cake, with each stage a little smaller than its predecessor. The plain parapet is later. The chancel has mostly Perpendicular windows, but the east window is Decorated. The porch is a good C19th version of a medieval timber model. There is evidence of early C16th restoration/reconfiguration (see certain brickwork, roofs and some windows). The interior was thoroughly and routinely revamped in 1878 by Phipson and is largely uninspiring, but the heavily timbered roofs, tie-beams and suspended wheels for St Catherine add presence and there are enough older survivals to maintain interest during a visit. In front of the tower arch, part of which may be Norman, stands the familiar shape of a C13th Purbeck Marble font, with characteristic shallow arcading on the bowl. The supporting pillars are Victorian. The chancel was restored in the C19th, but the C14th piscina, unusually situated in the east wall, was retained. The east and south windows in the chancel contain glass by Clayton & Bell, the figures, to some eyes, having a curiously unsettling appearance. The tiling, possibly by Minton, is very good, but has suffered through the depredations of bats. A plain, faded and wordy late C18th tablet for members of the Watson family is set high on the south wall of the chancel. On the nave south wall are obscure paintings from a medieval Seven Works of Mercy sequence. The graveyard contains several war graves with characteristic Portland Stone headstones.

An inviting prospect

From the north east

Lest we forget

South doorway

Interior looking east

Norman window, tie-beam

The chancel

Piscina

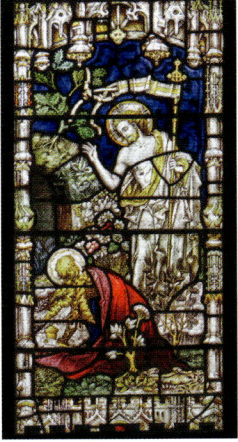
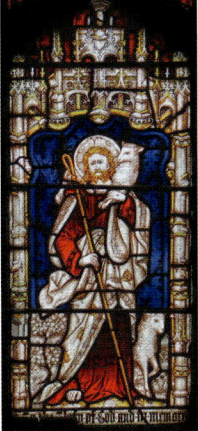
Clayton & Bell stained glass

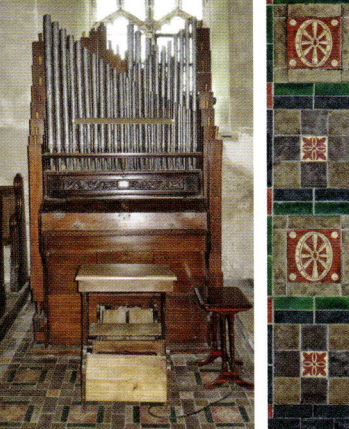
The organ

Chancel tiling

Watson tablet, late C18th

Chancel roof

West from the sanctuary

Seven Works of Mercy (part)

The font

189

RISBY ST GILES B2, TL 802 663

Evening falls at St Giles

Risby is off the tourist trail and little visited, but St Giles is a superb church that in a more popular area would see many times more visitors than it does. There is so much to see that it is difficult to know where to start. The building is very ancient, and Saxon origins are claimed for it in certain quarters, but the consensus today is that it is late C11th and post-Conquest. The evidence mostly lies in the rugged round tower, which has two tiny slit windows with heads formed from single blocks of stone; however, this early feature probably spans the Saxo-Norman overlap. The odd belfry openings towards the top are thought to be later, but still Norman. The high doorway above the tower arch inside gives credence to an early date, it may have been defensive. The tower arch itself is crudely made and archaic in design, and again it may have its origins in the Saxo-Norman interval. The nave too is at least early Norman on the evidence of the exposed portion of a deeply splayed round-headed window in the nave north wall, only visible inside. A C14th north chapel, now gone, was replaced by a C19th vestry. The modest porch is C15th. Much reconstruction took place in the early C14th. Thankfully, the inevitable Victorian restoration was light, leaving the interior with much of its ancient glory. The chancel arch was reconstructed in the C13th from possibly two C12th forerunners, and makes a fascinating study. The pointed arch reuses horseshoe shaped voussoirs on the east face. To the west the arch is flanked by fabulous C14th niches, beautifully restored. The C15th screen, though narrow, is magnificent, with lovely tracery. The exceptional C15th font owes its fine preservation to prudent plastering over when danger threatened, this was later removed to reveal undamaged bowl carvings. The north nave wall has a series of C13th and C14th wall paintings, in poor condition generally, but certain areas are clearer, including Mary Magdalene washing Christ's feet. Rood stairs and doorways are in place. The Jacobean pulpit is in fine condition, as is a George III royal arms. At the rear of the nave is a suite of medieval benches with brattishing and poppyheads. In the chancel the impressive C14th piscina and east wall niches are similar and contemporary. Windows here contain a wonderful array of medieval glass fragments, with lots of figurative pieces. Some reconstructions are completed by modern glass. Good later glass is by Kempe. There is much more, a visit is highly recommended.

From the south east, north east and east

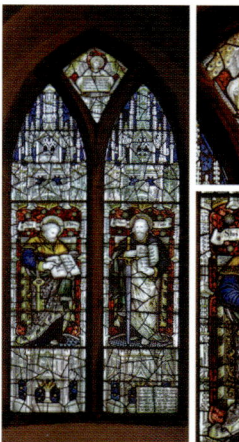

From the nave looking east · The pulpit · Chancel arch, screen, niches, rood doorways · St Peter & St Paul, by Kempe

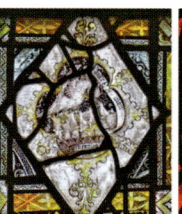

Chancel east end · Piscina, niche, rood doorway · C16th Flemish glass · Medieval glass

From the sanctuary · Mary Magdalen washes Christ's feet · George III royal arms, old benches · Font, tower arch

ROUGHAM ST MARY

B3, TL 912 625

St Mary is a grand church, set off with a good collection of gravestones

Once St Mary stood at the heart of its village, but then the Black Death arrived on its doorsteps in the mid-C14th and the villagers took the drastic decision to burn their settlement and move further south. Thus, St Mary was left stranded half a mile from the present village and isolated for many centuries thereafter, but these days the building is not quite alone, or quiet, anymore, for a modern primary school stands nearby. The church is big and bold and has the 'full set' of west tower, embattled nave and aisles, clerestory, chancel, extensions off the chancel to north and south and a south porch. Wool money was probably responsible for much C15th expansion, particularly the grand tower, an assertive and beautiful sight. The top of the tower has a wonderful display of flushwork, with a tracery frieze, and dedications to the builders, Marian symbols and neat panelling on the stepped battlements. Pinnacles stand at the corners. Much Perpendicular fenestration was added in the C15th, but the chancel retains its Decorated windows, though much renewed. Inside, a superb range of nave and aisle benches demands attention. Eight pairs are original early C16th work, but the later C19th copies are also excellent. All are distinguished by finely carved and imaginative ends, backs, and poppyheads. The font is old and gnarled, its octagonal bowl with panel and tracery designs. Damage to the rim was partly caused by the rough removal of the the medieval lock. The quatrefoil-piered arcades are delightful. The nave and aisle roofs are medieval with later restoration, the former is of hammerbeam type and is particularly fine despite its angels being decapitated. The wallplate is enhanced with quatrefoils and cresting. The aisle roofs have distinctive human corbels, typically medieval in appearance, but in such excellent condition that some or all may be much younger. The north aisle east window is partly obscured by a large Victorian memorial, but above it the window tracery contains medieval glass fragments. The C19th stained glass is of reasonable quality. Below the memorial is a C17th carved wooden panel. The nave aisles have an old piscina each and there is an exceptional piscina and sedilia set in the chancel. A fine, large early C15th brass for Drury husband and wife resides in the north aisle, an excellent copy of it can be seen elsewhere. Several distinguished wall tablets now find themselves overseeing domestic activities under the tower. A rood loft lower doorway survives, as does a niche by the pulpit.

The church from the south east and north east

Fine flushwork at the top of the tower

South east across the church

Nave seating details

Nave roof and decapitated angels

The chancel

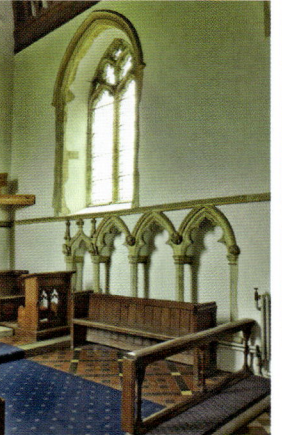

Chancel piscina and sedilia

Nave piscinas, chancel piscina angel

The nave looking west

North aisle east end, C17th tablets

Drury brass, early C15th

The font

Medieval glass fragments

193

RUSHMERE ST ANDREW   C3, TM 196 460

Old St Andrew from the south

All churches are different and have a variety of attractions to beguile visitors, but some are more different than others, and St Andrew is a case in point. It is an odd feeling to see it for the first time, and quite confusing, for it is a blend of old and new and much is not what it seems at first glance. In the beginning there was a Norman church here, probably just a nave and chancel. We know that because a Romanesque doorway is still here, it has been resited and much rebuilt, but still makes an impressive sight today in the south wall. A later medieval church was built in its turn and served the (then) small parish, but like so many in the C18th and early C19th it fell into disrepair and was in serious need of renovation. Enter architect E.C. Hakewill, supposedly retired to live in Rushmere, but persuaded back into action to put the old building back into order. His restoration of 1861 was drastic, the nave and chancel were demolished back to the foundations and rebuilt in Early English style, a favourite period with Hakewill. A north aisle was added to accommodate Rushmere's burgeoning population. The fine tower of the late C15th/early C16th with smart flushwork and stepped battlements at the top was left alone apart from the addition of an odd west window and pinnacles. In 1930 a bleak brick vestry was added to the north west, converted now to kitchen and toilets. There things stood until, with yet more people arriving to swell the catchment area of Rushmere St Andrew, a decision was taken in the late 1960's to expand – considerably. Hakewill's chancel was completely remodelled to become the focus for an altar, which became a central altar when a new, very modern, extension was built to the east. This was furnished with chairs looking west and north to the altar, a revolutionary concept in 1968, but with the seating in the old nave integrated into the plan, an open and very satisfying environment for worship was established. Also at that time a new vestry was commissioned to the north, running off the new nave. Finally, in 1987 a large church hall was constructed south of the new nave and connected to it, again very modern in conception. These additions and alterations clash with the old church, and the present-day ensemble of buildings may not please the purist. Any historical interest in the church centres on the old nave, which has some fine Lavers and Barraud glass, super benches, a substantial font by Hakewill, a few middling wall tablets (mostly oval) and a decent ledger slab of 1660.

The church from the north west and west — The Norman doorway

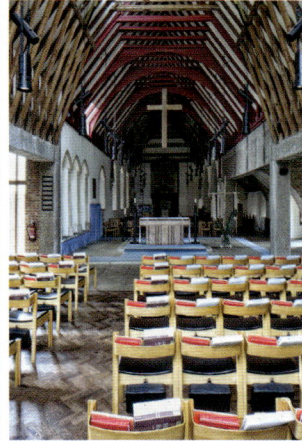

Views inside St Andrew

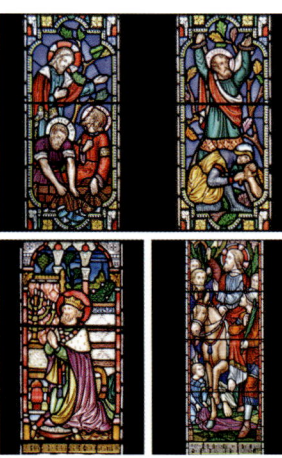

From the altar looking west — Arcade pier — Lavers & Barraud glass — Benches in the old nave

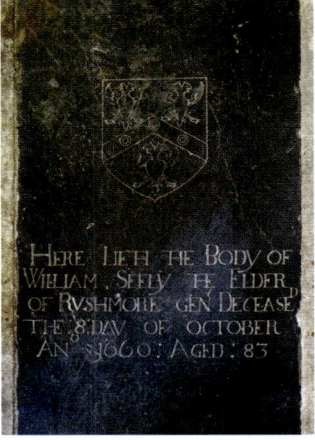

Bench end — Wall memorials — Seely ledger slab — The font

SANTON DOWNHAM ST MARY the VIRGIN B1, TL 816 876

A bleak day at St Mary the Virgin

An atmospheric site in the midst of darkling forest sets the scene for a fascinating church. East of the north porch is a half-arch filled with a window, next to it an external piscina; the porch east wall is unexpectedly thick, and the frontage asymmetrical. The explanation for these features is that a chapel once stood here. The arch formed the entrance from the interior, the piscina was internal and the west wall of the chapel became the east wall of the porch. The internal doorway, despite some later modification, is clearly Norman. Another blocked opening in the chancel wall may have been a doorway or lowside window. On the other side of the church the south doorway is Norman, as is the priest's doorway into the chancel. Above the south doorway is an enigmatic carving of a rapacious animal. Two Norman nave windows were later re-made as pointed lancets, but their true origin is revealed inside by their round-headed frames. The north and south doorways also retain their original Norman surrounds inside. The Perpendicular tower was built in the late C15th/early C16th, according to bequests. Unusually, the names of the donors who financed the building of the tower are recorded at its base, interspersed with flushwork panelling, sacred monograms and donors' initials. The interior was reconfigured several times, but in addition to the Norman doorways and certain windows, a length of coeval carving is preserved in the chancel. High in the south east nave wall is an exposed portion of a blocked aperture, with medieval painting in the reveals. Did it once open onto, or light, a rood loft? Other highlights of the interior include a battered C13th piscina in the chancel, accompanied by drop-sill sedilia. In or on the north chancel wall are a tomb niche, deeply splayed C13th lancet window, an aumbry and two old wall tablets, also the strip of Norman carving mentioned earlier. The east window contains high-quality glass by Clayton & Bell, of Christ in Glory. The lovely screen is a well-preserved example from the 1300's and has a tiny window-shaped squint; near to it is a delightful Jacobean pulpit. The font with plain octagonal bowl is probably C14th, its neat cover Jacobean. Near it on the west wall are two fine memorials for members of the Cadogan family. Three lancets contain Faith, Hope and Charity in glass by Kempe, and an excellent Annunciation by the same workshop fills the west window. During the years 1665-70 a deep drift of sand partly buried St Mary, along with much of the rest of Santon Downham.

Tombs, chapel site, donors

St Mary from the south west

South, north, priest's doorways

The interior looking east

Chancel screen

The pulpit

The chancel

Chancel piscina

Christ in Glory (Clayton & Bell)

Chancel north wall

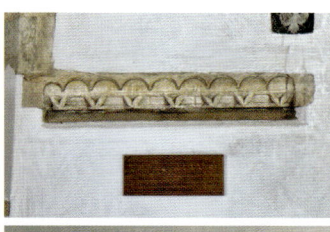
Norman carving, blocked nave window

The nave looking west

Hope by Kempe

The font

Earl Cadogan memorial

Annunciation by Kempe

SHADINGFIELD ST JOHN the BAPTIST   D2, TM 434 837

At its best on a sunny day, St John the Baptist at Shadingfield

Regular travellers on the A145 south of Beccles will be familiar with St John, for its C15th tower looms over the road at a tight bend. Its setting seems precarious, but as it has been there since the 1400's, there may be nothing to fear. The rest of the church has stood for much longer than that, two round-headed slit windows at the west end speak of Norman origins for the nave, and much of the rest of the church was in place by the end of the C13th. The form of the two nave doorways is transitional between Norman and Early English, the north has dogtooth embellishment in the arch. A large lancet in the chancel points to a C13th age; a single Perpendicular window is set in the nave north wall. The Y-shaped and intersecting windows to the south are restored or replacements, but they may be faithful ones, which is possibly also the case for the east window. The porch is a powerfully fronted C16th brick affair, which glows beautifully in afternoon sunlight. Two major Victorian overhauls left the interior a little short of character, but several significant features remain. The chancel arch was removed at some point in the past, also all traces of the rood loft, but two strange head corbels on the north and south walls in that area may once have supported some element of the loft. Both may once have been double headed, but the one to the south appears to have lost a head. Near it is a plinth for a statue and the resited bowl of a piscina, indicating the former presence of a chapel next to where a screen once stood. Over time, both north and south nave walls have been stripped in places to reveal wall paintings, probably of mixed ages. Much of the detail is obscure, but a scene where Christ is being whipped is discernible and there is some clear scrollwork. In the sanctuary the altar is flanked by two C19th niches containing the Ten Commandments. To the north of the C17th altar in the east wall is an aumbry and on the south wall a plain C13th piscina and drop-sill sedilia. Three well-maintained C17th inscription brasses lie in the floor nearby, with another from the late C16th on the nave south wall. The east window has an interesting assemblage of old glass. The border is made up of C16th–C18th fragments which frame a variety of roundels and a rectangular portrait of Christ at the Last Supper. A rare mid-C19th 'All flesh is grass' themed window in the chancel is painted in enamels. The splendid C15th font, lovely organ, Carolean royal arms and banner stave locker will also reward study.

The porch

St John from the north east

North doorway, Norman window

Interior looking east

Head corbels

The sanctuary

Christ at the Last Supper

Chancel south east

Brasses

'All Flesh is Grass', detail

Interior looking west

The Flagellation of Christ

The font

Early C19th organ

Carolean royal arms

SHOTLEY ST MARY D4, TM 237 360

St Mary is no beauty, but it is endearing

The site of St Mary on its hill in Shotley Church End is a wonderful spot even without the presence of a church of very great interest. The views over a stretch of the Orwell river, which include the vast docks at Felixstowe, are fabulous. No finer place then for the resting place of hundreds of sailors, who died in the two world wars of the C20th and at other times. Their graves lie in well-tended rows on a slope running down to the river. Then there is St Mary, a quite extraordinary building, although it would take a rare imagination to think of it as beautiful. Indeed, it looks like it was assembled from a kit of disparate parts, but charm and character are attributes it does not lack. The top section of the medieval tower fell long ago and now the remaining portion reaches no higher than the roof of the nave. The nave is also medieval and has a clerestory and two aisles, plus a porch much repaired. But it is the chancel that draws most interest. It looks like it was imported from a Wren or Hawksmoor church, although its date of 1745 is somewhat later than the works of those great master builders. It is a textbook Classical edifice and was the inspiration of the then incumbent the Rev'd Henry Hervey Aston, presumably to replace a decayed medieval original. The 'Venetian' east window is a standout. In contrast, the contemporary vestry is more utilitarian. Through the nave south doorway a much-diminished medieval interior is revealed, with two slightly different arcades. However, glancing upwards, the nave roof is a different thing altogether, a magnificent double hammerbeam example, sadly now lacking what once must have been a grand array of hammer end angels. Elsewhere there is a modest font of 1906, fine glass of 1907, a piscina in the south aisle, a murky George II royal arms high on the tower wall and an odd thin niche in an arcade pillar. Sealing the narrow tower arch is a Classical doorway. A few tablets and memorials adorn the walls. But it is to the chancel that all eyes eventually turn. At its portal is an outstanding chancel arch, in dark wood and embellished with typical C18th carving, the arms of Aston at the apex. On the west side, the arms of Hervey. The chancel is lined with dark wood panelling, with the altar table, surrounded by rails on three sides, being the focus. The table is wonderfully carved, with cabriole legs enriched with fine angels, while the stunning reredos with its paintings of Moses and Aaron extends the width of the east wall. A handsome coved ceiling enhances a delightful picture.

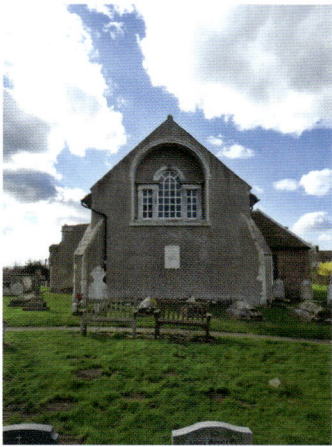

St Mary from the east and north east — **Requiescat in Pace**

Interior looking east — **Chancel arch, reredos beyond** — **Aston arms** — **Chancel east end**

Altar table, reredos detail — **Nave looking west** — **Nave roof** — **George II royal arms**

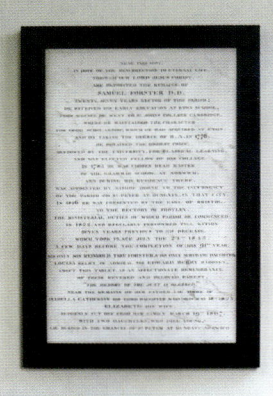

1907 glass, war memorial, niche — **Forster tablet** — **Font of 1906** — **The south aisle**

SHOTTISHAM ST MARGARET of ANTIOCH   D3, TM 321 447

The southern aspect of St Margaret

St Margaret is distinguished by a pretty approach from the west, up a short lane and then a flight of steps to emerge into the spacious churchyard, where the church has plenty of room to show off its attributes. A tall C15th tower is one of them, with a stair turret to the south, Perpendicular-style bell openings with, below, slim lancets. The west face has a doorway with flattened 'Tudor' arch and, above, a window emplaced, like the bell openings, during a sweeping C19th restoration by E.C. Hakewill, a familiar name in the realm of Suffolk Victorian church overhauls. The one here came in 1867 and much was changed; an Early English template was adopted. Externally the biggest project was a new north aisle, which was accommodated under a massive overall roof that also encompassed the nave. As often seen with Hakewill restorations, this roof was taken down almost to ground level. At the east and west ends of the aisle are curious windows, Early English in inspiration but of unconventional design. The east wall was rebuilt and given a classic Early English configuration of three lancet windows, with circular window above. The south wall of the chancel retains a C13th priest's doorway with a lancet functioning as a lowside window alongside. The lower half is now blocked, as is a Perpendicular window on the north side, its frame entombed in the filling. Other windows on the south side are replacements, two of them with plate tracery designs. The south porch is Hakewill's. The interior did not escape Hakewill's attentions, all the seating, complex nave roof and much more are his, but thankfully some older features and fittings were retained. The rood opening and stairs set in a south window reveal are very well preserved and open to view. The stairs don't rise far, the opening onto what was the loft is barely 2 metres above the lowest step. In the floor nearby is a good brass of 1620 for Rose Glover, with touching sentiments in rhyme. Two roses are engraved on the plate. Surviving in Hakewill's chancel are a restored medieval piscina and sedilia, as well as the aforementioned priest's doorway, lowside window and blocked window to the north. Also present is an attractive, ornate ?C18th chair and a good C16th chest. The glass of 1880 in the east window lancets is by Henry Hughes of London. The font is a typical C13th Purbeck Marble example, with the usual shallow arches on the bowl. The marble pillars supporting it are C19th. The modern water-drop chandeliers are a nice addition.

St Margaret from the west and north east

Lowside window, priest's doorway

North east from the nave

Rood stair

Rose Glover brass (1620)

The chancel

East window and detail

Chancel piscina and sedilia

Chancel south west

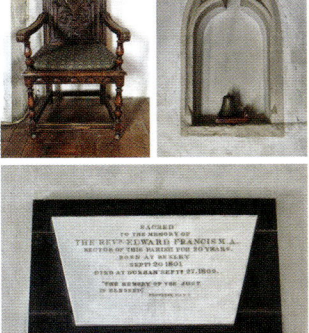
Old chair, piscina, wall tablet

North west from the chancel

The font

203

SIBTON ST PETER

D2, TM 367 695

This view illustrates well Hakewill's work on the south and east walls

Like the preceding church Shottisham St Margaret, Sibton St Peter was restored by E.C. Hakewill in the late C19th, and the two churches share certain of Hakewill's trademark Early English stylings. These include the familiar three-lancet window form for the east window (with circular window above), and plate tracery windows elsewhere. Hakewill's rebuilt chancel at Sibton incorporates slightly pointed, shafted and embellished lancets, both singly and conjoined; the priest's doorway is in the same vein but also takes some inspiration from the Transitional south doorway. The battlemented tower is early C15th, with flushwork designs (blind windows and diamonds) and gargoyles at the top. About two thirds of the way up a break in stonework indicates that the highest portion of the tower was rebuilt, perhaps by Hakewill. He also modified the north aisle with new windows and much else, but its west window is original C15th work. Yet the doorway into the aisle is C13th, as is the arcade within; both may have been recycled from the ruins of Sibton Abbey across the A1120 road. The south doorway is from around the turn of the C12th. Its semi-circular arch has plain roll-mouldings, whilst three of the four engaged shafts in the jambs have ornamented capitals. The front two have rings at their mid-point. Benches inside can be moved to create space for events, thus brasses and ledger slabs in the nave floor are often open to view. Brasses in the nave and chancel, and some excellent wall memorials, are highlights of the interior. Three brasses, for members of the Scrivener family (1574, 1582 and 1626), feature figures including children; the last dated is partly hidden beneath a choir stall. There are also several inscription brasses. Superb memorials for Sir Edmund Barker and his wife (1676), and Johan Scrivener (1662) adorn the chancel and nave respectively, and there are several other tablets of high quality, if not all in the best of condition. The chancel screen is composed of four panels of delicate tracery saved from a C15th original, whilst the font is a nice item of similar age, ornamented on the bowl with angels and evangelists' symbols; the stem has wild men and lions. The medieval hammerbeam nave roof, with ornate wall plates, hammers and angel corbels, is impressive. The church's glass by Hughes, Ward & Hughes and Lavers, Barraud & Westlake, is of fair quality. See too the fine Jacobean pulpit, remnants of floral wall painting, pairs of canopied niches either side of the chancel arch with original paint, and Stuart altar rails.

St Peter from the east and south — Transitional south doorway

Looking east — Pulpit, niches, rood stair doorway — Johan Scrivener memorial — Scrivener tablet and memorials

  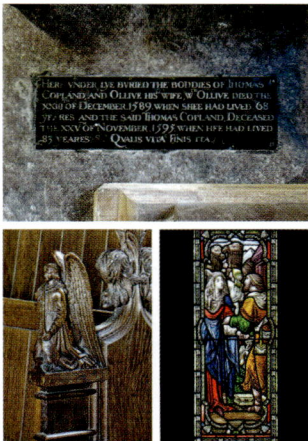 

Chancel, screen, ledger slabs — John Chapman and family (1582) — Copland brass (1595), angel, Hughes glass — Barker memorial (1676)

West from the sanctuary — Nave roof and details — The font — South doorway, painting traces

205

SOTTERLEY ST MARGARET of ANTIOCH   E2, TM 459 852

Just perfect. St Margaret from the south east

One of Suffolk's finest churches is sequestered in a medieval park near a picture-book C18th manor house, which succeeded a demolished medieval precursor. Little has changed here for centuries, and it is entirely appropriate that it requires effort to find and then reach this magical place, involving a very pleasant walk of three quarters of a mile or so through the park, following way markers. The nave north wall has characteristic Norman coursing, indicating an early foundation for St Margaret. Most of the building is C14th and C15th century, with restoration in the C19th, but the bottom half of the tower could be C13th. The tapering and slightly narrower top half sits rather uncomfortably on the older lower part, with a marked junction. The south porch is C15th and within is a medieval door, bleached with age and with typical Perpendicular tracery in the head. The interior requires detailed inspection, for it is a veritable treasure house. There is a grand collection of old brasses, one of the best in a Suffolk church, many with figures. Most are for members of the Playters family, who ruled the roost from the big house from the 1460's until the manor was sold to the Barne family around the year 1744. Particularly fine brasses are for Thomas Playters and his wife (c.1479), another Thomas Playters (c.1572) and Thomasina Playters (c.1578), but all are worth finding. Complementing the brasses are several memorials for Playters and others, the most ostentatious being a massive wall memorial in the chancel for Thomas Playters and his two wives, featuring three kneeling figures and effigies of their 22 children (some apparently misbehaving). The tomb chest of Wm Playters is from 1512 and a battlefield cross and memorial is for 1st World War victim Miles Barne. Medieval glass panels appear in several windows, but the best figurative work can be found in the east and west windows. Most of the east window is by Kempe (1899); detail and colouration is of the highest order. Below it is a tasteful reredos by Sir Charles Nicholson (1920). The font is a typical C15th East Anglian type with evangelists' symbols and angels on the bowl. The chancel screen is C15th but the tracery has been altered and the dado figures repainted. Behind the pulpit is a modified, sealed rood stair entrance. Characterful old corbels support the nave roof, at the west end of the nave is a banner stave locker and the choir stalls are partly medieval. See also hatchments, piscinas and stoups. There is much more, a visit is highly recommended.

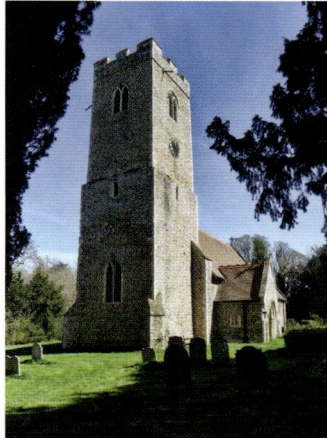   

St Margaret from the south west and north east — South door and north doorway

The screen — Medieval glass — Miles Barne battlefield cross — Corbels, font

The sanctuary — Sir Thomas Playters memorial (1658) — Detail of east window by Kempe — Sanctuary south east

Playters brasses (late C15th, 1578) — Wm Playters tomb chest, Barne tablet — North west across the nave

SOUTH COVE ST LAWRENCE E2, TM 499 808

A picture book setting to greet the visitor to St Lawrence

Despite the presence of the B1127 road just beyond the gate, once St Lawrence's churchyard is entered all is tranquil. In many ways St Lawrence is the perfect small country church, with deep roots in time. Both doorways into the nave are Norman and there are hints of an earlier Saxon church in the inner arches of these doors and the crude north east quoin at the junction of nave and chancel. The north doorway retains a C15th door with Perpendicular tracery, still braving the English weather after c.600 years. The south doorway is the more ornate of the two, with chevrons in the semi-circular arch. The sheltering porch was rebuilt in the C19th. The chancel is C13th and the tower, with flushwork on the buttresses and a battlemented parapet, was added in the C14th. The overall thatched roof is delightful. Inside, there is no chancel arch. A suite of neat benches with C15th carved ends and fine poppyheads, sets off the nave nicely. The tall Jacobean pulpit is the remaining section of an original triple-decker. Beside it is one of the church's finest attributes, a narrow door, late C15th, sealing the rood stairs. It bears a painting of St Michael dealing with his dragon. It is a remarkable survivor, which would have a long and fascinating tale to tell, if it could talk. A set of old oil lamps, now converted for electricity, are mounted on the church's internal walls and add a homely touch. The southern section (dado only) of a C15th chancel screen still exists, now with seating attached. The tracery of the panels is painted in red and green, but the painting stops abruptly a little lower down, suggesting that they were never painted because an altar stood in front or that ?figures were removed. The roof is restored medieval and there is a C13th grave slab near the south door. The C15th 'East Anglian' font is in a parlous state following iconoclast attack and is one of the worst in East Anglia for such damage. In the north west corner of the nave is a banner stave locker, one of several in the Lowestoft and Great Yarmouth area. Oddly, these are unknown from outside this small patch of East Anglia. The chancel has two attractive features, one being the very fine east window glass, dated 1924. The theme is 'suffer little children' but the artist is unknown. The other is a C13th angle piscina in nice, mostly unrestored condition, with drop-sill sedilia to the west. Nearby is a good old chair, in the Jacobean style. Further along the south wall is a simple pointed aperture, probably an aumbry or candle recess.

Tower and porch from the south

The church from the north east

South doorway

St Lawrence looking east

Pulpit and rood stair door

Screen dado, bench end

The chancel

East window glass (detail)

Angle piscina

Old chair

Looking west across the nave

Old lamps

The font

Banner stave locker

SOUTH ELMHAM ST JAMES D2, TM 322 812

St James from the north west

St James is one of several churches in north east Suffolk prefixed by the settlement name South Elmham. These churches are often considered together as a group with those of the Ilketshall villages nearby. The area is characterised by scanty settlements and a remarkable atmosphere. St James has much to offer apart from its evocative surroundings. The unbuttressed tower stands strong and stark, the plainness relieved by neat flushwork arcading on the parapet and Y-shaped belfry windows. The base may be very old, the fabric is clearly different from that which follows. It is similar to fabric in the north nave wall, which is thought to be Norman. The north doorway is certainly Norman, its original billeted semi-circular arch later altered to a point. The Perpendicular windows in the nave were added much later, in the C15th. Lancets in the chancel indicate a C13th origin; the south aisle is probably the same age. By the C13th south doorway is a flamboyant stoup, its ogee head extravagantly worked. There was restoration and refitting, including the east window, in the C19th. St James has a sparse service pattern, therefore in the winter especially a musty but evocative pall pervades the interior, adding to the thrill of exploration. The C12th square font (with nice C15th cover) is an early 'Purbeck Marble' example. The long years, and possibly exposure outside, have eroded the characteristic arching on the bowl, leaving just faint traces. The C17th pulpit is a highlight of the interior, tall and stylishly carved. In the nave walkway is the church's best brass, of a civilian couple, lacking its inscription but probably C16th as she wears a kennel headdress. The church also has two inscription only brasses, one dated 1601. In the north wall is a blocked Norman window. There are medieval piscinas in the aisle and chancel, the latter a good restored angle type. Above the priest's doorway is an ancient statue of St James. The rood stairs are visible through the bottom doorway, the top one is blocked. A little medieval glass can be seen in certain nave windows. The very indistinct royal arms are for George III. Round and half-round blocked windows either side of the tower arch are suggestive of Saxon work. An old screen has been resited to enclose a vestry at the west end. In the same area is an old chest and the dove that used to be the font cover counterweight. An early C20th carpentry project led to much local work being used in the church, including two fine owls carved by the vicar (later stolen, but replaced).

North doorway

St James from the south east

Holy water stoup, south doorway

South east across the nave

The pulpit

Figure brass

Rood stairs and doorways

The chancel

Angle piscina

Local carpentry, St James, aisle piscina

South west across the nave

Medieval glass, nave

George III arms, ?Saxon windows, owls

The font

Old screen, chest, dove

STANSFIELD ALL SAINTS
B3, TL 783 525

Medieval glory, All Saints from the south east

Stansfield is a small village that straggles along north to south trending minor roads in the south west of Suffolk. The landscape is open rolling farmland, hereabouts reaching over 100m elevation in places, high for Suffolk. It's an exhilarating, deeply rural area and it is home to a very good church. Much of the building is Decorated and shows some typically expressive features of that period, like good windows in the chancel, two external image niches either side of the east window and three in the west face of the tower. The external rood stair turret to the north is inflated into a veritable tower which extends above the nave, allowing access to the roof. The turret is topped by battlements, complementing those on the nave parapets, tower and porch. The C14th tower has massive angle buttresses to the west, which considerably modify its outline. At its base is pretty chequerwork. C15th upgrading resulted in several Perpendicular windows being emplaced in the church and tower. Despite the lack of aisles, the interior is capacious, but the nave is diminished by long rows of dull Victorian benches. A pretty red and black tiled floor, with diamond pattern, improves matters. The pulpit is another handsome Jacobean example, how rich Suffolk is in these lovely furnishings! This one is tall and stately, with the usual elegantly carved panels. Behind it and to the south is the dado of what must once have been a marvellous C14th rood screen. What remains is still impressive, with excellent tracery on the panels, the whole sensitively restored. The higher rood loft doorway is sealed, the lower has a door. In the chancel is an angle piscina with flowing tracery in the head, and the usual accompanying drop-sill sedilia. Two chancel windows have collages and borders of medieval glass, but the best work of that period is in the nave. Another chancel window has distinctive Victorian glass, thought to be rare work by Cox, Son & Buckley. Two excellent mural tablets grace the chancel, both from the early C18th, and another one from the early C19th is mounted on the chancel west wall. Also in the chancel is a hoary old chest (another in the nave) and C19th stall ends enhanced with figures of saints. The font has had its corners (heads?) hacked away, leaving a very distressed picture. An image niche and piscina in the nave south east mark the site of a chapel, and there is a pointed stoup near the south door. The nave roof is early C16th and features remarkable spandrel carving. On leaving, pause to admire the fine porch roof.

Porch interior

All Saints from the north east

Nave south wall gargoyle

Interior looking east

The pulpit

Medieval glass in the nave

Screen and chancel

Tablets of early C18th (2), late C18th, 1809

Glass by ?Cox, Son & Buckley and detail, c.1884

Sanctuary south east

Old chest, stall end saints

Chancel piscina, stoup, nave piscina

West from the sanctuary

The font

STRADBROKE ALL SAINTS D2, TM 232 740

In the heart of Stradbroke, the church of All Saints and its magnificent tower

The large village of Stradbroke (pop. c.1500) has never been turned into a showpiece or become fossilised, as has happened to other Suffolk settlements of similar size, always it has moved with the times and remains a busy, everyday village with excellent amenities. One suspects that few of its houses are second homes. The village is most fortunate to have the large and handsome church of All Saints to beautify its centre. The church has a crispness that testifies to thorough renovation and refitting in Victorian times followed by years of dedicated stewardship. Much medieval work must have been disposed of in the C19th and earlier, but a few selected items were kept, making an exploration of the spacious interior a rewarding exercise, not just to seek out the surviving older fittings, but also to admire the quality of the Victorian work. The vigour of the latter has much to do with the evangelical fervour of Rev'd J.C. Ryle, who masterminded major restorations in the 1870's. Dominating the village and surrounding area is the wonderful C15th tower, all 30.5m (100 feet) or so of it. The west face is impressive, with flushwork, a fine doorway, niches and four windows of various sizes. At the top are battlements, flushwork and tall pinnacles. A bold, crenelated stair turret ascends the south face and rises above the battlements. The rest of the church is a little dwarfed by the tower but has an expansive plan of aisled nave, C15th clerestory, C14th chancel with C15th chapels, C15th north and south porches (restored C19th) and C19th north vestry. Inside, the arcades and some other details are C14th, but Victorian restoration overprinted much else. The font is an excellent C15th 'East Anglian' example with Evangelists' symbols and angels with shields around the deep bowl, angels beneath and a well-preserved set of lions and woodwoses on the stem. In the sanctuary is an exquisite, tall C14th niche with a trellis pattern in the canopy. The smart angle piscina is probably C19th, but the sedilia alongside are original. Near the north door is a medieval niche, also medieval are some wall post corbel figures. Two detached C15th screen panels featuring kings are fine work, as is the C19th sentimental monument for Elizabeth White and her uncle in the chancel. Good windows are by Clayton & Bell and the O'Connors; another, by an unknown hand, is armorial and dedicated to Queen Victoria. The C19th 'improving texts' on the nave roof tie beams and chancel arch are delightful. A rood loft doorway survives high in the south aisle wall.

From the west

Through the blossom

South doorway

Interior looking east

Nave roof

Interior from the sanctuary

Sanctuary, general views

Sanctuary niche

The font

Angle piscina

Aumbry, corbel, angel

White/Duill and White memorials

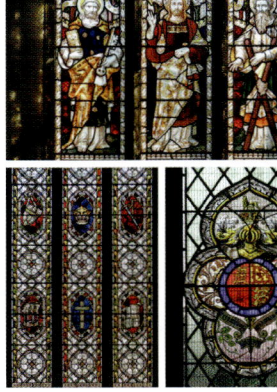

Glass by Clayton & Bell & unknown

Two screen panels

Old ?communion table

STRATFORD ST MARY

C4, TM 052 346

A glorious sight, St Mary from the south

The exterior of St Mary is one of the finest in Suffolk, an extravaganza of Perpendicular form and expression, further embellished by the expansive work of architect Thomas Woodyer in the late 1870's. Several local cloth merchants were involved in the beautification and enlargement of the C15th and early-mid C16th via bequests, and some of the work they financed was exceptional. Significant areas of the church were renewed and some built new, like the clerestory, in that time, and most feature wonderful flushwork. Some of that takes the form of inscriptions, particularly on the north aisle, which commemorate certain of these donors and also include a very rare alphabet. Woodyer rebuilt and modified much of the old church, but sometimes his enthusiasm led him to over-elaborate his designs, particularly the window tracery of the south aisle and north porch, and the tower stair turret. Yet it has to be admitted, these features are eye-catching. Woodyer was also responsible for the spread of battlements around the building. The Victorian interior, mostly the work of Woodyer, is quite opulent, but, overall, lacks allure. Yet, in detail, some of the Victorian work is admirable. For example, see the lovely marble shafts of the chancel arch, the flamboyant pulpit, the nave roof angels, the neo-gothic niche in the south chapel and the Powell & Son glass in the east window. The font of 1858 is busy and not to everyone's taste, and the damage to the biblical tableaux on the bowl hints at vandalism or carelessness. Above the font across the tower arch is a gothic style balcony with painted shields. Paintings of biblical scenes by Alexander Jamieson (1904) can be seen above the north chapel arcade. The pretty credence table in the sanctuary is a copy of one in Oxford All Souls chapel. The older features include two sweeping arcades with ogee apices to the arches and no capitals, a well preserved C14th tomb lid with a Cross of Lorraine in the south chapel, fragments of an old screen in the same area, medieval glass fragments in the north aisle west window which include Old Testament figures and an excellent St Jude with his boat, and medieval piscinas in the chancel and south chapel. The church has two brasses, one beneath the nave carpet whilst on the north aisle wall a figure brass for Edward and Elizabeth Crane is mounted on wood and dated 1558. Both rood stair openings survive, but are now blocked. The south chapel houses modest wall tablets. Constable included the church in certain of his paintings.

St Mary from the south west and north west — Porch west wall

South east across the church — Pulpit, rood stair doorways — North aisle medieval glass — Nave roof angels

 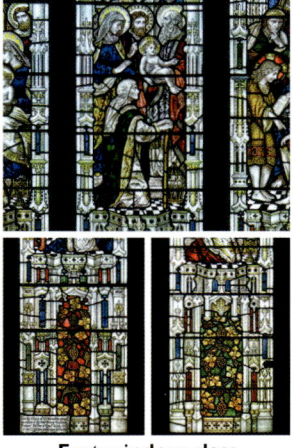  

Chancel south, chancel arch marble shafts — East window glass — South chapel wall tablets — Crane brass (1558)

     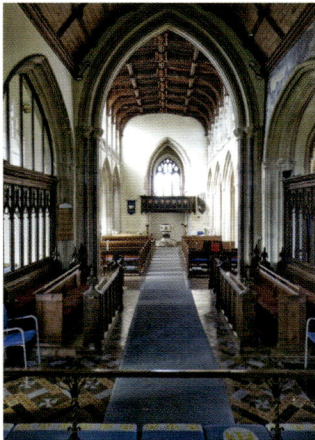

Chancel piscina & credence table, S. chapel niche — S. chapel, screen pieces — C14th tomb lid — The font — West from the sanctuary

STUSTON ALL SAINTS   C2, TM 134 778

All Saints from the south east

Like many of East Anglia's churches, All Saints is largely alone and embowered by trees. What little constitutes the village of Stuston lies to the north west, very close to the Norfolk border. Visiting All Saints is certainly rewarding, an intimate atmosphere envelops the church and its graveyard, and despite the lack of significant items inside (with two exceptions, see later) the interior is an engaging space. The round tower is difficult to date accurately, it has been modified over the years, but it seems reasonable to assume a Norman age for most of it, with a later octagonal top stage and even later brick parapet. However, if the small, slightly pointed west lancet near the base is original, that would imply a C13th date. The rest of the church was the subject of restoration in 1861 by Thomas Jeckyll, a brilliant, but sometimes controversial architect. The chancel was rebuilt, and north transept and vestry built from new. Jeckyll was also responsible for the polychrome brickwork inside and some strange window tracery. Apparently other features were remade as they were before, so, overall, the restorations of 1861 did not overwhelm the pre-existing C13th–C15th architecture. The great treasure inside is a very large and grand early C18th monument in the chancel. It is for the Castleton family, of whom Sir John Castleton was head. There are busts of him and his wife, and their three children are depicted in medallions. The design is Classical and stylish. There are few other memorials in the church, apart from war memorials only a plain early C19th marble tablet for Robert and Mary Clarke is worthy of note. The other special feature inside is the C19th stained glass, which fills several windows. This is of uniform high-quality and is chiefly the work of Heaton, Butler & Bayne and William Wailes. See especially the east window by Heaton, Butler & Bayne and the Wailes windows in the nave. The use of red, black and yellow bricks for the chancel arch and the frames of all chancel and transept openings may not meet with everyone's approval, but others will see a bold patterning that enhances the prospects around the church. The pulpit of 1861 is a neo-gothic showpiece. The rood stairs are extant and both doorways are open, the upper lined with bricks. The font is plain and may be C14th or C15th. Behind it the narrow tower arch is of archaic form, arguing for an early age for the tower. There are medieval piscinas in the chancel and nave, the latter accompanied by a niche in the nearby window embrasure.

From the north east and north west • The south porch and nave window

Interior looking east • Rood stairs and doorways • Nave piscina and niche • Chancel roof

The sanctuary • Castleton monument (C18th) • Chancel north transept

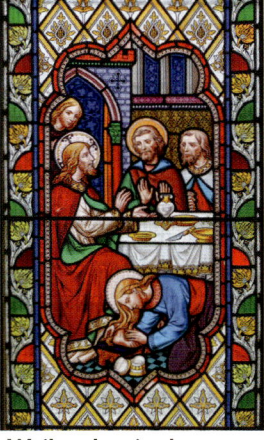

From the chancel looking west • Wailes glass in the nave • Pulpit, Clarke tablet • The font

STUTTON ST PETER C4, TM 161 345

St Peter from the north east

Suffolk is full of delicious corners and St Peter is situated in one of them, set off a quiet lane close to the banks of the River Stour. The church has an intriguing history as well as a rather unusual layout. There is one clue to a Norman church having stood here, in the form of a composite window in the east wall of the south transept. Its parts include a semi-circular arch made of a single stone and short lengths of interlace work. It has been suggested that there was once a Norman round tower. The present-day C15th tower stands to the south west. On top are attractive battlements, with chequerwork, and its base is both a porch and the main entrance. A handsome outer doorway ushers in visitors, with original C14th door set within. The nave is medieval and has a Decorated west window, but the rest of the church consists of Victorian rebuildings and additions, represented by a rebuilt chancel, a large north transept, another transept to the south housing organ and vestry, and a large north chapel. These days the chapel and north transept are enclosed and used as a meeting room. The area is not open to visitors. The font is a typical C13th Purbeck Marble example, in nicely restored order. The church's C19th and later stained glass is noteworthy, some of it by a rarely encountered artist, Charles Clutterbuck. 2nd World War bomb blast destroyed much glass and deterioration is noticeable in some of the remainder, but the windows by Ward and Hughes are very good. Striking modern glass by Thomas Denny is set in the west window. Two large and splendid C17th monuments are mounted on the wall at the west end, broadly similar in design although they are 40 years apart in age, one from c.1623 and the other c.1664. They are for members of the Jermy family and both show husband and wife facing each other across a prayer desk. Another good monument, for Bridget Allan and dated 1777 is mounted on the north nave wall further east. A brass inscription for John Smythe (d. 1534) near the chancel step was crudely hammered by iconoclasts to obliterate offending 'papist' phrases. On the chancel arch above is a royal arms for George IV. Recent reordering in the chancel has seen the screen reset in front of the sanctuary, while the altar has been moved in front of it. By the screen is a pretty triptych on a table. The lower rood stair doorway is in place, but blocked. See also a hatchment of 1827 for Anne Mills, wooden angel corbels, chancel piscina, slate vault cover and an hour glass holder.

Tower from the east   Norman window   St Peter from the south   Tower & nave doorways

North east across the church   Roof angel, hatchment, George IV arms   The chancel   Triptych, Smythe brass (1534)

    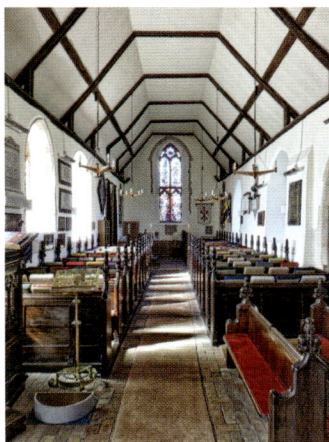

Vault, piscina, Allan memorial (1777)   Screen and reredos   Through the screen to the nave   Nave looking west

  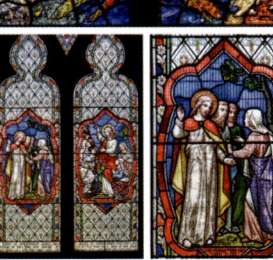 

Jermy monuments, c.1623 and c.1664   Glass by T. Denny and Ward & Hughes   The font

SYLEHAM ST MARGARET

C2, TM 204 789

The church from the south east

Syleham is a small, attractive village near the River Waveney, which forms the border with Norfolk. St Margaret is some distance north east of the village in a delightful, isolated setting just a field away from the river. For many years the church was officially known as St Mary, but in 2008 the local long-standing usage of the original name of St Margaret was ratified by the diocese, so St Margaret it is. Externally the building is rather curious, for the steep-roofed chancel stands higher than the nave, which seems paltry beside it. However, on the east face of the tower an older nave roof line can be seen, and if extrapolated, this would meet the gable at the junction with the chancel, thereby confirming that once nave and chancel were of similar height. The tower is round with a much modified top stage, which is ornamented with borders of dark and light stone and brick battlements. The tower may be Norman or earlier, but the only evidence is some coursing at the base which may or may not be Saxon. More reliable as a pointer to age is some long and short work in the north west corner of the nave, also suggesting Saxon origins. The south porch is C15th and the hoary door within may be earlier; it retains remnants of its ancient furniture. To the right of the door is a holy water stoup. Lancets in its walls indicate a C13th age for the chancel. At the west end inside, near the blocked north doorway, is a most odd font, with a long, narrow, octagonal bowl, clearly old but difficult to age. It is set on the inverted stem and bowl of a Norman font. On top sits a rustic C17th cover. A time-worn C13th chest stands near the font and C18th Decalogue boards hang above the north doorway. The pulpit is a tall Jacobean example, panelled as usual, but with only the top panels carved. The altar rails are a fine late C17th or C18th set with barley twist balusters. The sanctuary piscina is old and dilapidated, with a plain pointed arch. Only a little way below it since the chancel floor was raised is an inscription brass for William and Anne Fuller of 1634. In a corresponding position to the north is one for Anthony and Elizabeth Barry of 1641. Nearby is a ledger slab recording the tragic demise in quick succession of three young brothers in the late C18th. On the east and south walls of the chancel are three memorial tablets, the best a mid-C18th example for the Lambe sisters. The others are early C19th. Rood stair doorways remain, both blocked. Before leaving, pause to take in the tranquil surroundings.

View from the south west

Commemorative tablet in the nave south wall

The porch

The interior from the west

Pulpit and lower rood stair doorway

The sanctuary

Lambe sisters memorial

East window by Heaton, Butler & Bayne

The interior looking west

Sanctuary piscina

Barry brass, Mann ledger, war memorial

The font

South doorway

223

TANNINGTON ST ETHELBERT D2, TM 242 674

St Ethelbert, splendid in its isolation

St Ethelbert is an unusual dedication, one of just a handful of churches in East Anglia so named. King Ethelbert of Kent helped establish Christianity in Anglo-Saxon England, and after his death in 616, canonisation followed. Tannington St Ethelbert's attractions are enhanced by an serene setting. An early foundation is established by the late C12th round-headed north doorway, which has fleshy leaf carving in the capitals. The C15th tower has a stumpy outline, as if it was never finished, but there is good chequerwork at the base, battlements, four strong diagonal buttresses, a stair turret to the south, and west doorway and window with wooden bars. The restored east window with intersecting Y-tracery is the oldest window on show, from around 1300, the others are later Decorated and Perpendicular types, some quite ambitious. The late C15th porch has a pretty frontage, heavily embellished with flushwork, also battlements, a niche above the doorway and roses in the spandrels of the doorway. The church was restored in 1879. A most pleasant interior awaits the explorer, with a surprise at the east end of the C14th nave roof. Here is a rare, medieval canopy of honour, or celure, placed above where the rood loft would once have been. It was restored in the recent past, and its monograms, roses and bosses are nicely seen. On the wall below is a considerable wall memorial for Jane Barker of 1820, with a lady weeping over a grave marker surmounted by an urn, below which is an inscription, with a sarcophagus at the bottom. Jane Barker's hatchment is mounted above. A little further west in a window embrasure steps to the rood loft are preserved. The window in the north wall opposite contains vivid glass of 1976 with an attractive rustic theme, depicting a church, field workers, birds, rabbit, etc. On the sanctuary north wall is a colourful early C17th memorial tablet which catalogues members of the Dade family. Many shields and an achievement enliven an agreeable piece. Nearby in the floor are contemporary brasses for some of the people on the memorial. The C13th angle piscina opposite was later modified. The royal arms are for Elizabeth II, a very rare example. At the rear of the nave is a suite of C15th bench ends, with handsome poppyheads and the vestiges of what once must have been a marvellous set of figures with sacred and secular themes. The C13th font is a Purbeck Marble example of standard design, mounted on an older stem.

Tower and porch

St Ethelbert from the north east

North doorway

Interior looking east

Rood stairs

Barker hatchment and memorial

Modern glass (1976)

Brasses for Thomas, Marie and Ann Dade, all early C17th

Dade family memorial, early C17th

Chancel angle piscina

Old chair

Looking west from the sanctuary

Celure, C15th bench ends

The font

225

THORINGTON ST PETER

D2, TM 423 741

Romantic and pleasantly wild, St Peter at Thorington

At Thorington the setting and the church building combine to give an exquisite experience for the church enthusiast. In the churchyard Nature is largely allowed free rein and the natural history in all seasons is delightful. The building is a little gem too, not least the marvellous tower. Around its midriff is blind, round-arched arcading cut into the fabric, suggestive of Saxon origin for the tower. Later, the Normans added slit windows to the north, south and west in three of the recesses of the older arches. They also rebuilt or raised the top stage and inserted characteristic belfry windows. The Tudors finished off the whole delightful ensemble with a singular brick parapet and stepped battlements. More evidence of the Norman input can be seen above the south vestry, where there are parts of a once-considerable Norman arch in the nave wall, with chip-carved ornament. It may have framed a window and gives a Norman age for the nave, which also has very thick walls. Some of the later Decorated windows have outstanding tracery. The north porch is set off-centre to the inner doorway, apparently because the doorway was very close to the west end of the nave. The interior was given a large-scale Victorian reworking, but the older work that was left and the Victorian innovations are of some interest. The font, housed under the tower, is a strange hybrid of a typical C13th Purbeck Marble bowl with shallow arches, wedded to a later C15th stem, with lions and dogs. Three hatchments are for members of the Bence clan, who are also commemorated on several of the mural tablets. One of the latter in the chancel is a substantial and very wordy representative. The royal arms is for George II. The C13th chancel piscina has a cusped ogee arch with finial, two pinnacles with finials, and unusual flushwork-type roundels between the arch and pinnacles. The nave roof retains medieval elements, including angels and braced wall posts ornamented with shields and brattishing. In the porch and at the west end are old benches, with poppyheads. The Norman-inspired tower arch is C19th, but whether the design follows an original is unknown. Above it is an original, re-exposed opening, probably a doorway. In the fabric below it is an arch formed of recycled ?Roman bricks, and a Norman voussoir. High quality C19th glass in the east window and the chancel is by Heaton & Butler and Thomas Baillie. The choir stalls incorporate tracery from the old screen. In the nave is a 1st World War wooden battlefield cross. Fine reredos of 1882.

 The tower from the south
 View from the north east
 Windows and head stop
 Inside the porch

 Interior looking east
 The church's roofs
 War and family memorials
 The chancel

 East window detail
 Chancel piscina
 Glass by T. Baillie
 Bence family memorial
 George II royal arms

 West from the sanctuary
 The west end
 Hatchment, 1st World War cross, old bench
 The font

THORNDON ALL SAINTS

C2, TM 141 696

All Saints south west tower peeks out in this view from the north east

Thorndon is a thriving village, with good amenities and a self-sufficient air. Its church of All Saints has stood since the early C13th, and has been reconfigured many times since, not least during major Victorian restorations in the late C19th. Immediately conspicuous is the early C14th south west tower, which, as is customary, doubles as a porch and the main entrance to the building. Strong buttresses run up the south frontage and between them is an impressive doorway with four chamfered mouldings forming a continuous frame. In the angle between the doorway and the east buttress is a battered stoup. Above the doorway is a niche, above which is a lancet; the parapet is of jumbled brick with stone crenellations. Low in the tower west face is an original splayed lancet. The nave is C13th with C15th modifications, and has original north and south doorways, with a C15th west doorway. The latter is quite ambitious and has a square head with shields in the spandrels. The south doorway is set within a larger arch similar to the external porch doorway. The chancel is probably C14th and appears to have been raised at some point to a height conformable with that of the nave. It has C15th additions including a priest's doorway (above which is a large niche, framed by tiles and with a finial) and enriched buttresses. The north vestry is medieval, with lancets, later brick buttresses and a blocked east window with brick frame. An outside tomb niche at the west end of the chancel south wall contains a stone coffin. Most of the church's windows are C19th replacements. Inside, the C15th font is a well-restored 'East Anglian' type, with the familiar lions and angels with shields on the bowl, angels with outstretched wings beneath and lions around the stem. Set in the recess of the sealed north door is a very good George IV arms. Next to it and on the opposite wall are reset brasses for Grimeston father and son (1599 and 1610). The restored pulpit is a beautifully carved C17th example. In the wall adjacent are rood stairs and both doorways. Nearby, the pretty C19th lectern features winsome lion supporters at the base. In the chancel is an ornate C14th ogee-headed piscina with square head; sedilia are alongside. A fine collection of C14th-C16th glass fragments and roundels, including figures, is set in a chancel north window. A very well executed C19th tableau of the Last Supper forms the centrepiece of the reredos. Commandments, Creed and Lord's Prayer plaques are mounted on the east wall.

All Saints from the south east

Holy water stoup

From the west

Interior looking east

The sanctuary

Chancel south east

Chancel piscina

Old glass in the chancel

Last supper, lectern, lion

Pulpit, rood stairs & doorways

A closer view of the pulpit

Interior looking west

Grimeston brasses

George IV royal arms

The font

THORNHAM MAGNA St MARY MAGDALENE C2, TM 103 714

St Mary Magdalene from the south east

A short distance from St Mary Magdalene is the notable church of Thornham Parva St Mary, with its important wall paintings and C13th reredos. Parva's treasures have tended to overshadow Thornham Magna's attractions, which is a shame, for there is much here to please church enthusiasts. At heart, St Mary is a C14th Decorated church, which saw extensive modification in the C15th and again in 1851. The latter restoration effectively established the look and feel of the church today, with high-quality furnishings and excellent stained glass. Little has changed in the 170-odd years since 1851. The tower is tall, with flushwork west buttresses, stair turret, battlements and a neat west doorway, with head stops. Most windows are Perpendicular replacements, restored or renewed in the C19th, but two nave south windows are reticulated Decorated in style, whilst the east window has a rather fanciful Decorated-inspired design. The frontage of the C15th south porch is impressive, with elegant niches, shields in roundels and flushwork panelling. The highest niche is particularly ornate, with a canopy and a cheerful mask at the base. The doorway arch is embellished with a variety of paterae. The interior is a Victorian showpiece, with fine benches, pulpit, reading desk and chancel fittings. The powerful Henniker family were closely associated with the church, especially during the C19th, and their memorials and hatchments occur throughout. Especially noteworthy is the large early C19th standing monument by the chancel north wall for John and Emily Henniker. It was designed by Joseph Kendrick and features two willowy ladies mourning by an urn and pedestal. A big wall memorial of 1842 for Major Henniker reflects his life as a soldier, with plumed hat and sword. Robert Killigrew, who died in 1707, is commemorated on a decorous cartouche. The many windows with fine stained glass feature the work of William Miller, who has several windows, W.G. Taylor and Morris & Co. (one with designs by Burne-Jones). The latter and the Taylor window are very distinctive and effectively engage the senses. The screen is an excellent C19th version of a late medieval type, with admirable tracery. Similarly inspired are the angels in the chancel roof. The delicate angle piscina in the chancel and a small piscina near the pulpit are two of few medieval survivals. Another is the rood stair and doorways near the reading desk. The font has a C15th design, but is most likely Victorian. Above the tower arch is a murky royal arms of George II.

Tower and porch   St Mary from the north west and south, west doorway, churchyard angel

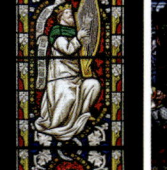

Interior looking east   Glass by Morris & Co., Miller, and Taylor   **Chancel screen**   Memorials (1707, 1842, 1912)

Nave south east   **Nave north east**   Chancel, angle piscina, Riddel post angel   Henniker monument (early C19th)

Nave looking west   Benches, roof angel, hatchment   **The font**   **George II royal arms**

231

TOSTOCK ST ANDREW   B3, TL 960 636

Autumn at Tostock St Andrew

Though on the surface St Andrew might be thought to be just another modestly attractive church, it has a special claim to renown. That is a set of remarkable medieval benches in the nave, plus two more in the chancel. More on these later. St Andrew consists of a 'standard set' of west tower, nave with south porch, chancel and north vestry, but there are a few surprises externally. One is the presence of two large niches in the east wall of the nave, north and south of the junction with the chancel. Another is the unusual tracery in the C14th porch side windows, mostly filled in but with two open mouchettes at the top. The C13th chancel was thoroughly restored in 1889 and other modifications were undertaken elsewhere, such as replacement windows, mostly in Perpendicular style (see the big nave windows, with the same design on both sides of the church), but with a Decorated-type east window. The C14th tower is of no great height but is nicely detailed with flushwork buttresses, stair turret, battlements and a good west doorway above which is a window with a bold Decorated design. The C15th benches are the highlight of the interior and are in very good order, notwithstanding minor damage to some of the bench end carvings. The latter are an outstanding collection, featuring a wide range of animals real and imagined on either side of fine poppyheads. Figures include a rare cockatrice, unicorns, dogs, sheep, angels, eagle, seal and several with animal bodies and humanesque faces. The bench backs have pretty tracery. Eight benches at the front of the nave are excellent Victorian copies, also with a fine array of bench end figures. The font, thought to be early C14th, is distinctive and somewhat mysterious, with a deep bowl carved with foliage and leaves, a theme complemented by the inclusion of a Green Man. Both rood stair doorways are extant in the south east of the nave, the lower accompanied by an aumbry. Nearby is an unusual and decorative war memorial, featuring a sentimental painting. To the north of the chancel arch are a matching pair of distinctive wall tablets, others are gathered on the chancel north wall. The C15th nave roof is finely wrought and embellished. There is medieval glass in the east window, with nearby a small, ogee-headed piscina. The altar rails are a fine C17th set. The parish chest is plain but has five locks. Several Victorian mural banners survive around the church.

St Andrew from the west and north — Inside the porch

  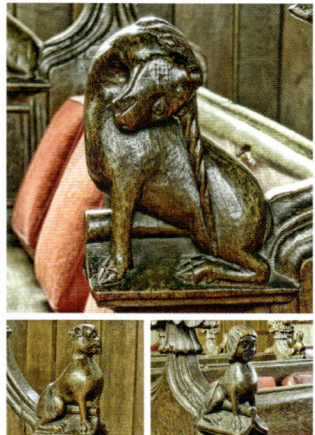 

Interior looking east — Nave benches — Bench end carvings — Benches, old chest

  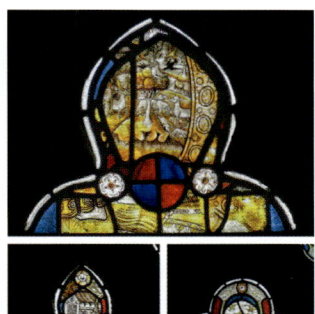  

War Memorial — The east end — East window glass — West from the sanctuary

Chancel tablets and piscina — West along the nave — Rood stair doorway & aumbry, tablet, Green Man — The font

TUNSTALL St MICHAEL & ALL ANGELS D3, TM 363 551

St Michael and All Angels from the south

Tunstall lies on the western edge of a distinctive area of Suffolk called The Sandlings, an expanse of heathland and sands. The region is slightly other-worldly, and secretive. The churches tend to share this 'difference', more in their atmosphere than in physical details, but St Michael does indeed stand out by dint of its singular interior. The tower is late C14th and has had at least two major repairs; the first, with brick, following a lightning strike in the C18th and the other in the late C20th. There is flushwork at the base, a nobly weathered west doorway and a stair turret to the south. The south porch frontage overlaps the body behind and looks rather odd, but the flushwork, doorway and niche are excellent. Within, the inner doorway retains its original C14th door. The priest's doorway into the chancel is C14th and most windows are Perpendicular in style, the ones in the nave forming a uniform set. The north doorway is blocked and partly obscured by the roof of the old coal hole. It is the interior that sets St Michael apart, chiefly the set of handsome C18th box pews that fill the nave. These are an attractive light yellow-brown in colour, which imbues a delicate pastel feel to the surroundings, an impression reinforced by the beautifully painted and shapely pulpit. The nave windows are large and admit plenty of light to further enhance the interior. The brick floor adds a touch of rustic warmth. The font is a characterful hybrid of a Purbeck (or sometimes said to be Sussex) Marble bowl married to a C15th stem and base. The bowl is ornamented with the usual arches; here they are round-headed, indicating a C12th age. The C15th parts carry much quatrefoil embellishment. Exposure of an area of wall in the north east area of the nave has revealed a plethora of graffiti, dominated by depictions of boats. Not an unexpected subject, with the sea close by. The inscriptions are quite clear, but fairly crude, and are probably the work of children. Two notable items are set on the nave wall. One is a top-quality George III royal arms, dated 1764, and the other an upright war memorial by Munro Cautley, who published the first comprehensive survey of Suffolk churches in 1937, as well as being Ipswich diocesan architect for many years. A nave window contains dingy fragments of medieval glass. The finely realised east window glass was designed by Eric Dilworth in the 1950's, whilst the piscina nearby is C14th. Another, plainer, in the nave may be somewhat later. An inscription brass for John Haughfen is dated 1618.

| The approach to St Michael | South porch | Tower from the north east | West doorway |

 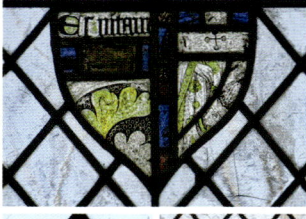    

| East and west along the church | Medieval glass fragments | The pulpit | George III royal arms, graffiti |

   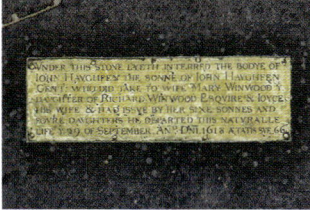  

| The font | War Memorial, wall tablets | Haughfen brass (1618), piscinas | The chancel |

| Altar rails | East window | Roll of Honour | South doorway |

WALBERSWICK ST ANDREW   E2, TM 490 747

Part romantic ruin, part active church, St Andrew at Walberswick

Walberswick is one of Suffolk's most visited spots, a result of its pretty maritime surroundings and a long history as a favourite spot for artists. A visit can be delightful, but beware of the crowds in the season. If the throng is too great, then escaping to St Andrew is highly recommended. For here is a wonderfully diverting building, part evocative ruin and part working church. The ruins should be seen first, and it is fun trying to work out the layout when the church was whole and in its heyday. The history is fascinating and involves the decline of Walberswick in the C16th and C17th when its viability as a port was seriously compromised. The villagers found that their large and extravagant C15th church could no longer be maintained, and they were forced to partly ruin it to save money. That involved taking the chancel, nave and north aisle out of commission, and abandoning them to their fate. They then made good the south aisle and tower, and that became the church, one that could be maintained within budget. The tall tower is particularly impressive at the top, where there is flushwork, stepped battlements, shields, tracery and pinnacle figures. One of the best things to survive the downsizing was the C15th south porch, a formidable but attractive two-storey construction with a palpable tang of the past inside, with ancient benches to the side and a fine vaulted ceiling with bosses of angels, crowns and Tudor roses. The vast reduction in size did nothing to diminish the atmosphere of the interior, which has an intimacy that could never have been present in the old building. There is much good, old woodwork including several benches in the chancel, with poppyheads and some carved ends. Also, the base of the screen from the old church, with doors and tracery, and a simply splendid, ornate, and rare, C15th pulpit. An intensively carved and highly individual old chair in the chancel should not be overlooked; note the carving of a ravening wolf. The battered C15th font may have lost some of its lower parts, leaving the typical East Anglian bowl carved with lions and angels looking oversized. The step is formed of half an arcade pillar base, salvaged from the abandoned sections of the church. Another more complete pillar base supports an old grave slab in the chancel, the latter adopted for use as a credence table. In the centre of the communion table is an ancient 'mini' mensa, complete with consecration crosses. The only wall tablet of note dates from the early C20th and is for the Rose family. The roof is original.

Tower through the old east window

St Andrew from the north east

The active church of today

Interior looking east

The pulpit

Rose wall tablet

The chancel

Screen, benches and poppyheads

Old chair

Mensa

Pillar base and credence table

Grave slab/credence table

Reading desk

Interior looking west

The font and step

WALDRINGFIELD ALL SAINTS D3, TM 282 442

All Saints brick tower catches the sunlight

Standing on a modest elevation off narrow Mill Lane a little way from the main village of Waldringfield is the distinctive church of All Saints. There is some suggestion that the Anglo-Saxons were active on this ancient site, but the present All Saints offers no evidence of that. In fact, the Victorians were very busy here, and thoroughly restored the church, leaving very few old features. The handsome C16th red brick tower dominates the building, the rest of the church is housed under one roof and cowers in its shadow. Blue brick diapering in diamond patterns beautifies the tower and there is a prominent stair turret to the south which terminates a little over half way up, with battlements at the top. To the south is a plain porch (at heart C15th, but later modified) with eye-catching white painted gates. To the west and east of the porch are two late C13th or early C14th lancet windows. The lower part of the one to the east once served as a low-side window; this section is now filled in. Another lancet is set to the north. The interior is very pleasantly fitted out, comfortable and attractive, but there is almost nothing on view of any age. What there is attracts attention immediately, as it faces the south doorway. That is a sturdy and well-preserved C15th font, designed in typical East Anglian style with angels holding shields and saintly iconography around the bowl, and delightful flying angels beneath, but with unusual deviations from the standard. In amongst the familiar bowl figures are griffins holding banners, and, around the stem, slightly disturbing satyr-like creatures alternating with seated figures who may be priests. Behind the font is the blocked north doorway. The font may be the only medieval item inside but there are some worthy fittings from later years. The pulpit is an C18th example with shapely base and traceried panelling, studded at the top with small paterae, one of which is carved in the shape of a creature with its tongue out. There are just a handful of wall tablets, one a benefaction board of 1853. Under the tower are C19th gold-lettered boards for the Decalogue, Creed and Lord's Prayer. Almost the only stone tablet is for William Kersey who died in 1887. Stained glass is confined to the east and west windows and comprises fine work by Lavers & Barraud and Powell & Sons. A highly polished brass commemorates Thomas Waller (d. 1920), a rector who formed part of an unbroken line of four Wallers who ministered here from 1862 until the death of John Waller in 2013.

All Saints from the south east, south and west   **East window**

    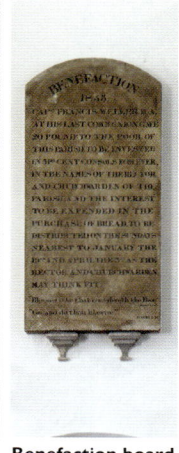

Interior looking east   **The pulpit**   **Pulpit detail**   **Lancet window**   **Benefaction board**

  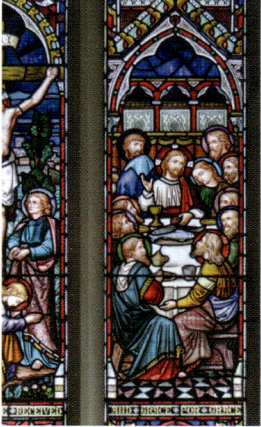 

On the walls   **The sanctuary**   **East window detail**   **Sanctuary south east**

    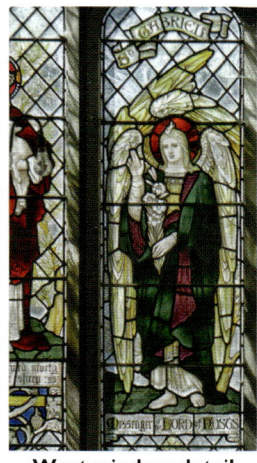

Interior looking west   **The font**   **Decalogue, Creed, Lords Prayer**   **West window detail**

WEST STOW ST MARY

B2, TL 819 705

St Mary from the south

From the outside St Mary has all the hallmarks of a typical medieval church of the C14th and C15th, with a mixture of Decorated and Perpendicular windows, some renewed, and a mid-C14th tower with chequerwork at the base and on the buttresses, and a full length stair turret to the south. The Decorated windows are largely in the reticulated style, best expressed in the east window. Much older roots are demonstrated by a Norman north doorway with a single roll moulding in the arch, tympanum and early ornament. This doorway now faces into the Victorian vestry. Layered flint coursing at the base of the nave south wall may also be Norman. C13th work is represented by a lancet window to the north. The modest porch is C15th. It is inside that St Mary departs significantly from its medieval template, for here in the middle of the C19th the renowned Gothic Revival architect William Butterfield undertook a root and branch restoration, the results of which still dominate the interior. Many East Anglian churches that were heavily modified in Victorian times retain the furnishings fitted at that time and the unique atmospheres that were generated, but at West Stow the shadow of those years is particularly strong. It is curious then that a single artefact remains which reminds us of what a glorious interior this church must have possessed in its pre-Reformation heyday. That is a remarkable C14th angle piscina in the chancel, an extravaganza of gables, crockets and oversize finials. It is almost the only medieval fitting on show, apart from its accompanying sedilia. The font, which has blank shields in quatrefoils around the bowl, may also be old, but an accurate date is hard to establish. A late C16th brass for William Boyce is inconveniently concealed beneath the pulpit. Two C18th wall tablets can be seen under the tower and another is mounted next to the C19th organ. The west window contains a few scraps of medieval glass, but it is the C19th glass that draws attention. Four windows are by the firm of Hardman but the east window and others are by Ward & Nixon. The modelling and draughtmanship of all are of a high standard, and the colours of the east window are rich. The Victorian woodwork is well-made, though not inspiring, but don't miss the bristling, foliate poppyheads on the chancel stalls and graceful angels in the chancel roof. Nave and chancel roofs are impressive and there may be some old brattishing in that of the chancel. The tower arch almost reaches the roof, above it is a sanctus bell window.

The south porch

The church from the north east

West doorway

Interior looking east

Woodwork and organ

Wall tablet of 1794

The chancel

Sanctuary south east

C14th angle piscina

Chancel angel

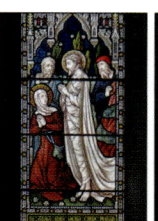

Glass by Hardman and Ward & Nixon

Interior from the sanctuary

West end and tower arch

The font

Hubbard and Swift tablets

241

WESTON ST PETER   D1, TM 429 871

Late afternoon at St Peter

Weston St Peter lies just a short distance east of the A145 road south of Beccles, but the contrast between its setting and the hectic main road is very marked. Mature trees shade the churchyard and the slightly elevated church, and all is peace and serenity, with just a touch of deafness required to filter out the faint traffic noise. The churchyard has a good complement of gravestones, which adds further enhancement to the surroundings. St Peter received the usual C15th and C19th reconfigurations but a single blocked Norman window in the north nave wall points to early foundation. Two open and two blocked lancets date the chancel as C13th, and the positioning of the two open ones suggests they served as low-side windows. The C15th tower has a brick parapet and buttresses with shields at the base and niches filled with brick, as are the former flushwork panels beneath. The distinctive north doorway is constructed of Tudor brick, disused now but retaining its door. There are no aisles and the interior is small, so that the C15th seven sacrament font on its massive Maltese Cross base opposite the south doorway becomes a significant object. The panels have suffered the usual iconoclast attacks but all seven sacraments are discernable, and the eighth panel depicts Christ's baptism, a rare subject. The church has a single medieval wall painting, said to be the Entry into Jerusalem, but it is very difficult to decipher, as are three later goodly texts, one of them just below the painting. The James II royal arms is a rare example and in fair order, one of only three in Suffolk. Opposite on the north nave wall is a very rustic, dark and probably C18th Lord's Prayer and Creed board, surprisingly overlooked for replacement by Victorian restorers. Even less clear is a wall tablet for the Rev'd Clowes and his wife in the chancel. Some nave benches have medieval carved backs and ends with poppyheads and carvings, but the latter are all damaged, though identifiable. Amongst them is a rare cockatrice, a priest in a pulpit, a windmill, a dragon, and a seated priest on a stall in the chancel. The sanctuary piscina is simple and unadorned. It is set relatively high in the wall, indicating that the floor was raised only slightly, or not at all, during light Victorian restorations. The patterned and attractive east window glass may be by Ward & Hughes; much older is a single foreign roundel in a nave window depicting Christ at Gethsemane. A large gouge in the nave north east corner is the site of the rood stair.

| View from the west | Norman window | St Peter from the south east | Tudor north doorway |

| North east across the church | James II arms, Lord's Prayer and Creed | Wall paintings | Site of rood stairs |

| Chancel lancet window | The chancel | Clowes tablet, goodly text | Chancel piscina |

| View from the sanctuary | Benches and bench ends | C17th ?Flemish roundel | The font |

WETHERINGSETT ALL SAINTS C2, TM 127 668

All Saints impressive south frontage

The approach from the west over a ditch crossed by a wooden bridge is the best introduction to the splendid church of All Saints. Its sylvan setting is entirely in accord with the attractions of the village of Wetheringsett in central Suffolk. As for the church's age, the C15th tower, porch, clerestory and most windows speak of an extensive reconfiguration in Perpendicular times, but a Decorated window in the south aisle, a lancet in the vestry and C13th north doorway give a more accurate indication of the church's origins. The south frontage of All Saints is impressive, the tower is not especially high but its clasping buttresses with chequerwork and niches lend a dignified solidity, and the big open arch in the tower west wall leading to a very good doorway into the nave is also noteworthy. The ornate porch with its flushwork, pinnacles, small niches and enriched doorway, and the superb 8-window clerestory, which is almost all glass, also enhance a charming scene. The south doorway is of similar morphology and age to the north, and shares details with the priest's doorway into the chancel. Inside, the regal arcades and chancel arch support a C13th attribution. The unusual font, which may be post-medieval, has small plain diamonds, shields, rectangles and one coat of arms around the bowl, and stands on C13th columns. The chancel sedilia are from around 1300 and form a fine set, the delicate columns have ring capitals, whilst the arches are trefoil with pointed mouldings above. On the trefoil cusps and hood moulds are leaf balls, and on the truncated end columns two facing heads. In contrast, the piscina alongside the sedilia is small and plain. The remains of a more elaborate double piscina can be found in the vestry, which clearly was once a chapel. Also in the chancel are two old misericords, whilst the east window has good C19th glass by Heaton, Butler & Bayne. Both aisle roofs have significant medieval components. Three rood stair doorways are present (with stairs still in place), two in the south aisle wall (near the fine organ) which served the loft above a parclose screen, and one just south of the chancel arch. A small number of modest medieval benches can be found at the west end, with poppyheads. There are few wall tablets but a re-made benefactions board originating from 1715 is mounted on the north aisle wall, as is a distressingly long list, for such a small village, of war dead from 1914-18, one family losing four brothers. See also a nicely lettered, early C19th tablet for members of the Bellman family.

Porch and clerestory

From the north

Tower doorway to nave

The church looking east

The chancel

East window, with details

Sanctuary south east

Misericords

Interior looking west

Organ, rood stair doorways

Nave rood stair opening

Nave roof

Benches, poppyhead, roof angel

The font

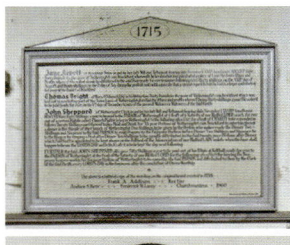

Benefaction board, tablet

WEYBREAD ST ANDREW

D2, TM 241 801

St Andrew from the north east

Weybread is an unusual name, and its origin might be supposed to be rather exotic, but it seems that the meaning is quite parochial, 'strip of land along the way'. Be that as it may, the village is a pleasant spot to linger awhile, as is its church of St Andrew. Whilst it was subjected to a formal and far-reaching restoration in 1865-6 by Richard Phipson, there is much here to admire. The lower section of the tower is usually said to be Norman, but if so the traces of chequerwork at its base and the brick-lined putlog holes would need an explanation. The top stage is C14th and has a ring of open and blind windows. The plain parapet is probably later still. There is nothing in the rest of the church earlier than C14th and the replacement Victorian windows reflect the Decorated origins of the chancel and the Perpendicular nature of the aisles and clerestory. Phipson added an organ chamber and vestry to the north. The highlight of the exterior is the C15th south porch, which has a marvellous panelled façade in flushwork and a groined niche housing a later statue of St Andrew. The bold doorway with its fine spandrels is a perfect complement. The interior is heavily Victorianised, but Phipson reprieved a few medieval items. The original C15th font stands forlornly near the open stairs of the lower rood loft doorway in the south aisle, its bowl missing the top half, which was roughly shorn away at some point. Its replacement at the west end is a curiously unattractive and stiff model of c.1865. There are two very similar C14th piscinas, one in the sanctuary and the other in the south aisle, both have pillars to the side and are accompanied by sedilia, those in the sanctuary with custom-built bench superimposed. Each side of the chancel arch are C14th niches with cusped ogee arches. Of the few wall tablets, the best are one in the chancel for John Ayton of 1836 and another in white marble in the north aisle for Lieutenant W.H.J. Jennings, who was killed 'whilst gallantly leading his men' in 1860. Excellent glass by the O'Connor brothers and their successor W.G. Taylor adorn several windows. Subjects include the Ascension, Nativity and the raising of Lazarus. A single roundel of old glass survives in the south aisle east window, a very fine eagle symbol for St John, perhaps C15th. On the west wall is a large and lavish mural painting of Christ in Glory, completed in the 1890's, possibly by Clayton & Bell. Good C19th corbels adorn the roofs, mainly saints and prophets, but with some grotesques.

St Andrew from the west and south west — The porch

 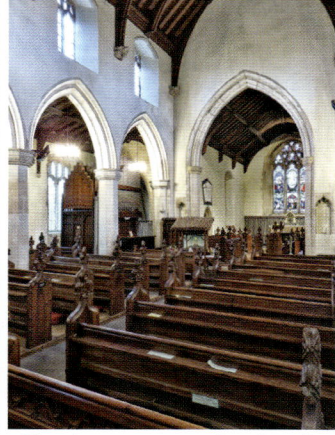  

Interior looking east — North east across the church — Niche, font, St Peter corbel — Jennings tablet

The chancel — Chancel piscina and sedilia — Glass by the O'Connors, ?C15th roundel — Ayton tablet, aisle piscina

Rood stairs doorway, old font — West from the sanctuary — North arcade — West wall painting

WHATFIELD ST MARGARET   C3, TM 024 466

St Margaret is a gem of a church in choice countryside

In south central Suffolk lie a number of charming villages, intimate and a little secretive. Whatfield is one of these. To get a flavour of what life was like in this area in the early years of the C20th, see Simon Dewes' wonderfully evocative book, 'A Suffolk Childhood', rural writing at its best. Echoes of those days can still be felt today. The church of St Margaret is completely in keeping with its surroundings, possessing an amiable, homespun appeal. Even the all-over rendering doesn't detract. From the Tudor brick porch to the quaint truncated tower with its pyramid roof, all is seemly and reassuring. Despite its small stature, the ?C13th tower has a prominent stair turret to the south and angle buttresses. To the south a rustic external rood stair turret with tiled roof occupies the angle between nave and chancel. As for the church's age, the windows, some replacements, range from simple Y-shaped to reticulated Decorated and suggest an age of late C13th to mid-C14th. The tower has a later Perpendicular west window. The C16th brick south porch has shallow niches flanking the outer doorway, above which is a modern sundial; there is an original roof inside and the floor is brick. The interior has something of everything and is a pleasure to explore. Just to the right of the door inside the church is a more elaborate holy water stoup than is usually seen, it is C13th and has a trefoil head and attached pillars with rings. The hoary old bowl of the font nearby is octagonal and quite plain, on a later stem and legs. It is generally thought to be C14th. The medieval roofs have plenty of character, the nave has a tie-beam type with king posts and in the chancel is a wagon roof with thin ribs, these have face bosses on foliate bases at their intersections. The pulpit is C17th and retains its tester and backboard; the panelling is boxy and plain. Opposite is the church's best wall tablet, for William Vesey, who died in 1699. It has a flamboyant achievement at the top, ionic columns and shield at the bottom. Above the north doorway is a white on black marble tablet for the Clubbe family, of 1776. A fine early C18th balcony survives at the west end, with a super front rail of balusters. Of similar age and design are the altar rails. The nave north side benches are C16th, of plain design. A single bench end is inscribed Jhon (*sic*) Wilson and dated 1589. There is also an excellent George I royal arms, an old piscina in the chancel and two C13th grave slabs in the sanctuary, one with double omega.

Tower and porch

Windows and rood loft turret

The east end

External memorial

Interior looking east

The pulpit

Vesey memorial

The chancel

Chancel roof

Chancel roof bosses

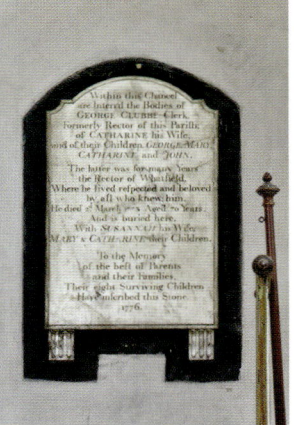
Clubbe tablet

C13th tomb lid, piscina, stoup

Looking west to the gallery

George I royal arms

Bench end of 1589

The font

WILBY ST MARY D2, TM 241 720

St Mary from the south east

It is remarkable that so many tiny settlements in East Anglia boast exceptional churches. Wilby is no more than a scattered hamlet, yet St Mary is a significant building containing many important artefacts and features. Whilst it is not a major Suffolk church, St Mary should be on every church enthusiasts' list for visiting. There is a suggestion that fabric at the base of the nave north and south walls could be C12th, but there is no unequivocal evidence to prove that. Most of what can be seen today is C15th, and Perpendicular designs dominate. The tower is tall and bold, with lots of nice flushwork and a decent west doorway with a plush late Perpendicular window above, with embattled transoms and flanked by niches. Matching it in impact is the grand C15th south porch, which boasts an extravagant frontage of stooled niches, stone panelling and cresting, plus a fine outer doorway. The interior has a wealth of fascinating features and fittings. To the left of the entrance is a large triple tomb with beautifully carved front panel for members of the Green family, who died in the C18th. On the wall to the south is an exquisite portrait bust of George? Green. The defaced C15th font has angels and evangelists with their symbols on the bowl, and niches around the stem containing saints. The glory of the church is the set of C15th benches in the nave, which have ends with double arm rests on which repose a riot of figures, animals real and imagined, grotesques, devils and more. Their medieval splendour is muted by iconoclastic damage, but they still make a powerful impression. A C19th set of very good copies gives some idea of what the originals looked like in their pomp. Some windows contain fine medieval canopy glass and other oddments, more complete than is usual, with figures. More recent glass is by Hardman and Clayton & Bell. The extravagantly carved Jacobean pulpit is one of the best in Suffolk, and has a tester. A St Christopher wall painting on the north wall is large but indistinct in parts. The church possesses several interesting C16th and C17th brasses, some in slabs set in the floor and others mounted on walls. The venerable parish chest is worm eaten and has been reduced in size, but is still impressive. Nave and aisle roofs are medieval, but have seen some restoration. The carved wooden angels in the aisle roof are excellent work of 1938. Inset in a frame on the top of the altar is an ancient mensa slab, probably surviving from the original church. Near it is a medieval piscina with credence shelf.

South porch

South side from the east

East wall

Interior looking east

The pulpit

St Christopher wall painting

St Mary from the sanctuary

Medieval bench ends

Recent bench ends

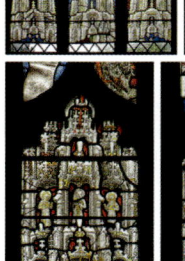

Medieval canopy work

Font and detail

George? Green d. 1739

WINSTON ST ANDREW C3, TM 180 616

A variety of windows on St Andrew's south side

Here is a wonderful little rural church in the sort of setting that makes the problems of the world seem very far away. It lies off a tiny lane and through a pretty gate. Once in the churchyard, peace is absolute. St Andrew is unpretentious, a little run-down and possesses no great treasures, but the atmosphere is priceless. The tower is plain, without buttresses and may be C13th, the battlements probably later. The simple, pointed arched west doorway has a fan of brickwork above it. Brick too is the C16th south porch which has an assertive, almost castle-like frontage fortified with buttresses that run up into sturdy pinnacles, with three niches and a stepped gable in between. The doorway is wide with a recessively moulded arch. In the north wall of the chancel is a blocked doorway which may have once opened into a chapel, vestry or sacristy. The interior is modest and filled with good, functional furniture, plus a few more notable items. The ranks of C19th benches in the nave are unremarkable except that they retain their original numbering scheme on the ends. The nave roof is ceiled, but the C14th arched tie beams are exposed beneath like the timbers of some great shipwreck. The octagonal font suits the surroundings and is unadorned. Such fonts are difficult to date, but the absence of evidence for a medieval locking mechanism on the rim of the bowl suggests a post-medieval date. Near the font are an C18th Creed board and a faded George III royal arms; the latter is set over the blocked north doorway. The most intriguing feature of the interior is a group of foreign painted glass panels, set onto the otherwise clear glass windows of the nave. These depict saints painted in a sepia tone and framed by variously coloured glass carrying attractive floral motifs. Both rood loft doorways are open, the lower enclosed by a door. Nearby is a very distinctive C18th pulpit with a nicely finished three-sided box with unadorned panelling, but, unusually, it stands on two clusters of five turned legs and one of four. It may, indeed, be a unique design. The chancel has a few items of interest. The piscina is a fine C13th example, with ringed shafts, carved capitals and a trefoil arch. The parish chest is a venerable affair, heavily reinforced with iron banding. Most of the C19th stalls are functional rather than beautiful, albeit with good poppyheads, but three bench ends are carved with tracery and one of those has a strange flying beast with a man's head on the arm rest. The neat organ is attractively painted white.

Brick porch

St Andrew from the north west

West doorway

Interior looking east

Pulpit, rood doorways

C18th? glass panel

The chancel

Blocked chancel doorway

Chancel piscina

Chancel stall

Old chest, chair, nave benches

West from the sanctuary

George III royal arms

The font

The organ

WITHERSFIELD ST MARY the VIRGIN   A3, TL 651 477

On its low mound, Withersfield St Mary the Virgin

Almost on the Cambridgeshire border in the south west of Suffolk lies the verdant village of Withersfield, many of its houses hidden behind high hedges or trees. The handsome church of St Mary is set prettily in a large churchyard on a low rise off Church Street. Already the tangled, rustic feel of Suffolk has been left behind and the open, flatter landscape of the county to the west beckons. St Mary's southern elevation, seen from the road, is mostly Victorian. A far-reaching restoration saw the chancel rebuilt and a new vestry, porch and south aisle. The tower is C15th and is distinguished by a prominent stair turret projecting beyond the battlements. Much of the rest including the north aisle is C15th too, but just a hint of an earlier church is given by the C13th door handle and backing plate on the south door. This door is set in a reused, square-headed, C16th doorway, with fleurons in the arch mouldings, spandrels with quatrefoils and a niche above. The treasure of the interior is a set of C15th benches in the nave. Those to the north are low, with buttressed square ends and no poppyheads, but those to the south have plain ends with intriguing poppyheads. These are large and intricately carved with subjects including St George dispatching a very singular dragon, St Michael weighing souls (note the demon interferring with the scales) and a bird feeding her young in a nest. Another, vividly carved, shows two curious creatures facing-up in a tangle of vines and grapes. St Mary retains a fine, gated C15th chancel screen with trefoil heads and tracery. In the C18th it was embellished with carvings, including heads, whilst the panels were decorated with fleurons on red and dark grey grounds. The medieval font is rather good, with shields and big flowers in unusual patterns. So too is the dainty early C17th pulpit, with its beautifully toned woodwork and classic Jacobean carving on the panels. A very unusual item can be found near the south doorway, the capital of a C13th pier adapted for use as a stoup. It was probably derived from the arcade of the first, medieval, south aisle, and it bears the notch for a parclose screen. Both nave and north aisle have fundamentally medieval roofs, the latter enlivened by striking bosses, including the twisted face of a ?lion with tongue out, an eagle and a Tudor rose. In the north aisle is a small brass for the sponsor of its building, Robert Wyburgh. A C19th wall tablet for the Mayd family and a nice benefactions board should be seen. St Cecilia in the north aisle east window (1972) is by Pippa Blackall.

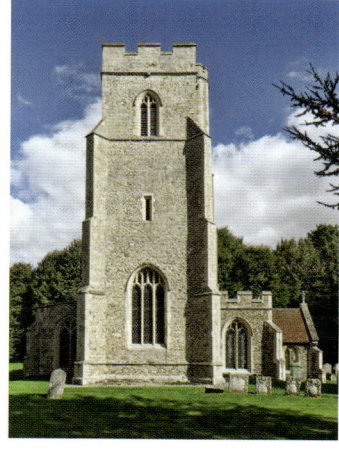

St Mary from the west, north and south west

Interior from the west and east   The pulpit   Chancel screen   Faces on the screen

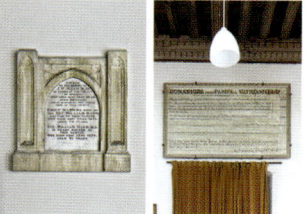

Screen panelling, roofs   North aisle roof bosses   The chancel   Wyburgh brass, Mayd tablet, charity board

St George and the Dragon   St Michael weighing souls   Capital/holy water stoup   The font

WORLINGTON ALL SAINTS — A2, TL 691 738

All Saints has a good range of gravestones in the southern churchyard

Right out on the edge of north west Suffolk lies the village of Worlington and its little known church of All Saints. Away from tourist areas, it is off the radar, but deserves to be better known. Some churches have an especially strong feel of times past, and this is one of them, despite late Victorian and early C20th upgrades. In fact these restorations were sensitive, and some interesting old artefacts were retained. The exterior has a number of features that attract attention. One is the C18th yellow brick porch, which from the south east looks a rather bland affair, but around the other side are surprising and unexplained recesses in the wall, two arches and a circular window, all blind and probably never open. On the nave east gable is a rare survival, a sanctus bell turret, which retains a guide ring in the wall below through which went the rope to pull the bell. In an unusual location at the top east corner of the nave is a niche. The C13th/C14th tower has a fine west front, with an excellent doorway with recessed mouldings, above which is a stylish Decorated window flanked by two ogee-headed niches. Much of the rest of the church is C13th. The chancel is short and its east window is a late version of the classic Early English three lancet design, with cusps. The clerestory is C15th and is present both sides, despite the lack of a north aisle. Much awaits the visitor inside. The square font is affectingly askew with age and could be Norman; it has piers at the corners and similar shafts, and is mounted on a section of the pre-aisle south wall. The pulpit is a solid C17th affair, in excellent order. Nearby is the lower rood loft doorway, complete with stairs. The original rood beam survives. Enigmatic slivers of wall painting remain in certain places. The rustic aisle benches are medieval and ricketty, with crude carving at the ends. The pride of the church is the abundant and varied early graffiti which covers large areas of the arcade piers and other areas of stonework. Circular designs are common, but the rarer shields are important and may reference the Crusaders. Several windows carry sections of medieval glass, much of it canopy type, there are no figures. Two or three of the fairly numerous wall tablets are worthy of inspection, and there is one inscription brass, mounted on the nave north wall. In the aisle is a small, crumbling piscina. The poorly preserved royal arms are for George III. The charming early C19th wall clock presented in 1921 is an 'Act of Parliament' type. Linger awhile to appreciate the rest of this super church.

Tower and porch

All Saints from the north east

Tower west wall details

Graffiti on arcade piers

Interior looking east and west

The pulpit

Lower rood stair doorway

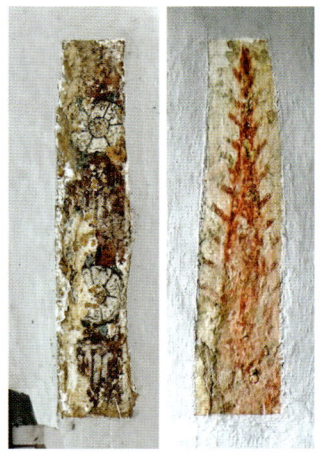
Wall paintings

George III royal arms

Old benches, wall clock

Aisle piscina

The font

The chancel

Medieval and recent glass

Mortlock brass, wall tablets

WYVERSTONE ST GEORGE   C2, TM 042 678

St George Wyverstone – a country church to savour

In a quiet corner of rural Wyverstone stands the charming church of St George. It has a lot to offer, quite apart from a seductive setting. The exterior has several notable features. The C14th tower has big buttresses but they are rather curious; the two easterly ones are at right angles to the tower while the westerly ones are at c.45°. All have chequerwork along their length and at the base, the battlements are also prettily chequered. Look too at the bell openings, on the south and west they are conventional, two-light windows, but on the north and east they take the form of odd, inflated loop-shaped openings with cusps. Below the bell openings on the south and west faces are very small, quatrefoil openings. The nave clerestory has four Perpendicular windows to the north and south, but there are no aisles. All the other windows are Perpendicular but some may have replaced Decorated originals, and some are probably Victorian. The church generally shows no architecture earlier than C14th. The old wooden porch has been restored, and was apparently built off centre to the inner doorway to avoid a nave buttress. Inside is a most unusual survival, the dado of a medieval screen with three-dimensional carved figures instead of paintings. In addition, these portray biblical scenes, not the usual saints, prophets or kings. To the south are just two carved C15th panels, depicting the Mass of St Gregory and the Visitation. These are now joined with two C17th panels, characteristically carved. To the north are two panels showing an Annunciation scene (St Gabriel and the Virgin), then a Nativity and finally, the Magi. All carvings are damaged, some severely. Next to the screen is a ricketty C16th pulpit with linenfold carving. The nave roof is C15th (later restored) and has hammerbeams alternating with arch-braces, also a rare pulley block, part of the apparatus for suspending lighting for the rood. Both rood stair doorways are extant in the nave north wall, whilst nearby windows contain medieval glass fragments, some with recognisable figures. The east window glass of 1926 by William Glasby is very striking. A fine carved wooden royal arms is for William and Mary. Another set, more conventional, is for George III. The altar rails are C17th and some of the old benches at the rear of the church have extraordinary poppyheads. One bench end has the date 1616 and churchwardens initials. The font is C15th and its cover C17th. The C14th chancel piscina has a cusped head. In the sanctuary is a very fine C14th chest.

West end from the south   **From the south west and east**

Interior looking east   **The screen and details**   **The east end**   **C15th and C20th glass**

Altar rails   **Interior looking north west**   **Around the rood doorways**   **The pulpit**

Two royal arms, chest   **Old benches**   **Font, piscina, Steggall tablet**

References and Select Bibliography

There is a good range of books and papers about Suffolk churches, from the general to the very specific, and only a selection of the best and most useful is given. Unlike Norfolk, the county saw little in the way of early research on the churches as a whole (but see Bryant 1912). It was not until the ground-breaking tome by Munro Cautley in 1937 that an in depth survey was published. This monumental work of scholarship provided the fundamental information on which later writers could build, although post-medieval churches were omitted and churches not deemed by the author to be of much, if any, importance were dismissed in a few lines or with a brief 'little of interest'. These were usually churches that had been much restored in Victorian times, and had lost most of their medieval fittings. The omission of Victorian churches was redressed in 1982 when a revised 5th edition emerged complete with a supplement by Anne Riches on them. Whatever the few failings of Cautley's book, it contains, as well as the individual church entries, lucid and comprehensible sections on church fittings and features, plus a wonderful selection of photographs which alone are of inestimable value. In the 1970's the definitive work on Suffolk's churches by Derek Mortlock appeared in three volumes. It has formed the bedrock of Suffolk church studies ever since, quite simply its thoroughness and detail are beyond praise. Every Anglican church in the county receives its due in lengthy entries which, while technical to a degree, are approachable and aimed at everyman. Without Mortlock's work as a guide it is doubtful this book could have been written and it seems scarcely fair to point out that illustrations are few and far between, and of poor quality. Joining 'the Mortlock' in the reference pile next to the computer were the two editions of Suffolk (east and west) by James Bettley and Nikolaus Pevsner (2015) which were an able support, although the information given on the churches is variable and again reflects the relative value accorded to each building. A mention must be given also to Birkin Haward's fine and erudite volume on medieval Suffolk stained glass (1989), indispensible for information on that art form. Of the other books in the list, all have merit and together form an essential library for any Suffolk church enthusiast.

Suffolk Churches

Agate, J.N. 1980. Benches and stalls in Suffolk churches. Suffolk Historical Churches Trust.
Aiken, P,. Winnifrith, J. & Ingham, S. 1991. Suffolk churches: day tours of Suffolk churches. Geerings, Ashford.
Barker, H.R. 1907, facsimile 2018. West Suffolk. Forgotten Books, London.
Bettley, J. & Pevsner, N. 2015a. Suffolk: East (Pevsner Architectural Guides: Buildings of England). Yale University Press, New Haven & London.
_____ 2015b. Suffolk: West (Pevsner Architectural Guides: Buildings of England). Yale University Press, New Haven & London.
Birch, M. 1998. A pocket guide to Suffolk parish churches. Richard Castell Publishing Ltd, Thwaite.
Blatchly, J. & Northeast, P. 2005. Decoding flint flushwork on Suffolk and Norfolk churches: a survey of more than 90 churches in the two counties where devices and descriptions challenge interpretation. Suffolk Institute of Archaeology and History, Ipswich.
Bryant, T.H. 1912. County churches. Suffolk (in 2 volumes). George Allen & Unwin, London.
Butcher, D. 2019. Norfolk and Suffolk churches: the Domesday record. Poppyland Publishing, Oulton.
Butler, A. & A. 1987. See Suffolk's churches! Suffolk Historical Churches Trust.

Cautley, H.M. 1982. Suffolk churches, 5th edition, with supplements by **Riches, A. & Northeast, P.** The Boydell Press, Woodbridge.
Dutt, W.A. 1927. Suffolk. 4th revised edition. Methuen & Co. Ltd, London.
Felgate, T.M. 1976. Knights on Suffolk brasses. East Anglian Magazine Ltd, Ipswich.
Haward, Birkin. 1989. Nineteenth century Suffolk stained glass. The Boydell Press, Woodbridge.
_____ 1993. Suffolk medieval church arcades,1150-1550: a measured drawing survey with notes and analysis. Suffolk Institute of Archaeology and History, Ipswich.
_____ 1999. Suffolk medieval church roof carvings: an exploratory photographic survey with notes. Suffolk Institute of Archaeology and History, Ipswich.
Hunt, D., Welhm, M., Allen, T., Tricker, R. & Wilde, M. 2013. 100 Years 100 Treasures. St Edmundsbury & Ipswich Diocesan Board of Finance.
James, M.R. 1930. Suffolk and Norfolk. J.M. Dent & Sons Ltd, London & Toronto.
Linnell, C. 1955. Suffolk church monuments. A preliminary survey. *Proceedings of the Suffolk Institute of Archaeology* volume 27, part 1 (offprint).
MacCulloch, D. 1971. Royal arms in Suffolk churches. *Proceedings of the Suffolk Institute of Archaeology*, volume 32, part 2 (offprint).
Mortlock, D. P. 2009. The guide to Suffolk churches. Lutterworth Press, Cambridge.
O'Donoghue, R.E.L. 2009. Medieval stained glass in Suffolk churches: let the stained glass speak. Authorhouse UK.
Pardy J. & Tricker, R. 2000. Suffolk church walks. Countryside Books, Newbury.
Pye, A.S. 2008. A photographic and historical guide to the Parish Churches of East Suffolk. ASPYE, Lowestoft.
_____ 2009. A photographic and historical guide to the Parish Churches of West Suffolk. ASPYE, Lowestoft.
Raven, J.J. 1890, facsimile 2019. The church bells of Suffolk, a chronicle in nine chapters: with a complete list of the inscriptions on the bells, and historical notes. Hansebooks.
Reynolds, G. D. & Maclachlan, P. (eds). 1990. Guide to heraldry in Suffolk churches. Suffolk Heraldry Society.
Rimmer, M. 2015. The angel roofs of East Anglia. The Lutterworth Press, Cambridge.
Salmon, J. 1981. Saints in Suffolk churches. Suffolk Historic Churches Trust.
Scarfe, N. 1960, 1962, 1966, 1976, 1982 (editions and revisions). Suffolk: a Shell guide. Faber & Faber, London.
Sherlock, D. 1980. Medieval floor tiles in Suffolk churches. Suffolk Historic Churches Trust.
_____ 2008. Suffolk church chests. Suffolk Institute of Archaeology and History, Ipswich.
Stanford, D. 2005. Suffolk churches. Frances Lincoln, London.
Sterry, J. 2005. Round tower churches on the Norfolk and Suffolk border: a series of detailed day tours. Jack Sterry.
_____ 2010. Round tower churches in mid-Norfolk, north Norfolk and Suffolk. Jack Sterry.
Tilbrook, R., Tricker, R. & Pipe G. 1998. Suffolk's churches great and small. Jarrold Publishing, Norwich.
Tricker, R. 1983. A selection of Suffolk churches, ancient & modern. Brechinset Publications, Ipswich.
Various Authors. 1977. Suffolk churches: a pocket guide. Suffolk Historical Churches Trust.

Suffolk Church Guides

Church guides are usually found in the churches that have produced them, but the supply is variable and can dry up. Sometimes churchwardens can get hold of them for interested parties. Quality also varies from single sheets to lush brochures, but the vital point to make about them is that they often contain titbits of information gleaned from local knowledge that don't appear in the wider literature. The following list is made up of guides that were available at the time of the author's visits, no claim is made that they still will be. On the other hand, new guides and editions will always appear as time goes on.

Alderton. Angels and Pinnacles Organisation. N.D. Alderton St Andrew leaflet.
Alderton. Angels and Pinnacles Organisation. N.D. Angels & Pinnacles Church Heritage Trails. No.6 in the series: Shottisham cluster.
Aldringham. Anon. N.D. St. Andrews Church, Aldringham.
Alpheton. Mullens, A. 1997. St Peter and St Paul Alpheton. Revised edition.
Ampton. Redman, A.J. 1994. St Peters Church Ampton. A brief guide and description.
Bardwell. Anon. N.D. The Parish Church of St. Peter and St. Paul Bardwell. Church Guide.
Barking. Herring, S. 2015. St. Mary's Church Barking Suffolk. Guide. Reprint.
Barnham. Anon. N.D. Welcome to St Gregory's Barnham.
Barningham. Lingwood, W.M. 1990. St Andrew's Church. Barningham, Suffolk. 3rd edition.
Barningham. Anon. N.D. The Benefice of Stanton, Hopton, Market Weston, Barningham and Coney Weston.
Barrow. Murry, K.M. 1998. An invitation to All Saints Church Barrow Suffolk. Illustrated by J. Wall.
Bedfield. Tricker, R., Easton, T. and Martin, E. 2011. A Guide to the History & Architecture of St Nicholas Church, Bedfield, Suffolk. 3rd edition.
Bildeston. Andrews, S. 2006. The Church of Saint Mary Magdalene Bildeston, Suffolk.
Blaxhall. Goodchild, N. 2012. St Peters Church Blaxhall. A guide to the Church and it's history.
Boxford. Boxford. 1999. St Mary's Church Boxford. A brief history.
Brampton. Nelson, P. 2011. A walk around Brampton Church.
Brent Eleigh. Fitch, J. 1986. Brent Eleigh Church. An Illustrated History and Guide.
Brettenham. Anon. N.D. Saint Mary the Virgin, Brettenham.
Brome. Anon. N.D. The Church of St. Mary Brome.
Bromeswell. Anon. N.D. St Edmund's, Bromeswell.
Brundish. Tricker, R. 2005. The Parish Church of St Lawrence, Brundish. A Guide for Visitors.
Brundish. Tricker, R. 2016. The Parish Church of St Lawrence, Brundish. A Guide for Visitors. 3rd edition.
Burgate. Anon. N.D. A Brief Account of Burgate Church.
Burgh. Tricker, R. 2003. Saint Botolph's Church Burgh.
Butley. Tricker, R. and Harrap, V. 1990. Church of St. John the Baptist Butley Suffolk. Brief guide.
Buxhall. Kendall, C. N. 1972. St. Mary's Church Buxhall. First impression.
Buxhall. Clayton, T. 2007. St. Mary's Church Buxhall.
Charsfield. Elliot, M. 1984. Saint Peter's Church Charsfield, Suffolk. A short guide.
Chediston. Anon. N.D. St Mary's Church Chediston, Suffolk.
Creeting St Mary. MacBeth, N. and Glazebrook, J. N.D. Creeting St Mary Church Suffolk. A short history and guide. Revised edition.
Debenham. Tricker, R. 2002. A Guide to St Mary Magdalene Church Debenham, Suffolk.

Debenham. Tricker, R. 2002. How old is the church? An extended history to accompany the church guide.
Earl Soham. W.V. and N.M. 2009. St. Mary's Church Earl Soham. PCC of St Mary, Earl Soham.
Easton. Warner, R. 2008. All Saints' Church Easton Suffolk. A Short Guide and History. R. Warner, Brandeston, Suffolk. Sixth printing.
Falkenham. Tricker, R. 2011. St Ethelbert's Church Falkenham Suffolk. History and Guide.
Felsham. Barber Jackson Ltd. N.D. Welcome to St. Peter's Church Felsham, Suffolk.
Freckenham. Anon. 2015. St Andrew's Church Freckenham Suffolk.
Glemsford. Hemphill, P., Hill, R., Perkins, S. and Newell, D. 2014. A Guide to St Mary's. A tour around the Parish Church of St. Mary the Virgin, Glemsford. St. Mary's Church, Glemsford.
Gosbeck. Brief guide to Gosbeck Church.
Great Ashfield. Anon. N.D. Great Ashfield Church.
Great Bradley. Anon. N.D. St Mary's Church Great Bradley. Notes by R. Tricker (1975), pictures courtesy of K. Ireland.
Great Glemham. Tricker, R. 1995. All Saints' Church Great Glemham Suffolk. 2nd printing.
Great Saxham. R.S. and D.S. 2014. A short guide to Great Saxham parish church.
Hawstead. Hillman, A.E. N.D. Hawstead Church.
Helmingham. Anon. N.D. The Benefice of Debenham and Helmingham welcomes you.
Helmingham. Anon. N.D. A Short History of St Mary's Church Helmingham.
Helmingham. Anon. N.D. The Helmingham Church Monuments. The Seven Baronets. A journey through history.
Herringswell. Holman, A. 2015. The Story of Herringswell, Suffolk. Reprint.
Hinderclay. Fulton, J. 2016. A Guide to the Parish Church of St Mary – Hinderclay – Suffolk. Revised edition.
Horham. Harvey, J. and Streeter, D. 2010. The Parish Church of St. Mary Horham, Suffolk. Revised and reprinted edition.
Iken. Tricker, R. 1996. St. Botolph's Church Iken. Revised edition.
Ilketshall. Anon. N.D. The Parish Church of Ilketshall St Andrew. The Benefice of Wainford Suffolk.
Lawshall. Holmes, F. 1975. The History of the Parish Church of All Saints and the Parish of Lawshall.
Lidgate. Foreman, A. 2014. A Guide to St Mary's Church Lidgate.
Little Cornard. Cotton, S. 2016. All Saints Little Cornard.
Little Cornard. Anon. N.D. Bell restoration. All Saints Church, Little Cornard.
Little Waldingfield. Paine, C. 2015. St Lawrence's Church Little Waldingfield. A Suffolk 'Landmark' Church. History and Guided Tour. Parochial Church Council, Little Waldingfield, Suffolk.
Metfield. Metfield Parochial Church Council. 2006. Saint John the Baptist Metfield.
Nacton. Thuell, M. 2010. St Martin's Church Nacton, Suffolk. Revised edition.
Nayland. Weston, J.D. 2004. St James' Church Nayland, Suffolk. Revised edition.
Nettlestead. Tricker, R. N.D. St. Mary's Church Nettlestead.
Newton. Willis, R.W.G. 2011. All Saints Church Newton nr Sudbury Suffolk. A short history and guide. D. Crimmin, Cragston, Newton, Suffolk. 2nd edition.
Pettistree. Whitehand, R. 2012. St Peter & St Paul Pettistree. Church Guide.
Preston. Wilkins, J. 2016. St. Mary's Church Preston St. Mary. A Guide and Short History of the Church and Village. Preston St Mary Parochial Church Council. 3rd edition.
Raydon. Reeves, D. N.D. A Walk around St. Mary's Church Raydon.

Risby. Paine, C. 2015. A Guide to St Giles' Church, Risby. Risby Parochial Church Council.
Redisham. Anon. N.D. Saint Peter's Church Redisham.
Reydon. Jigsaw Design & Publishing. N.D. Sole Bay Churches.
Rougham. Paine, C. 2015. St Mary's Church Rougham. The History & Guide.
Rushmere. Lines, P. 2001. St Andrew – Rushmere. Church Guide. Revised edition.
Santon Downham. Fitch, J. 2007. The Church in the Forest. St. Mary the Virgin Santon Downham, Suffolk with some notes on All Saints' Santon, Norfolk. Revised edition.
Santon Downham. Anon. N.D. St. Mary the Virgin Santon Downham "The Church in the Forest".
Shadingfield. Shadingfield Parochial Church Council. 2003. St John the Baptist.
Shotley. Warner, M. 2012. Parish Church of St. Mary the Virgin, Shotley. Guide. Revised edition.
Shottisham. Angels and Pinnacles Organisation. N.D. Shottisham St Margaret leaflet.
Shottisham. Angels and Pinnacles Organisation. N.D. Angels & Pinnacles Church Heritage Trails. No.6 in the series: Shottisham cluster.
South Elmham. Anon. N.D. St James South Elmham Suffolk.
South Elmham. Anon. N.D. Saint Margaret's Church South Elmham.
Stuston. Anon. N.D. All Saints Church Stuston.
Stutton. Paine, C., Browne, P. & Bull, E. 2014. St Peter's Stutton.
Tannington. Anon. 2012. Brief notes on the history of Tannington Church Suffolk. Revised edition.
Thorndon. Paine, C. 2011. All Saints Church Thorndon.
Thornham Magna. Anon. N.D. The Church of St Mary Magdalene Thornham Magna, Suffolk.
Thornham Magna. Anon. N.D. The Five Churches of Saint Mary. St. Mary Magdale, Thornham Magna.
Tunstall. Anon. N.D. St Michael and All Angels Tunstall.
Walberswick. Tricker, R. 2013. St Andrew's Church Walberswick Suffolk.
Walberswick. Jigsaw Design & Publishing. N.D. Sole Bay Churches.
Wetheringsett. Tricker, R. 1998. All Saints Church Wetheringsett-cum-Brockford. Church History & Guide. Illustrations by R. Pearson.
Withersdale. Anon. N.D. The Parish Church of St. Mary Magdalene Withersdale. A Short History & Guide.
Withersfield. Bent, A. 2008. St Mary the Virgin, Withersfield. Church Guide.
Wyverstone. Hungate Rood Screen Trails: No. 8. Eye, Yaxley, Westhorpe, Wyverstone.

General books on churches

Betjeman, J. 1980. Collins guide to parish churches of England and Wales. Collins, London.
Cox, J.C. and Ford, C.B. 1961. Parish churches (rev. edition). Batsford, London.
Cunnington, P. 2005. How old is that church? Marston House, Yeovil.
Fewins, C. 2010. The church explorer's handbook. Canterbury Press, Norwich.
Goode, W.J. 1994. The round tower churches of south east England. Round Tower Churches Society.
Hart, S. 2003. The round tower churches of England. Lucas Books.
Jenkins, S. 2009. England's thousand best churches. Penguin Books, London.
Jones, L.E. 1965. The Observer's book of old English churches. Frederick Warne, London.
_____ 1963. What to see in a country church (3rd edition). Phoenix House Ltd., London.
_____ **and Tricker, R.** 1992. County guide to English churches. Countryside Books, Newbury.

McNamara, D.R. 2011. How to read churches: a crash course in ecclesiastical architecture. Herbert Press, London.
NADFAS. 1993. Inside churches. A guide to church furnishings. NADFAS.
Sharpe, G.R. 2011. Historic English churches: a guide to their construction, design and features. I.B. Tauris & Co Ltd, London.
Smith, E., Cook, O. and Hutton, G. 1977. English parish churches. Book Club Associates, London.
Taylor, R. 2003. How to read a church. Rider, London.
Winn, C. 2014. I never knew that about England's country churches. Ebury Press, London.

Websites

The internet has revolutionised data dissemination and is an essential tool for researchers. Without it and access to the websites below, the task of building the factbase for this book would have been immeasurably more difficult. Information that would have taken hours to extract in a library or research facility is now available instantly. The most useful and informative websites about Suffolk churches are the British Listed Buildings, Suffolk Churches, Diocese of St Edmundsbury and Ipswich and Church of England A Church Near You sites. Most churches also have their own website or share a benefice website. Some of these are excellent. The list below is just a small selection of the websites out there. The two volumes that constitute the only completed parts of the Suffolk Victoria County History are available to read on the British History Online site, but despite containing a wealth of information, neither of them cover the churches.

http://www.suffolkchurches.co.uk/
http://britishlistedbuildings.co.uk/england/suffolk#.XOZTgYhKhPY
http://www.achurchnearyou.com/
http://www.cofesuffolk.org/
http://www.british-history.ac.uk/
http://www.english-church-architecture.net/suffolk%20a/aa_index_suffolk.htm
http://shct.org.uk/suffolk-churches/
http://www.visitchurches.org.uk/
http://www.explorechurches.org/
http://www.britainexpress.com/counties/suffolk/churches/index.htm
http://www.literarynorfolk.co.uk/Literary%20Suffolk.html
http://www.nationalchurchestrust.org/
http://www.roundtowers.org.uk/
http://www.crsbi.ac.uk/

Final words – the top 12

These are my 12 favourite churches in Suffolk at the time of writing, the list may change! Being my choice does not make them the best, please go out and decide for yourselves. Also, please don't forget to leave a donation in the churches you visit, and sign the visitors book.

In no particular order:

Hawstead, Boxford, Great Saxham, Thorington, Alpheton, Ousden, Barking, Helmingham, Sotterley, Ampton, Brent Eleigh and Bardwell